THE GREAT LEADHERSHIP AWAKENING

RACQUEL BERRY-BENJAMIN   ALIX BIONDO

KATE BIRMINGHAM   JENNIFER BURNHAM-GRUBBS

ARYANA CHARISE   LISA CLAPPER   ADAPIA D'ERRICO

CECILIA DAHL   LINDA FISK   EILEEN COSKEY FRACCHIA

SHIRI GABRIEL   NIKKI GREEN   MARY E. GREGORY

PEGGY HEDGEPETH   KASIA HEIN-PETERS

RACHAEL MAIER   KELLY MCCARTEN   CINDY MOLINA

KAYLEIGH O'KEEFE   KRISTIE ONDRACEK

GERI PACHECO   TERRE SHORT   LAUREN TATRO

SHIRLEY WANTLAND

Contents

Print ISBN: 979-8-9873454-4-3

Ebook ISBN: 979-8-9873454-3-6

Introduction

The era of the "good girl" is dead. The era of the "true girl" is dawning.

Chances are a "good girl" lives inside you, even as the world sees you as an intrepid leader in corporate, founder of your own company, or rising star in your profession.

This "good girl" is the unseen, unheard, unhealed part of you that often wonders, "Am I worthy?"; "Am I enough?"; "Am I lovable?".

The "good girl" overcommits your energy, silences your voice, causes dis-ease in your body, serves everyone else first, and does so with a tight smile.

What's more is that the "good girl" has been beloved by the business world, which has exploited her hard work ethic and maintained the perfect environment for her insecurities to metastasize.

For those of us that grew up in corporate America, we entered into a system that was designed to honor the masculine way of business and leadership. There is nothing necessarily wrong with that, it just meant that as women we had to accept that we would be:

- lauded for our results more than our process
- encouraged to dismiss our intuition or emotions because they appeared to slow down progress
- judged for our appearance more than our talent

And sometimes worse. Verbal abuse. Discrimination. Sexual harassment. You will hear about these experiences from the authors in this book.

Driven to perform a role, the "good girl" has overextended herself. And yet, the pandemic created a rupture in our collective psyche and revealed just how much women had sacrificed their truest selves at the altar of societal expectations.

In this liminal space, the "true girl" inside each of us must step forward and become the most authentic, unapologetic woman.

The "good girl" within you will tell you to just prioritize differently, take a vacation, or work on your boundaries. But the solution to this universal pain is to shift the paradigm entirely. Only a completely new perspective will do.

The Divine Feminine Leadership Paradigm

What is *The Great LeadHERship Awakening*, exactly?

The Great LeadHERship Awakening is a movement of women in leadership positions who are fully embodying their truest essence and heralding a new era of consciousness in business.

These women are the way-showers among us who have woken up from the fear-driven illusions that have so heavily influenced the world we live in and chosen to break the cycle one thought, word, and action at a time.

The Great LeadHERship Awakening is about a deeper awareness of—and a renewed appreciation for the *inner way of leadership.*

On the outside, nothing has changed.

You still show up to the Board meeting, work on strategic plans, and even submit expense reports!

But on the inside, you feel the difference. You have now become more fully human, more fully connected to all parts of yourself and what makes you a unique, powerful woman. You are aware of your automatic reactions, and even though the triggers still show up, you now know to take a pause, breathe, notice your thoughts, and choose a response from a calmer place.

This book is a reckoning that yearns for us to see ourselves—and others—as inherently worthy, lovable, and purposeful by virtue of our existence.

I have been where you are. The straight-A student, the worker bee, the all-star, the MBA student, the ideal corporate consultant, and the scrappy tech start-up commercial leader. I was the "good girl" who made it her mission to "be the best" and prove her worth constantly.

And I have spent the last three years unbecoming the version of me that contorted to fit the typical corporate environment and fully embracing my gifts as a creator, catalyst, and way-shower. In the unraveling, my company Soul Excellence Publishing was born, helping over 350 leaders become published authors in best-selling leadership books like *Leading Through the Pandemic: Unconventional Wisdom from Heartfelt Leaders, Significant Women: Leaders Reveal What Matters Most, The X-Factor: The Spiritual Secrets Behind Successful Executives, Black Utah: Stories from a Thriving Community, Greener Data: Actionable Insights from Industry Leaders,* and *STEM Century: It Takes a Village to Raise a 21st-Century Graduate.* I've brought people together in community to reflect, write, publish, and spark new movements into existence.

Driven by nothing more than an inner desire for expansion, I leapt into the unknown.

The divine feminine leadership path requires faith, after all.

∼

May you feel a stirring in your heart as you read the stories of the women who have written in this book. Let their wisdom wash over you.

Lean back in your chair, feel grounded here on earth, place your hands on your heart, close your eyes, breathe in deeply, and become present to this moment. What if by virtue of picking up this book and engaging in the task of reading it, you set your soul on fire and your life in a new direction?

Every time a woman stands up for her true self, her inner magnificence, and asserts herself in the world, she shifts the course of humanity. She embodies *The Great LeadHERship Awakening*. She becomes her "true girl".

There is no wrong or right way to read this anthology. Let a chapter title inspire you and dive in! Or read through each author's profile to sense a connection before reading their story. Read it front-to-back or pick it up and put it down as you seek guidance and inspiration along your journey.

I invite you to connect with the women in this book by reaching out to whomever speaks to you via the contact information they've shared. This new paradigm seeks reciprocity and mutuality; if someone moves you, acknowledge them and let our bonds strengthen.

Together, let us embody the feminine leadership paradigm.

Are you ready to live into your expression of *The Great LeadHERship Awakening*?

With love and admiration,

Kayleigh O'Keefe

Founder and CEO, Soul Excellence Publishing

ONE

Racquel Berry-Benjamin

CALLING ALL LEADHERS

Who Run The World? Girls!

"If you want to save the world, help the women" –Nelson Mandela

Women leading is not a new phenomenon. For centuries, women have broken barriers, surpassed boundaries, set records, and made advancements in industries of every kind. The Bible offers many stories of inspiring women leaders, and world history records the great works of countless more. The common theme found throughout these stories is that there are women of each generation who have recognized their time to lead and tapped into the courage to do so.

To all the beautiful women reading this book, now that you know women have been leading with impact from the beginning of time, are you ready to take the leap into leadership? Look around you. What are you seeing? Is there a problem you are often called on to solve? Is there something lacking in the household, the workplace, the community that should be invented? Do you feel the urge to lead? Is there a persistent nudge for you to share your ideas with the world? Do you feel a push to use your gifts to serve others? If you are a woman called to lead, this chapter is for you!

There are countless studies that show the benefits of women in leadership. *Women in the Workplace*, a study by McKinsey & Company and Leanin.org (2021), offers the most exhaustive research on the state of women in corporate America. While there are some studies that show women performing equivalent to or better than men in other areas of leadership, the *Women in the Workplace* study specifically highlights that:

- 11% of women spend more time contributing to diversity, equity and inclusion efforts in comparison to 7% of men;
- 29% of women are better at helping employees navigate work-life challenges in comparison to 24% of men;
- 31% of women are better at providing emotional support to employees in comparison to 19% of men;
- 61% of women are better at checking in on the wellbeing of employees in comparison to 54% of men; and
- 21% of women take action to prevent or manage employee burnout in comparison to 16% of men

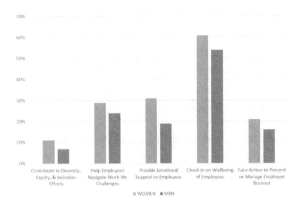

VISUAL 1.1: Women in the Workplace Bar Graph

These statistics should provide some measure of comfort to women who are delaying their much deserved and desired move into leadership because of fear. Moreover, the results should serve as reassurance for those of us already at the helm that leading with care and empathy can have a significant positive impact. In her book, *When Women Lead*, Julia Boorstin tells the inspiring story of Toyin Ajayi, a medical student who went to the small West African nation of Sierra Leone and was not yet able to officially practice medicine but used her head and heart to impact the world around her. Toyin led with empathy, and thus improved the quality of life for the people, despite not having an official leadership title as a healthcare practitioner. I implore you to read this stirring book by Julia that will help you see the positive impact of femininity in leadership.

By its very nature, leading—or being that quintessential 'girl boss'—does, in fact, require women to tap into what is traditionally considered *masculine energy*: action-taking, risk-taking, doing, and decision-making; however, as the earlier statistics indicate, there is much room for women to bring their more feminine traits—softness, empathy, being, understanding—to the workplace and into every aspect of life.

Ladies, to be clear, my push for you to lead is not a push for you to take the role of the men in your lives. Rather, I am encouraging you to be courageous and boldly take action toward achieving your heart's desires—i.e., opening that business and monetizing your gifts, managing that family business, supporting your spouse or partner's business, managing that firm or non-profit organization. You are encouraged to put your natural strengths to work and lead where you are called. You may be called to lead as a homemaker, as the family archivist who collects family photos or organizes family gatherings, in a community organization or as a world leader. Whatever your calling, there is a need for women in leadership. In the words of Simon Sinek, "If your actions inspire others to dream more, learn more, do more, and become more, you are a leader."

What Is Your Why?

"Find your why and you'll find your purpose" —*Simon Sinek*

To lead with purpose, you must first know your why. I believe God created all of us with uniquely innate gifts to be of service to ourselves and to others. I also believe that our personal and professional life experiences, acquired knowledge, learned skills, and interests, coupled with our God-given talents will tell us our *why*.

Take a moment to consider that the aforementioned make up your superpower—the thing that only you can do in the way that only you can do it. Collectively, these innate capabilities also bring to the surface that *thing* inside all of us that simply won't let us go. We feel restless when we ignore it. It keeps coming back, until we take some action toward it. That *thing* is your purpose. It is the one thing others always call on you to do; that one thing that is constantly with you. Your purpose can derive from a negative incidence you never want to experience again or a positive inspiration you know you must do, even without payment or public accolades. Your purpose is unique to you and only you can fulfill it.

For me, that nagging thing that refused to leave me alone was the desire to rise out of poverty and never return. Breaking the chains of poverty, building an empire, and helping others to do the same was my *why*. As a child, I had had one too many experiences that were the result of growing up poor and I'd made up my mind that I would have better.

Even back then, I imagined being independent, running several businesses, and traveling the world. It is an image I held on to. I wanted to elevate my mind to unimaginable heights that was so different from the reality I experienced as a child. This is not to say I have not had innumerable positive family experiences throughout my childhood and the instilling of values that continue to guide me today. I am specifically speaking of the setbacks of poverty that have plagued vulnerable families, including mine, for generations. These include dependency on government-subsidized food and housing programs, parents living paycheck to paycheck (and offspring growing up to do the same), inability to afford family vacations, inability to maintain utilities, little to no access to healthcare, witnessing of physical, sexual and drug abuse, normalizing of criminal or deviant behavior that ensnare many poor families in the criminal justice system, and the lack of education around economic and financial literacy, entrepreneurship, and more.

I wanted the comforts of life I believed could only come from the level of education and courage it would take for me to become financially free. Ladies, you must know your *why*. Your *why* keeps you motivated and gives you direction and focus. It is a gravitational pull so strong that it fuels you forward every time the familiarity of the past tries to pull you backward. What is your *why*?

The Courage To Lead

"Courage is the most important of all the virtues because without courage, you can't practice any other virtue consistently" —*Maya Angelou*

Having courage simply means acting in the face of fear. Leading yourself and leading in the world requires you to be fearless. Yes, you will always have moments of fear, but the key is to get past those moments. Truth is, once you've practiced being courageous long enough, you soon realize that your fears are those things you tell yourself without knowing what is on the other side of your actions. It is the classic 'fear of the unknown' syndrome. Once you take that leap of faith and come out on the other side, you soon realize that all is well, and things are not as bad as *fear* told you they would be. Fear will always show up at every new level you strive to attain. To get over fear, look back at the times you, or someone else, overcame it and use that as motivation to move forward.

Throughout my life, I have had many instances in which I've had to exercise courage. The same is true for you. Take some time and reflect on the different phases of your life. For the purposes of this chapter, I will share with you the very first, and last times, to date, that I have had to exercise courage in a big way.

BIG COURAGE #1

The first time I had to exercise courage in a big way was at the age 15 when I told my mother I was leaving high school and enrolling in Job Corps to get a General Education Diploma (GED)...and I did. One could argue that I was too young to have made such a decision; however, I would argue that I was not, and if I had not made that decision, I would have been doomed! If I had stayed in a traditional academic setting, I would have eventually dropped out or been expelled, only to become another statistic at the hands of traditionalists who believe there is only one path to achievement and success. I would have absolutely rebelled from boredom in school because I needed to be actively engaged in the things I found both interesting and challenging; frankly, I was not finding those experiences in school. There were far more exciting things in the real world.

That singular decision to leave school was the catalyst that changed the trajectory of my life. After obtaining my GED, I was fully in control of my life and it took off like a rocket.

- At 16, I enrolled in Job Corps and earned my GED;
- At 17, I was enrolled in college;
- At 18, I started my career in education;
- At 22, I became an elementary teacher;
- At 27, I was teaching at the university level;
- At 28, I transitioned to educational administration;
- At 32, I transitioned to educational leadership;
- At 39, I was a serial business owner; and
- have experienced many other accomplishments outside my professional career that will take us beyond the scope of this chapter.

BIG COURAGE #2

The last time I had to exercise courage in a big way was following the resignation from my position as commissioner of education. When my commissioner and superintendent colleagues from across the nation heard of my resignation, they immediately began to call and text with a myriad of offers. You see, education is an industry that will always need professionals. Children are born every day and education plays an essential role in the sustainability and growth of any society.

My inbox and voicemail box looked and sounded something like this:

- "Hey, what is your next move? I could really use your experience on my team."
- "You know, there's a superintendent position in so and so district that would be perfect for you."
- "Racquel, I was so impressed with the Community Council you organized to lead the transformation of your educational system. Can you join my leadership team and lead that initiative from concept to implementation?"
- "I am going to tell Dr. Smith to give you a call. Just last week, we were talking, and he mentioned his need for an experienced regional superintendent. His district has over 200,000 students with the same demographics as your student population. You would be a great fit."
- "I just learned of your resignation. Are you already positioned for your next job? I remember you sharing the Portrait of a Virgin Islands Graduate that you and your team developed to guide your transformational strategic direction. I would love to have you on board to lead this for my district."

The list goes on and on. There was no shortage of opportunities available to me, all with significant pay increases from what I made as commissioner. The flood of offers was a good problem to have, as most people don't aspire to be unemployed. Ironically, however, those same offers caused my spirit to become deeply troubled. It felt like I was being pulled right back into what I had worked so hard to ascend from all these years. Giving away my time and talent and working for another paycheck were simply no longer attractive. I was being called to do more purposeful work. My *why* was tapping me on the shoulder. Immersing myself in work that would get me one step closer to my dreams of owning my own businesses and traveling the world was ringing loud in my head. Deep within, I knew now was the time to embark on full-time entrepreneurship and business ownership. I had to find the courage to say 'NO' to all the (very) attractive job offers and 'YES' to my dreams.

The year 2024 marked the time I planned to complete my career in public service. Contrary to my plans, however, God had plans of his own for my life. In 2022, a series of events began to take shape that led to my eventual resignation as the head of the Virgin Islands public education system, and the subsequent launching of my education and business consulting companies.

I remember sitting at my dining table sadly drafting my resignation letter because I wanted to fully implement the great work accomplished by me and my team during the COVID-19 pandemic. At the same time, however, my insides were leaping for joy, as I knew the time had come to give birth to the twin babies I had been carrying for the last eight years—my consulting companies. It was during that bittersweet moment at my dining table, I finally understood the saying, 'If you want to see God laugh, tell him your plans'.

Over the last eight years, I have had to exercise courage at levels I'd not known before. Education consulting comes naturally for me, as it has been my profession for close to three decades. However, building a business to help other businesses grow was my challenge.

Entering the business and finance industries was very different for me. I was already credentialed and leading in the education industry, and here I was, preparing to enter full-time into industries of which I had no prior knowledge. Most people go to school for four years, earns a degree in business and/or finance and eventually finds a job or creates a business in either or both fields. In my case, I spent the last eight years of my career in education studying the two industries though a series of self-education, seminars, conferences, hands-on experiences, and professional education and training in preparation for my 2024 transition from public service.

It was sometimes scary sitting among classmates who were already well educated in these fields. I had to exercise courage to speak up in class and ask questions when I could not grasp concepts. Moreover, I had to build relationships and understand the diverse product offerings in business and finance. While understanding educational products is second nature to me, learning financial products offered by various financial institutions to help businesses grow proved to be challenging. However, the more I was exposed to the material and engaged with it, the easier it became. The moral is: courage or the lack thereof is the determining factor of our success or failure. Today, I own a company that helps businesses acquire financial resources. Do you have the courage to face your biggest fears and lead?

Who Inspires You, and Who Makes Up Your Network?

"You are the average of the five people you spend the most time with"
—*Jim Rohn*

Your network is your net worth. As such, having the right network is an essential part of leading. In its simplest form, Rohn's statement reminds us to choose better friends and associates that will enhance the quality of our lives. If you hang around with chickens, you will only fly as high as they can. For those of you who know anything about chickens, they can only go so high off the ground and for a very short time and distance. On the other hand, if you associate with eagles, you will soar to heights beyond your imagination.

People can only give you as much as they know and have. If your friends and associates do not know more intellectually and experientially than you, they cannot feed you. If they have a negative perspective and even a narcissistic disposition, they will take from you and decrease the quality of your life. Choose to let go of the ideas, people, places, and things that do not serve you and embrace everything that does. Be mindful that every idea, person, place, and thing from your last season simply cannot go with you into your next season. They have served their purpose and you must recognize that and be courageous enough to let them go.

Who inspires you? Who do you look up to? How do you see yourself? The people who you most admire have something in common with you, that is why you are fond of them. There is something in them that you see in yourself. Where do you see yourself in the future and with whom?

I believe in the power of the vision board. To date, I am on my third board, as I have achieved everything placed on the previous two, including jobs, fruitful mentorships, personal finances, and the like. As I did with my first two vision boards, I have included the ideas, people, places, things, finances, businesses, investments, and philanthropy, on my third board that I would like to realize in this season of my life. I have used a simple strategy to manifest the things I want, and it continues to work for me today. First, I envision it in detail, I then pray and ask God for it, I next take action toward it, and finally, I let go and let God. Scripture tells us in James 2:14-26 (NKJV) that "Faith without works is dead." I am a firm believer that you get what you believe. What do you believe about you?

WHO ARE YOU?

"Don't let anyone imprison you with titles; don't let them lock you up with titles that are beneath your level of gifting." —Bishop T.D. Jakes

Who are you without a title? Who are you without the make-up? Who are you when your values are being tested? Who are you at your core?

We are more than we believe ourselves to be. Personally, I believe we are multidimensional and ever-evolving. The Trinity Broadcasting Network (2022) published a powerful message, on its YouTube Channel, by Bishop T.D. Jakes entitled, "How are you Talking to Yourself"? The Bishop reminded listeners that it is what you say to yourself that heals you. So frankly, what others call you doesn't matter. You are whatever is inside you; you are whatever it is you think about at night; you are whatever you dream; you are more than what people call you; you are more than the job title you have; you are more than the company you work for; you are more than everything you have experienced up until this point!

During my tenure in public education, I have held many titles, the most prominent being commissioner of education. Despite the high-profile nature of the role, I never lost myself in the title. I knew the commissionership was not permanent, as I saw commissioners come and go throughout my career. I understood how the process worked and knew there would be an expiration date to my time in the position. During my time as the leader of the V.I. public education system, I remained true to my core beliefs, principles, and standards. I knew who I was, and I knew my *why* in life.

Like any other job, I could not solve every problem in the Virgin Islands public education system as commissioner. This was advice my mentors offered me from the onset and what I had witnessed with every commissioner before me. While I gave it my full effort and commitment, I knew it was impossible to build a team strong and talented enough to achieve the impossible. The reality of business, especially in the realm of public service, often amounts to when one problem is solved, another takes its place. Life is about making progress and the same is true of work. It is for each leader to solve the problems they encounter with the aim of moving the agency forward. That was my focus, and I am content with having moved the educational system further during my tenure. When that chapter was complete, I moved on to my next chapter with my character and core principles intact. Do you know who you are?

BE THE LIGHT

"For there is always light, if only we're brave enough to see it, if only we are brave enough to be it" – Amanda Gorman

In leadership, everyone looks to you for answers. As such, you must be that source of light to others. Addressing issues with positivity and inspiration is always a winning approach. Afterall, you catch more bees with honey than lime.

When you are on the path to achieving your dreams, it is a feeling like no other. When you've scaled the peaks of great mountains and experienced the depths of the deepest valleys, you enter another dimension that can only be experienced to be understood. Take action to lead; take action in the direction of your dreams. Use your unique gifts to be of service and be an inspiration to others. Share your experiences with them. When you lead and tell your story, you set another woman free; free from all the fears holding her back from living her full potential.

This single chapter does not allow for my whole story to be shared, but I hope I have been able to share some of my life experiences in a way that shows we have more in common than we have differences. We have similar experiences that came from different circumstances that occurred at different times. I have benefited from standing on the shoulders of phenomenal women and understand the call to do the same for other women.

Saying no to working for others and saying yes to my dreams propelled me on a path where I am now pursuing my heart's deepest desires. Taking action toward my dreams, being a mentor to other women, and sharing my journey with you is me being the light. Are you going to take action toward your dreams? Are you going to be the light? To gain more insight on my story and learn how to leverage yours, read my new book, *Your Story, Your Millions: Use your PAST to Fund your FUTURE, releasing May 2023.*

YOUR FUTURE AWAITS YOU!

"The best way to predict the future is to create it." — Abraham Lincoln

We are creators of our world. Until you realize that, you will forever live in the world of others. God knows your heart and greatest desires.

Ask and it shall be given. Although I had a plan to be finished with public service in 2024, God said, 'Nope, 2022 is your year'!

Be ready for when He answers. There will always be a need for creativity, new ideas, inventions, and leaders at home, in the community, government, and in business. Take your courageous step toward leadership and your dreams; you will inspire another woman to do the same. The future is a blank canvas; create the world you want to see. I can hardly wait to curl up in my library, with a cup of coffee or bush tea, and read your amazing and courageous story. Are you ready to lead?

REFERENCES

- Boorstin, J., (2022). "When Women Lead". New York. Avid Readers Press
- Jakes, T.D. [Trinity Broadcasting Network]. (2022, March 31), How are you Talking to Yourself? [Video]. YouTube. https://youtu.be/RYVeSSW7BXM
- McKinsey Global Institute and LeanIn.org (2021). *Women in the Workplace.* https://www.mckinsey.com/featured-insights/diversity-and-inclusion/women-in-the-workplace

About the Author

A woman of faith, mother, wife, bestselling author, educator, educational leader, speaker and businesswoman, Racquel Berry-Benjamin hails from the United States Virgin Islands and takes great pride in sharing her rich Caribbean history and culture with the world.

Racquel has lived a life of service as a 20-year career educator and educational leader and has always been a part of the great mission to help others elevate through education. She has risen through the ranks in education as a paraprofessional, teacher, mathematics coach, district administrator, state director, part-time university professor, deputy superintendent, and has concluded her decorated career as commissioner of education in the U.S. Virgin Islands.

In what Racquel defines as her next chapter, she has been intentional about living life very differently from her first chapter. Racquel is the founder and CEO of consulting firms Berry-Benjamin & Associates and Infinite Commercial Capital. She is a contributing author in the Amazon bestseller, *STEM CENTURY - It takes a Village to Raise a 21st Century Student* and served on a national delegation to South Korea to further the conversation on the importance of STEM Education. She is also the author of the new book, *Your Story, Your Millions: Use your PAST to fund your FUTURE, releasing May 2023.*

Racquel remains committed to her mission of helping others elevate through education, but this time, through business and philanthropy. In her chapter, Racquel hopes to inspire women to find the courage to lead and tell their story. She shares provoking personal and research-based nuggets to challenge readers to face the fears holding them back from leading in their own lives and leading in the world. Her candid insights show women they have more in common than not and that everyone has something they are called to fulfill.

Racquel is honored to be a part of the movement to empower and elevate women and encourages you to do the same.

FIND RACQUEL'S BOOK

Your Story, Your Millions: Use your PAST to Fund your FUTURE! – available May 2023 on Amazon, Bookshop, Barnes & Nobles, Apple Books and other online retailers!

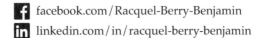

facebook.com/Racquel-Berry-Benjamin
linkedin.com/in/racquel-berry-benjamin

TWO

Alix Biondo

DOING REAL BUSINESS AT THE NUNNERY

What I Learned from a Nun

*H*ow does a non-Catholic businesswoman, wife, and mom wind up at a nunnery in self-inflicted silence? It may sound crazy, but it happened to me.

What drove me there? To be honest, there are parts of it I may never unravel. But since then, I've learned that true, authentic leadership can be developed in unexpected ways.

What if leadership's purest form comes from allowing people to see you flail, fall flat on your face, and rise back up as a stronger version of yourself?

The Business: From Podunk to Promising

Here's a little background: I work in the uber-competitive recruiting industry. In 2008, my two partners broke off from our previous firm after a buyout and started Talance Group. Shortly after the birth of our identical twin girls (and with a two-year-old son at home), I joined them, setting out to build a contract consulting practice. Little did we know then, but the Great Recession loomed. I was a team of one, and the scene was bleak, to say the least. Picture a tiny room in a business incubator center, phones that were not ringing, and a looming fear of failure permeating the air. I called it "Podunk, USA" at the time.

The hiring market was abysmal, and I began questioning if I had the chops to create something from scratch. I knew I wanted to help people, but there were so few jobs. Every "no" felt like another nail in the coffin, and my self-doubt was suffocating. Slowly, momentum started to build, clients were added, and I was able to hire my first team member. We became a dynamic duo doing whatever it took to make job placements. We typed up resumes, set up interviews, and even handled our own invoicing and collection calls to ensure we were paid. Despite the dreadful survival rate of startups in our field, we were determined to beat the odds.

From the beginning, my partners and I were intentional about the type of "in-service" organization we wanted to create. With every cherry-picked new hire, we set the expectation to always do what was best for the client, candidate, and the team. We had all previously experienced co-workers who wreaked havoc on others to get ahead. "Headhunters" are often associated with doing whatever is necessary to shove a candidate into a job, get a fee, and move on. We set out to be different, striving to build authentic, long-term relationships.

Potholes

Two years in, our business was growing at a steady clip. I was starting to think I might actually have what it takes to lead a team and attract new clients, all while being a great wife and mom to three tiny humans. Keeping all the balls in the air took a lot of energy, but it was a wonderfully fulfilling ride back then.

And then I hit a massive pothole.

My stepfather passed away from cancer. Six months later, I discovered my mom had early-onset Alzheimer's. She was a retired trailblazing businesswoman and my rock. There aren't enough words to describe the devastation I felt as I started losing my mother a little more each day. Mourning the realization that my children would never *really* know their grandmother took me to my knees.

It became an all-consuming job learning to navigate the havoc Alzheimer's dishes out. I untangled overdue bills, located bank accounts, and unscrambled finances for someone who had been meticulously organized. I moved her four times, first to my own home and then to different care facilities as her disease progressed.

Every day, I took on the problems of others and internalized them as my own, all while going through the motions of my normal life. And like so many women, I told myself I was "half-assing" all of it daily.

Wake up. Anxious thoughts. School drop. Commute. Pump up team. Smile for clients. Solve problems. Make sales. Handle marketing. Network. Check on Mom. Race in high heels to (insert after-school activity of your choice here). Kids to bed. Sit in the dark. Drink copious amounts of wine. Listen to depressing music until your husband gets worried. Complain about social obligations.

Cry out to God.

Rinse. Repeat.

The Meltdown

Years of shoving down insecurities, guilt, and grief ultimately turned into bitterness and anger. So, you'd think it would come as no shock that my self-sabotaging coping skills would cause me to crash at some point.

Nope. It was still a shock, and I hated myself for it.

One day, I realized I could no longer live the life I had built for myself. Not for ONE. MORE. MINUTE.

And all the while, I couldn't stop wondering WHY. Why can't I move forward? Why am I flailing now after all I've already conquered?

After all, I am a self-proclaimed "overcomer" turned "high achiever" who has prevailed over life's hardships!

I grew up broke but put myself through college. I was a child of divorce who was now happily married. We struggled through infertility, IVF, and the accompanying depression but now have three children. I'm an entrepreneur, part of a successful business and partnership. I created a life surrounded by an inspiring mentor, supportive family members, and long-lasting friendships that I cherish.

Hadn't I done enough to prove I am a survivor?!

But that's not how life works, is it?

A Mortifying Moment

To begin "fixing" myself, I first sat my partners down and tried to explain to them what I could not understand myself. The only thing I could propose at the time was to take a sabbatical. However, I wasn't sure how long that would be or what it would look like.

They responded with kindness, concern, and wholehearted support, taking over my responsibilities and managing my team.

Being a female in the business world, I've always set one non-negotiable rule for myself. There is no crying in the office!

As you've probably surmised by now, I blew it that day. Bigtime!

Looking back, I understand the tears came from the utter embarrassment of needing to take a break.

Meanwhile Back at the Nunnery

A work friend mentioned that I should investigate the Ruah Spiritual Center.

How did I never know that this giant, fast-paced city housed a nature oasis as part of a convent just outside downtown? The website touted acres of massive oak trees, and a beautiful labyrinth meant to "promote the re-creation of the human spirit." Sold! Sign me up!

Upon arriving, I sat down with an elderly, wonderfully witty Irish nun who found herself committed to a convent at just eighteen. When I asked her how that happened, she winked and said she asked God that very same question every day!

I set out in silence with a giggle and hopeful optimism, thinking that if a nun could question her life, I must be in the right place. My intention was to spend all day walking through the tree-lined paths, listening to birds, journaling, praying, meditating, and swinging on an old wooden swing like I had as a child.

Walk the labyrinth. Check.

Journal in the swing. Check.

Time to leave. Double check.

I couldn't take the silence!

I made it five whopping hours before returning to my car, dialing my phone repeatedly, and blaring music to kill the quiet.

The Road to Recovery

Then something shifted.

In the following days, I realized that I had forgotten how to just be somewhere along the line.

I went from stimulus to stimulus (insert your favorite distractions here: Netflix, podcasts, Audible book binges, wine, etc.).

I lived an anxiety-riddled existence and tried to force, shove, and hustle my way through each day. More sales, more metrics, more responsibilities. Always more.

If I wanted to grow a business, I thought I had to keep my "dukes up" and be mentally tough. I was living the life of my dreams, yet I'd beat myself up every minute of every day.

And it still wasn't enough. I wasn't enough.

I had previously read countless books on how to get rid of negative self-talk. But guess what? Nothing worked before my meltdown. Want to know why?

Because somewhere deep down inside, I believed that if I gave up the self-beratement, I'd lose my edge. That mean girl voice inside kept me at high-achiever status. Giving myself even the tiniest bit of grace meant success would surely slip through my fingers. And if that happened, I'd be a complete failure. Or, even worse, mediocre.

So instead, and virtually unbeknownst to me, I used candy-coated sarcasm, defensiveness, and judgment to disguise my deep-seated resentment and sense of victimhood. Both at home and at work.

Doesn't that sound fun?

My clients often ask if I'm always high-energy and smiling?

My answer is a resounding, "No! Just ask my husband." (He often asks if my inner child is named Chucky)!

Before, I would sit in work meetings, smile, and try to force everyone to get along, work together, be accountable, and so on. Then, if I didn't get the cohesive reaction I expected, I'd walk out of the room, wanting to scream in frustration.

Was my career the cause of my burnout as a leader? No.

My growing resentment of trying to "manage" my mother's daily decline, homework, and after-school activities, coupled with a complete lack of boundaries and inability to say "no" eventually took its nasty toll.

I also discovered I'm an empath. This means I take on the emotions of others and feel them as deeply as if they are my own. Unfortunately, after years of taking a daily dose of everyone else's feelings, I somehow lost the way to manage my own.

I work alongside an amazing group of people I want to be around. I can now see that every person, including our candidates and clients, walks through life with their own set of past wounding, negative self-talk, and pre-judgments.

There are triggers a-plenty in the baggage they carry, whether they realize it or not. I just had to learn how to stop unpacking their "poop packs" and adding them to my own!

Do I still get triggered? Absolutely and on the daily!

The difference is that I now notice when it is happening. At that very moment, I can stop myself and ask, *What part of me is upset by what just happened?* I can take a deep breath, get curious, and use my hard-earned discernment skills to work through it without anyone else in the room even realizing it!

One realization that was especially tough to swallow was that I am not a good manager. Ouch! This one hurt me to my very core. I've always hated being told what to do, and in turn, it sucks the life out of me trying to "force" the actions of others. As a professional and an adult, I expect people to do their job and communicate back if they need support. I have come to see that I'm not good at managing simply because I don't like it.

On the flip side, what gives me solace now is that my team has told me that I am an inspiring, supportive leader who truly cares for them. In trying to find a way to recapture my energy, I came to realize that what fulfills me most is helping others see their own potential, especially when they can't see it for themselves. Nothing lights me up more than finding out what people want and then encouraging them to find a way to get it. I love seeing someone transform into a better version of themselves and learn how to recharge their batteries through those efforts, whether developing a healthier relationship, achieving an income goal, buying a new house, or taking a much-needed vacation.

The Repair Kit

For me, healing came in the form of tiny actions.

Some I do every day, and others I return to if I start to feel the negative energy rising. The list below came from my personal coaches, podcasts, and various authors.

- GRATITUDE: Before my feet hit the floor in the morning, I use my fingers to do a gratitude count. Big things on my left hand (my kids, my husband) and small things on the right (clear sky, a needed call from a good friend). Affirmations have never worked for me. You have to truly feel grateful for things to change.
- HIGH FIVE: I give myself a "high five" in the mirror. (Yes, it's as cringeworthy as it sounds, but it works.)
- MOVE: Moving my body helps me release emotions and changes my energy.
- JESUS: I read my *Jesus Calling* book or App.
- MEDITATE: Even if it's just for five minutes. I mostly use the Insight Timer app or YouTube.
- SLEEP: I use sleep buds at night and listen to meditations to help me stay asleep. Yoga Nidra is my favorite!
- JOURNAL: I write to get to the bottom of triggers. I rant through the highs and lows of my emotions to allow them to pass.

Life Truths I've Come to See

Grief is tricky and can rear its ugly head in the most inopportune moments!

It is not just the loss of a beloved person. It comes in the form of something that didn't happen, something that should have happened but didn't, or something that will never happen.

You can be surrounded by people you love and who love you and still feel agonizing loneliness.

Sadly, most people cannot understand the depths of your grief until they inevitably experience it for themselves. I have learned to forgive people for that. It's simply not their fault.

When you start to heal yourself, you will be surprised by how much others respond in kind. Once I realized how defensive I was and dropped my "dukes" in conversations, I noticed others being more open in return.

If given a chance, people will rise to be the best versions of themselves.

Seeking the external "magic pill" is an illusion. I have learned that true healing is an inside job.

The energy you put into the world is precisely what you get back. So if you feel a negative spiral starting, find some tools that work for you! Once you learn to start "allowing versus forcing," you will see things begin to flow to you.

The concept of "what you resist persists" has also been a tremendously hard lesson. The more resistance you feel, the more you need to take the leap!

It still takes lots of practice, but I can now use the perceived negative things that happen as another opportunity to grow.

My Hope For You: Progress Over Perfection

Are my tools fool-proof? Not even close.

I have found that grieving doesn't really end. It just evolves.

There are still days when I succumb to the lure of a bottle of bubbly, a pint of cookies and cream ice cream, or a Netflix binge. What good businesswoman doesn't love watching the sassy Beth Dutton pull out her crazy on *Yellowstone*?!

But you know what's different now? I give myself grace. The grace to mess up without hating myself for days after.

Things have changed a lot since my time at the nunnery. The COVID-19 pandemic hit, we could have lost our business, and both my parents passed away. They divorced when I was four, so you can imagine my surprise when I lost my dad in August 2020 and my mom the next August. I've continued to grieve the losses, handled two funerals, resolved estates, rebuilt revenues, and made fundamental changes to how I do life and business.

The hardships still come at me, but I now choose to appreciate my progress over unattainable perfection.

Our entire team experienced similar circumstances to mine, and some still endure far worse. Yet, each person continues to pull one another forward as needed, and we are all charging ahead. Somehow, we've even managed to have a record-breaking year company-wide! I have a renewed sense of pride in myself and this amazing group of professionals who found a way to survive (again) and thrive. I no longer live or lead from fear, and I hope others recognize that too.

Paving the Way

At my mother's funeral, I described her as a Renaissance woman, a delicate mix of grit and grace. One thing she enjoyed most was winning verbal debates using her wit and the sarcasm I inherited! But over the years, she lost the ability to communicate verbally, and I, in turn, lost my lifelong cheerleader.

I spoke about her love of butterflies and how I'd been seeing them everywhere since she passed. She was trying to tell me she was finally free! At her burial, tears ran down our family's shocked faces when a giant yellow butterfly kept swooping down on her casket. I was crying and sweating in the hundred-degree Texas heat, smiling in awe, saying, "Ohhhhh, now you believe me, don't you?! I told you she's been doing this!"

Someone very dear to me once said, "I think your mom is trying to show you that it's her turn to take care of you again."

In 2022, my colleagues nominated me for a business award that the *Houston Business Journal* gives out: Women Who Mean Business.

My inner mean girl immediately started throwing a hissy fit of resistance, pummeling me with doubts about my worthiness. What have you done to deserve an award?

It took firing up my mental tools at high speed to quiet her down. Still, I told my story and answered the questions, turning them in just two hours before the midnight deadline.

I felt satisfied that I had honored those who nominated me by sending in a response.

Weeks later, I was walking out of a lunch meeting when I saw an email stating: *"CONGRATULATIONS! You have been selected as a 2022 HBJ Women Who Mean Business Honoree!"*

No way!

Then it hit me. Exactly one year ago, on this very day, I had been exhausted, sweating in a hazmat suit, and sleeping on a blow-up mattress at my mother's bedside. After eleven long years of battling a horrific disease, she had peacefully left this earth.

Seriously, Mom?!!

Earlier that day, I promised to spend the day being grateful that she was no longer suffering, but I also thought it would be nice for her to show herself in some small way.

There was nothing small about that award to me, and she always loved to have the last word!

It's as if she was saying, "I see you. I see all you did for me and others around you all these years, and I know it wasn't easy. Now keep going, girl! I've got your back. But, more importantly, God's got your back."

What if being sandwiched between building a business, maintaining a marriage, and raising contributing members of society while grieving my mom's disease and the death of both parents was all part of the plan? What if hitting rock bottom and dragging myself back up was necessary to equip me to lead others through the same?

That's what I choose to believe.

Surrendering to things outside of my control, doing the work to move through the things I didn't want to face, and seeing myself come back to my own power has been more than just an accomplishment. At times, it feels like a miracle.

But take heart; you don't have to end up at a nunnery to find the miraculous in you.

About the Author

As an entrepreneur and Managing Partner for Talance Group, a boutique recruiting firm focused on Accounting, Finance and IT, Alix Biondo is on a mission to change negative perceptions of her industry. On any given day, Alix, her partners, and her team wear the hats of career coaches, market educators, and at times, personal counselors.

Alix and her husband live in the Houston area with their seventeen-year-old son and fifteen-year-old identical twin girls who are typically better behaved than their 70 pound Aussie-Doodle and 6 pound Schnoodle!

Alix enjoys traveling, speaking to groups about all things recruiting, and serving the community with her daughters in the National Charity League. Soon after this book comes out, she will also embark on 10-week campaign to raise money for the Leukemia and Lymphoma Society.

After being a businesswoman who endured corporate buyouts, infertility and mother's Alzheimer's diagnosis, she has developed a wholly different view on what being a leader truly means. Encouraging and equipping others to face their fears, get past their own limiting beliefs and come into their own power is now her main motivation.

Her chapter is just a small piece of a larger story she hopes to write one day. If just one person reads it and finds it helpful in pulling themselves up off the ground, then her goal was accomplished.

~

Follow her for more information and to help her #FIRECANCER for LLS!

https://talancegroup.com/

linkedin.com/in/alixbiondo

THREE

Kate Birmingham

GHOSTS & OTHER TEACHERS

Part I

Women have sat indoors all these millions of years, so that by this time the very walls are permeated by their creative force, which has, indeed, so over- charged the capacity of bricks and mortar that it must needs harness itself to pens and brushes and business and politics. —Virginia Wolfe, a Room of One's Own[1]

It's April of 2020 and I'm living in Brooklyn. My apartment is a 300- square foot studio on the second floor of a historic brownstown. It has a beautiful balcony with some lavender flowers on the banister. I appreciate these plant friends. They are hearty, indestructible warriors, able to survive my haphazard approach to watering. These are tough times. There is an omnipresent, ominous void in the city. It's the lack of urban sound. It's the endless, lifeless sidewalks, empty save the birds.

I buy binoculars to better observe the bird activity and begin to make up a fictional story, a love triangle, involving the three magnificent cardinals on my balcony. The alpha male, Ferdinand, holds daily morning debriefs for the block. He makes his presence known to his two female admirers who are dazzled by his bright colors and distinct song.

I'm a remote worker now, and I don't own a desk. I try to shop online for one and search "small cute functional white desks for studio apartments," and then realize I have nowhere to put it. If the desk of that description exists, perhaps it would fit in my bathroom? Or the balcony? I wonder if I can type well enough, with gloves on, to work outside in forty-degree weather. I give up on the ergonomic desk idea. I sit on the thin, worn-out cushions of my sofa, using my coffee table as a perch, pretending to listen on video calls by nodding my head up and down.

I decide to re-read *Driven to Distraction*, a book I last read at Boston University's School of Education while doing my student teaching work. The book causes me to reflect on my life and my childhood. Edward M. Hallowell and John J. Ratey write, *"I can think of no more precious resource than the spirits of our children. Life necessarily breaks us all down somewhat, but to do it unnecessarily to our children in the name of educating them—this is a tragedy. To take the joy of learning—which one can see in any child experimenting with something new—to take that joy and turn it into fear—that is something we should never do."*[2]

ADD and ADHD is frequently kept hidden within family units, a manageable neurodivergence made worse through secrecy and shame. Surely, I must have known on some level that I had an undiagnosed attention disorder myself. I went into education hoping to heal and educate myself, though I didn't know it consciously at the time.

Ferdinand chirps again on the closest branch. I can't finish the book because I'm looking out the window, staring at the bird love triangle. I stand up at five-minute intervals to get a glass of water or to top up the water I just poured, pacing the room aimlessly, looking for trinkets on the shelf to dust, pacing, pacing. I'm tired and uninspired and feel claustrophobic, as though my studio's four walls are getting closer together each day. It's like a box that is changing dimensions. It's like a slinky that is crawling back to its original shape, as though when I first rented the apartment the walls were at their extended capacity and they have now retreated back to stasis. I can't sleep, thinking perhaps there's a ghost in the apartment. The fire detector has eyes that actually blink. The coffee table/nightstand/desk (a table of many uses) is making eerie noises at 3:00 a.m., as though someone or something was standing on it, peering down at me.

Part II

It's a quiet comfort to sit at my desk today reflecting on this challenging time in my life and on all the people who supported me. During that spring and summer of 2020, I became part of a women's group that met during full moons and new moon cycles. It was facilitated by an amazing coach, a friend who is an astrologer, artist, and all-around great human to spend time with. When new women joined these online sessions, we would go around in a circle sharing something about ourselves. Each time I was asked to introduce myself and my work, I cracked a joke, usually at my own expense, something self-deprecating to the point of self-harming, like, "I have very little ambition" or "I'm not creative, that's why I work in finance." I pretended that my cup was full by having hobbies and friends, enough to make up for any feeling of sadness I had over my career and dissatisfaction at work. If there really was a ghost in my apartment, peering out of the fire alarm, I'm certain she saw right through my self-deluding. My peers and mentor certainly did and were helpful in helping me learn to tell my personal and professional story with self-respect and honesty.

Up until a year and half prior to the pandemic, I had worked as a teacher and an administrator in K–12 education for fifteen years. I became a teacher for the same reason that a lot of people "choose" career paths; I sort of fell into it. I started by working in adult literacy as an ESL tutor to help pay for college, and then I decided to become a certified high school history teacher. Working as an educator is a noble profession, and I'm proud of the time that I spent in schools helping children grow. I lived in Europe (Hungary and Belgium) for a total of seven years, both teaching and building an international English curriculum across all school subjects. I eventually returned to the

United States and continued to work in NYC schools, helping support students with special education needs.

One of my favorite movies growing up was Disney's *The Little Mermaid*. I channeled my inner Ariel when I made the bold decision to strike out of public education and into learning and development for adults in 2019. I wanted to see "a whole new world," spread my fins, and shed my familiarity and school pencil shortages behind. I was in search of something bigger and, frankly, better paid.

I found a position working in learning and development at a financial services company. It was the kind of place that, in retrospect, seemed to offer more job perks and trendy office decor than *actual* career development. Unfortunately, from day one, it seemed clear that my manager did not like or respect me. I was given very little feedback or guidance; my job description to "transform learning culture" was fuzzy at best. I received a review where I was told I was underperforming. Nebulous phrases in my review, such as "we had hoped you would bring more to the table" or "you don't really fit in here," were confusing and demoralizing. During video calls with my manager, I tried to hide my tears and then gave up the effort, hoping the Zoom pixelation would make my face fuzzy and my emotional distress undetectable.

Following each difficult call I would recommit myself to improving. On one particular occasion, I received an assignment to build a presentation. I checked in with my manager regularly before delivering it to her. She reviewed the assignment and said, "This isn't what I wanted." She denied that she had asked me to build a presentation with those components in the first place, despite having had multiple conversations (and entire email chains) with me about this topic. I looked up the word "gaslighting" in the dictionary, oddly satisfied that I could now really define for myself what this term meant and, more importantly, what it *felt* like.

Increasingly, my interactions with my boss reminded me of hurtful aspects of my childhood; namely the feeling of not being seen, heard or respected. The unspoken message was to be quiet and take up less space. In my confused, distracted state, ruminating late at night in my cramped apartment, my mom and my boss morphed into a gigantic two-headed monster, staring at me through the fire alarm, a real ghost, mocking me for not having power in my relationships.

As much as I tried to set boundaries with my manager and to reclaim my power, I found it *so* difficult. Naturally self-aware, I knew I had always looked toward women in positions of authority as pseudo-mothers, desperately hoping they would pay attention to me, be kind to me, and guide me. This mother wound deeply impacted my interactions with women over the course of my career. It led me to feel continually disappointed and disempowered.

Part III

"What may appear to be an arrow or a sword we can actually experience as a flower. Whether we experience what happens to us as obstacle and enemy or as teacher and friend depends entirely on our perception of reality. It depends on our relationship with ourselves." —Pema Chodron[3]

My stories of women in leadership from my working life defy clean structures or simple morals; they can't be put in a box or given a label. These women are neither heroes nor villains; they are just ordinary people who did the best that they could with the resources (spiritual, emotional, financial) available to them.

All the female leaders I worked with, regardless of whether they were "good" or "bad" managers, have led me to see the world differently. They have been a mirror, showing me where I was stuck and where I needed to grow. My manager throughout 2020, through those Zoom calls on my dilapidated sofa, taught me to love myself more. She pushed me to such a level of discomfort, a feeling of being actually haunted, that I had no choice but to *listen*. Listen to the ghosts of the past, listen to the discomfort in my body, listen to my attention difficulties, listen to my peers and friends and chosen family who offered kind advice. This attention inward led me to seek out treatment for my ADHD, to quit my job, and to find a new position on a more collaborative team.

I propose that leading is a very *ordinary*, rather than extraordinary, act. There are many books, podcasts, movies, and other art forms dedicated to depicting leadership, and for good reason. It's an important human action. But leadership isn't just grand gestures made by politicians and CEOs. It's much more subtle than that. Each time we walk down the stairs to feed our trailing cats, we are leading. Each time we vote, we are leading. Each time we offer a friend advice, we are leading.

What matters most and what's really worth discussing is the ripple effect that leadership creates, the virtuous cycle of healing and transformation. If we are led *astray*, as I often was by both family members and past managers, we can choose to see that as interesting information we need to learn from, and we can transform our lives through that experience. If we are led to places that bring us great happiness, that's also interesting, and we can get curious and call in more wonder and joy into our lives.

We learn our own leadership style through both positive and negative interactions with others. My flavor of leadership ice cream is to practice magnanimity and to put things in perspective. I aim to confront something difficult while smiling because I know it is not the final act. Reactivity and impulsivity are roadblocks I steer clear of, striving instead to be a steady, dependable, and approachable leader. I know that life is full of passing joys and painful moments, "great" managers and not so great ones, sand castles in the sands of our lives that change and evolve as time passes. True leadership is the ability to lead *yourself*. No authentic management or collaboration, whether personal or professional, can come from a place of personal lack. I'm grateful to be on this leadership journey, cultivating love and respect for myself and then radiating it outward.

---

1. Woolf, Virginia. (2015) 2015. *A Room Of One's Own (Annotated)*. HarperCollins. https://www.perlego.com/book/3183580/a-room-of-ones-own-annotated-pdf.
2. *Hallowell, Edward M. Driven to Distraction. New York :Pantheon Books, 1994.*
3. Chödrön, Pema, *When Things Fall Apart: Heart Advice for Difficult Times*. Boston, Shambhala, 2002.

About the Author

Kate is an educator and learning and development professional with a big imagination. Her background is in K-12 education but she now works with adult learners, including HR teams, life science professionals, and corporate compliance teams, building blended learning programs that are memorable and engaging.

Kate is also a certified meditation instructor. She leads guided meditations for small groups with the aim of helping people feel grounded and centered. In all of Kate's endeavors, both personal and professional, she leads others with humility, curiosity and generosity.

Kate's friends describe her as someone who is truly "in the moment." She frequently loses track of time and is fashionably late. Her personality is friendly and quirky with a healthy dose of New York pragmatism. Above all, she sees life as truly abundant. She is passionate about the ecosystem, bird behavior, spirituality, and the human condition. She enjoys yoga, hiking, ceramics and watching funny cat videos.

Kate also speaks fluent French and loves to travel. Some of her favorite places to travel include Vietnam, Borneo, the South of France and Colombia. She lived for 7 years in Belgium and Hungary at the start of her career, helping write international curricula, teaching children and building school communities.

Kate lives with her partner, Jonathan, in the Hudson River Valley in New York state. Her preference is to clean up afterward, rather than to cook.

~

To get in touch with Kate, reach out on LinkedIn and say hello.

in linkedin.com/in/kate-birmingham-0b750660

FOUR

Aryana Charise

CHOSEN: HOW CAREGIVING IS AT THE CORE OF FEMALE LEADERSHIP

We e all make choices in life and choices make us. Ever wondered, *why me?* I once wondered the same yet now I say, "yes, it is me." I choose my destiny.

Hearing the words of my mother saying, "the pain is gone" brings a smile to my face. After years of chronic pain, she awakens on Christmas day pain free. This is one of the best Christmas gifts ever. I am ecstatic and so very grateful. The journey to recovery has been long and filled with lessons that I deem priceless. It started five years ago when my mother went to her primary physician for a check up. Additional tests were done, and she was informed by her doctor of an aneurysm near her left kidney. She decided to have surgery to rectify the challenge with the intention of saving the kidney. The aneurysm was removed as well as the kidney in the procedure. Months later, Mom was scheduled for left knee and left hip surgery all within the same year. She loved traveling the world and wanted to get back to enjoying going to countries on her bucket list, including Israel and Italy. What seemed like the answer to relieve pain ended up being the beginning of a long journey that worsened over time.

Mom was diagnosed with rheumatoid arthritis, osteoporosis, and cachexia after discovering a severe mineral deficiency. She began losing weight, and her body became extremely frail. She dropped twenty pounds and then lost the use of her left foot. She went from being active to using a walker and then a wheelchair. I took her to many doctors in search of a solution to give her the quality of life she deserved and desired. I refused to give up. I encouraged her daily by asking her, "Mom, what are three things you are grateful for?" She would say, to be alive, her family, and her strength. Mom is a fighter; she always has been. I reminded her daily that she is happy and healed. I even created a sign and placed it in the bathroom where she can see it. We prayed together and asked God to heal her body. I have faith and so does she. We believed that all things are possible for those who believe and are called according to God's purpose. My mom has always been my hero, and I considered it my duty to do all and everything possible to assist her in this journey. It has been amazing what happened along the way.

Each day was and still is an adventure. Mom loves music, so I played her favorite songs throughout the day. We watched her favorite television shows: *Family Feud, The Andy Griffith Show, Gomer Pyle, U.S.M.C.,* Chicago *Fire, Law and Order SVU,* and *Deal or No Deal.* I encouraged her daily as we planned her next travel adventure. I asked Mom, "So, where are we going? If you could go anywhere, where would it be?" She chose Israel and Italy. We talked about each city and dreamed about what we would enjoy. I discovered the importance of creating a support system for her. Friends would call and ask about Mom, and I would call them back with her nearby, which cheered her up. Friends brought her flowers and promised to bring her more as she continued exercising. I arranged to have physical therapists come two to three times a week. Mom resisted getting up in the morning, and I decided to create games to get her up and out of bed. One game was "Roll, Mama, Roll" in which she would roll out of bed and land on her feet. She would tell me anything she could think of to stay in bed as long as possible. She would ask for just ten more minutes, and I would give her ten. I then asked her to "pinky promise" that she would get up and roll out the bed. I reminded, "Mama, you pinky promised." She would grin then finally roll over and get up.

One day she got up and then turned around and went back to bed. I reminded her that her doctor advised her to get up and stay up as long as possible to get her muscles moving. I hugged her and told her how much I loved her and kept her focused on healing. I prepared her favorite foods and teas. She loved the smell of salmon and liver and onions. Many days I would wake up early to get as much work done prior to waking Mama up… After waking her up, we did our daily prayer followed by our exercise routine, and I realized in order for this to work, it required doing it with her. She complained at first, and we did it anyway. I focused on results instead of feelings. Afterward, I asked if it worked, and she replied, "yes, it's better."

Some days the pain intensified, yet we pushed through and followed the routine. I found ways to reward her for her persistence. She loves green tea with honey and lemon. So, I often promised her a cup after she completed her cardio exercises or lifting her two-pound weights to build upper body strength. It was suggested that Mama take epsom salt baths, though she prefers sitting in the steam shower. We alternated until I saw the results from the bath outweigh the shower. She had difficulty at first getting in and out of the tub. I requested the assistance of a physical/occupational therapist who showed us a technique to make it easy. She recommended we install a mount on the tub as well. Team work is greatly appreciated. It truly took a team to get Momma back on her feet literally. When I needed assistance, I reached out to Josy who became Mom's aide when I was away. She bonded with Mama and took care of her with love and patience. I will always remember how she did kind gestures for Mom, including painting her fingernails, which Mom loved. Josy prepared her meals and encouraged her to exercise. It is such a blessing having people in your life who can be trusted to help out as needed. It was a breath of fresh air because caregivers are human, although we often appear supernatural.

Self -care is important and highly advised in order to stay fueled up and ready to serve. One activity that helps me most is connecting with nature. I take daily nature walks first thing in the morning to start my day. I exercise daily. I enjoy walking, cycling, swimming, and rebounding. Variety is ideal, so I change my routine up frequently. Music is an integral part of my life. I love to sing, dance, and play. I find music uplifting and peaceful. It has helped me in so many ways to maintain my happiness.

I am so grateful that Mom is a great cook who took the time to teach me how to cook along with my grandmothers who taught me how to make the best salmon croquettes and grits, homemade banana pudding, iced tea sweetened perfectly, and lemon pound cake. As a child I would watch and ask a lot of questions and then do what Mama and my grandmas told me to do...add a pinch of salt and trust your instincts. Now I get to cook daily for Mama all the recipes I have gathered over the years. It has been a fun adventure creating new recipes for her, and I have to share that she loves my liver and onions.

Funny, growing up I never cared for that recipe, and when she asked me to cook it at first I found a local restaurant to assist me. One day they were out of liver, so I went to the grocery store and bought some. I prepared it and Mom said, "Who made this liver?"

I replied, "Mama, I made it just for you."

She said, "Baby, it's delicious."

It boosted my confidence and I made some more, adding gravy to go with it and her favorite corn bread. My cooking skills have dramatically improved thanks to Mama. I now plan out the weekly menu in advance on Sunday to add variety and ease to the week when buying all the ingredients and preparing the meals. I discovered through research that certain foods aggravate arthritis, including trans fats, processed foods, and sugar, so I altered Mom's diet. She was eating sweets and processed food, which was replaced with baked, roasted, and grilled dishes as well as fresh vegetables and fruit. She hydrates with fresh filtered water and green tea. Daily supplements replaced prescription drugs. Her liver was strengthened. Trace minerals, exercise, and adequate sleep were taken daily, and epsom salt baths were taken weekly. Patience, consistency, hugs, kindness, caring, and sharing all contributed to Mom's miraculous recovery. When I first discovered the diagnosis, there was great concern, especially for her severe mineral deficiency. I wondered why she was dropping weight in spite of eating and having a hearty appetite. I took her to doctor after doctor searching for what was needed to restore her body. I am grateful for all the tests, recommendations, and advice received along the way.

Love is key. Everyday is filled with triumphs and challenges. I choose to do what is necessary to reach the goal. The goal of being happy and restored would not have been possible by focusing on how the circumstances appear. Stop looking and take action; daily actions create habits, and habits lead to transformation. My life has transformed as I helped my mother transform. I did what I knew to do and asked others when I did not know what else to do. I am unstoppable. I am determined. Persistence paid off greatly.

"I am no longer in pain." To hear those words from my mother on Christmas Day after years of chronic pain brought joy to my soul. Those words made all that we endured worth it.

On this journey I have discovered that simple habits make a significant impact. Sunlight has done wonders for both Mom and me. When I started walking daily, I noticed an immediate boost in my energy. I love the fresh air and being outside with the squirrels, deer, ducks, and dogs. It has become something I look forward to each day. In fact, I walk rain or shine. After experiencing these benefits personally, I suggested Mom go outside. She refused. As she observed my consistency, I suggested we have breakfast on the porch. She agreed. I prepared her favorite healthy foods, including soft scrambled eggs with cheese, turkey bacon, fresh fruit, avocado, and juice. I set the table with flowers and invited her to join me. She loved it. While she was enjoying breakfast outside, she was soaking up natural vitamin D. It boosted her mood and energy level. Amazing results with patience and persistence.

Mom's doctor recommended she move to alleviate the stiffness. I called to request physical and occupational therapy for her. The therapists started coming three times a week, which was helpful. It motivated

Mom to wake up knowing company was coming to see her. The exercises got her moving in the direction of less pain. In between therapy sessions, I encouraged her to exercise daily by walking, cycling, and lifting light two-pound weights to build upper body strength. These daily exercises made it easier to get in and out of the tub for Mom's epsom salt baths. Though Mom prefers showers, the baths were beneficial in easing constipation and reducing stress and pain. When Mom resisted, I reminded her of how she feels after the bath. Always focusing on results makes the difference.

Being a great caregiver requires strong leadership skills. I realized now that I was chosen to do this and do it to the best of my ability. My father taught me when I was seven to strive for excellence always. Once, it was my week to do the dishes, and I decided to go to bed before finishing my chores. Daddy worked the evening shift, and when he got home around midnight and saw a sinkful of dishes, he woke me up! I received a valuable lesson that night to never half do anything. To this day, I still hear Daddy's voice when I ever consider half doing anything. Excellence is the key to success.

After graduating from Emory University, I accepted a position with the Coca-Cola Company. I worked my way up to a management position, though I encountered challenges. One of the challenges was managing a team that lacked motivation. While some employees would show up, others arrived late. Some employees did not show up or call in to work. I found it frustrating to have to call adults who were irresponsible and unappreciative of having a job. I asked myself, *What can I do to resolve this issue?* I believe it is important to look internally first for a solution. I checked my attitude. I want to create an atmosphere where employees can thrive. I observed what other managers were doing to increase morale. I looked for opportunities in the midst of the frustration. I interviewed the employees to find out what was working and what was in need of improvement in our workplace. I discovered that they were coming to work to pay the bills and were not happy being there. Some employees felt underpaid, and others shared that they were not challenged in their position. I created a recognition program in the department to reward and inspire employees to do more and be more. I believe we all have gifts and talents uniquely given to us that if developed can significantly impact those around us and perhaps transform life as we know it. What is that gift? It may be something small or it may be developed already. Let's explore on this journey the gift and create unlimited possibilities of its usage.

Training and life experiences prepared me for the journey to nurture my parents as a caregiver. I love my family. I was often asked by my great grandmother, grandparents, and parents to assist them along their journey as they entered their seventies and eighties. I was there for them just as they were there for me. I am so thankful for their many contributions that have matured me into the woman I am today. My parents, grandparents, and great grandmother taught and trained me to be diligent, persevering, generous, and caring. My mother and grandmothers taught me how to cook. My grandmother made the best banana and pineapple pudding from scratch and bought me my first double boiler when I was nine. To this day, I scrutinize every banana pudding to her standard of excellence. I spent quality time with my family. My dad taught me how to be a defensive driver. Mom taught me how to multi-task and get even more done simultaneously by delegating tasks to others. My mom excelled with the gift to sell. She was successful in sales and inspired me to become a salesperson as a teenager. Thanks to her I became a successful marketing director at Eagle International. We traveled to different cities and countries promoting health products and helping people feel better. My grand father was a poet. He inspired me to share my words and showed me how the fewest words can go the furthest. My great grandmother Clyde was an entrepreneur. Her gift was using a needle and thread to create extraordinary clothing.

One day she shared her concern with me that she did not want to be the only one in the family who could sew, so she offered to teach me and I became a seamstress. These lessons taught me patience, perseverance, and attention to detail. My grandmother Gertrude was another remarkable role model. Her gift was to love everyone. She was excellent and taught me the power of forgiveness and the importance of loving the unlovable. I could call on Granny any hour of the day, and she would answer and share wisdom that made a significant impact on my situation. She always reminded me that everything was going to be alright. My great grandmother Beatrice was a disciplinarian. Her gift was being stern and enforcing obedient behavior. I will never forget that when she was a baby her crib caught on fire and she was rescued. I am truly grateful for her life and the lessons taught by her tough love.

Life is beautiful. It is filled with people who are gifted beyond measure. I believe in the gift and encourage others to cultivate and expand. Share the gift and watch what it produces.

Taking care of my parents has been the most challenging yet rewarding task I have accomplished. Growing up, my father and mother always supported me in my academic and extracurricular pursuits. I excelled in school and sports because of the values and determination that both my parents instilled in me at a young age.

When challenged, I remind myself of the power of love. I practice daily affirmations, self-care, and focus on the goals I set for myself and for those to whom I give care. I make choices knowing that I am chosen. Being chosen is an honor. It is demanding. It is often challenging, yet it is remarkable in so many ways.

About the Author

Aryana is a leader who has applied her leadership skills in an extraordinary way to nurture and heal others. She is a graduate of Emory University and wellness coach. Aryana has been mentored by, trained and shared the stage with legendary Motivational speaker Les Brown. She was chosen to nurture, love, and care for her great grand-mother, grandparents, and parents. The choices made by Aryana have inspired others to live life with intentionality. These choices resulted in creating a beautiful life and happiness beyond measure. She resides in Atlanta, GA and enjoys traveling, hiking, cycling and sailing . Aryana speaks, coaches, and inspires people to live a rewarding life while being of service to others.

For speaking and/or coaching, contact Aryana Charise via
www.sleepmbiohealing.com/aryana

in linkedin.com/in/erika-mckay

FIVE

Lisa Clapper

FINDING YOUR YAY: EXTENDED PLAY

*I*ntro: Welcome in!

Join me on this deep meander. It's broken into nineteen album tracks and interludes and goes nicely with your own magical musical beats.

You could power through this chapter with the remains of your power suit or you could drop into sections and pull them apart—gooey, chewy. Take breaks. Find your pace. Yours alone. Play it with your favorite list. Bring snacks. Look for signposts and cobblestones.

It's packed.

And you might lose track—I do, all the time. It usually wraps around and sometimes what's left flapping in the wind is the in-exacting of interacting.

Poetry is no trivial pursuit—as I learned at the beginning of a pandemic.

It's lyrical and musical and deep and wide. It's an unending source of combinating connection. It's random writing from thoughtful prompts that turns into sweeping swaths of being swept up into joy and belonging through the sacred portal of Zoom week after week.

It's women calling you a poet and learning you always were one. Apparently. Even before we all took an unscheduled break from endless expectations of extroversion. It was exactly what you needed to write into the middle of your life.

This is one of the tales I wish to tell before the fairy circle of the redwood tree encapsulates me for the next generation—feeding all of you through roots and shoots, hugs and many *many* pairs of kick-ass boots, while you feed me.

Confirmation that who we are and what we do matters.

Especially if we do what we do as who we are.

Track 1: About this

Step inside this Yayful ride
My work's alive
It doubles as art
It's the leadership of falling apart
Putting each other back together again and again
in full view
Pleats and darts
Pretty smart
You can break it apart

Anywhere is the place to start
Jump right in
Jump around
Get ready to play
outside the lines

Interlude: What is Yay?

Yay is how and why I do my thing
It's your very core
the thing you are
when you're not keeping score

Elevation inside revelation
Escalation
Arms in the air
Wave 'em like you just do care

It doubles up when you share yours with mine
And ripples out as pebbles creating good treble
in a pond of venn
diagrams of how, where, and when

By the simple act of you being here now
the work I create becomes a cohabitation
Even more than it already was
An impartation of meaning and meditation
A deep bow to your wow
A double Yay

Now back to our previously scheduled poetic ramble…

Track 2: Refrains of begending

This track is about the ways
we make our way
through
to each other
into the very depths of ourselves

In converse
reverse
rarely terse
this is not a curse
it's a whole universe
inside verse

It's love of self off the shelf

Unfrozen cores that thaw
melting all over the floor

Sometimes even in hidden corners of
glass-lined offices and u-shaped cubes
In awe of shells cracked
gobsmacked

It's the past
It's the here after
It's the prelude to an interlude
of a paper graph
You can do the math
Whenever you read this it's always now

It's the animated aftermath and the
powHER of reflection
no predilection for how it was before
or needs to be
rather a call to come back around to
the person you were
inside the person you are
no fuss about who you used to be

time and again
around the bend
befriending yourself
as each beginning
meets its end

Track 3: Retrospective perspective

this is me speaking
with the time and distance
to tune into
what's directly in front
brave enough to be swept up
blown back
into the
side wind of the
sidestep of
off treks
and crooked necks

finding true delights and
tender disciplines
all the way in the back of the cave
every trip in
up
left out
lost in the middle
wrong turn on the way in
back out

taking part
as a matter of course

Track 4: The fog transmogrifies

the labyrinth expands and
accepts your doubt
as you wonder about
transmuting
unmuting
low-falutin

let's keep on rooting down
and for each other

the fog says why
this is how you
transmogrify
the lessens into heights
that are the lessons that
learn you into next
resurrect
introspect
if it feels a bit circumspect
stay with the poet

this is a coming
at any age story
about
becoming your about

becoming about us

Track 5: Out East

did you know the candescent clown
used to work at a circus that traveled
town to town?

mostly between park avenue south
and the north shore
of a fishing lure
flights not so fancy
props propel us
sometimes we dance and hit the ceiling hard
after jr crashed on a similar path
you land safely shaken up

not the last time you're grateful
you didn't die on a business trip

in a place you scavenge and hunt
meeting kind witches on Salem tours
who remind you that different is beautiful

aura chakra
stop watching the clock
a tick
can be a shock when time stops

wearing a two-part shoulder padded
knockoff
skirt suit
pole climbers
horizon skyers

the condensation of that perfect storm
might cool you down
or warm your furrowed brow
and open your third-eye into a fourth try

or something resembling the upturn of your mouth

Interlude of gratitude

It feels so good to feel so much gratitude
it radiates out the woods
Into the coulds

We left behind the shoulds
I should say
we are on that never-ending journey
to chop that would
into the kindling
that lights
the controlled burn
of the uncontrolled learn

She's on fire
drop
stop
roll
butter us whole
alt
delete control

Track 6: Voices and Friends

I am not one voice
I am not one choice
I harmonize all the voices contained within me
the voices put there unwittingly and willingly
that are a part of the fits starts
profound
pro found
amateur town
all the parts that roll around inside my burial mounds
all the places and people
who couldn't contain me

All the countless Friends I found on the islands
I visited on my multi-stop tour
I played around singing in the round
Standing room only
Climb on board
She's a broad

Here in the legato of a vibration
I give you an ovation
the storied folk who
re-formed me in swirly seas

All of you who stayed with me —
even if you didn't realize it at the time

We are giants and specks
brain wrecks
full bodied on deck
in a myriad of decks

Lighthouses creating an
archipelago of
ever-changing tides
reachable in strong strides
changing each other
with every beam

Throwing each other more than a line
Showing up
Not by showing each other up
By filling our cups
wondering what's in yours

Interlude: What's in your cup?

What's in your cup?

Spill it
Write it up
Shout it out
This space is about your
Yay
too

Take note
of the dust motes

To annotate
might feel great
No need to wait
put down the weight
this space is for us to generate

I'm hear with you for the whole duration

Track 7: Scoping hope

Scopes of work can sow divisions
tiny incisions
so many revisions of
missions and visions

that time we gave him six hundred names
and he said not a single one
was as high as a six

we don't ask permission
to try a new pursuit
that tastes like persimmon
eighty six that empty suit

by the way
you can be and see in b2b
as long as you are free
to say and see
the people that be in the b to b
People in business
looking to be felt and known
bringing what they've sown to market
so it can shine
to dig it up inside that hidden mine we pack
headlamps
regaling friends with skills
cresting those hills
It's the people outside the lines who
wear reflective clothing
to be seen more clearly
my dear

My people
announcing the pain points of their
hierarchies of needs
Flashes of jumping off points
Equal-size
gaze into eyes up
for climbing the diving board ladder
And plunging well below the surface
We can come up for air
It helps if we share over and over

Track 8: Travel days

Delighting in the magic-quarium
inside apps and snaps
gritty graduation caps
mind-altering gaps
that rewire each synapse

Even the lapses
where we lose ourselves
in the sand traps
It takes a lot of clubs to get out of
the deepest mires
Some rewires
Quite a few new tires on our pull carts

We take lots of breaks and build in travel days
to celebrate and sweat it out
we carve seared steaks
drinking in pines and oak-colored stoke
with a full account of creative folk

Strategy queen reveling in the
kingdom of the in between
never reigning with iron fists
on iron thrones
sharing the love of the next episode
resting up on the way home

Sharing the love of sharing the load

In the throes of the pitches that
go without winning

learning the underpinning of
what's worth head-first swimming

Track 9: InteGreat

Joy points to the delight
of a shared insight
Sure beats an in-fight or
the need to be cool or right

still working on that one

giving up the need to be cool
to feed the need to be right

Giving that up to the night

As for building that plane in flight
refueling in mid air
I give up that ghost
it's a cliche with a
no host
bar cart

Iterate
Commiserate
You're good
not great

Isolate

The bell curve requires
we sort folks into buckets

silos make us feel so low

Why do we need to rank and rate?

Make your feedback
a feed forward

Let's move toward
intersect and integrate

now that feels great

Track 10: We go to eleven

Preternaturally Yay
quintessentially a solar array

Turning towards the wide open sky
I offer this glimpse of peregrine
it comes from within

the essence of leading is
following your essence

feeling into the ease of
unsure presence
shoring up
listening for resonance

as an unraveler
on a lifelong tour of
following the contrails that link
our trips around the sun
meteors break into shooting stars
one by one

trust your essence
choose effervescence

Track 11: Broken sticks on the tour bus

All facets reflect what we bring
into the broken light

The occlusions are what make us stand out
I repeat
the occlusions are what make us stand out

draw no conclusions
invite inclusion

There will be contusions
read the bumps on our head
they are slight protrusions
that show us our instead

steeping infusions
in good stead
what sticks with us
will amplify the tour bus

we play well in bands where we can
separate the strands and
hear the clear tones of our
own homing mechanisms

Jump in the car and be who you far
where wound becomes
many pointed star
not north of where you are
Right where you sit
dance
take a stand

Right where you be
is a slipstream of time and space
edit
don't erase

face to face

taste the grace

Track 12: Where are we now?

Right next to me
beside the 8-limbed
bent tree
the fork in the road says
"let's just see what unfolds"

take the wheel if you please
I'll follow your lead

Dropping fresh seeds
you water as needed
put a sign on the house plant
don't drown your roots
watch for new sprouts
we're traveling multi-parted routes
they converge and come alive
in the messy nest
of the understory

The fruits of mycelium are here
for the picking
walk through the forest
in the canopy
we are zipping

drop your crumbs from
an open weave basket
unmask it

face up
buttercup

This is the compost
of stardust

The friendly ghost
of sure trust

Track 13: The stops make the trip

We've so many more stones to lay
along the way
Let's try this way

the mortar matters
as much as the bricks
learn to mix the wax with flow

even what shatters can be melted
rolling bold never gets old
no such thing as too thick
stop for the ones
who hearten your quick

mile markers
tables of orientation
recalibrating is the
temerity of invention

the serenity of intention

If there's drama
we pause and talk to a baby llama
calmer
we add a comma
and bravely drink at the
well of our karma

We pack our bags and take the trip
traveling light or with a bevy
if it gets too heavy we can always
stop for a slushy up on the levee

how far have we come
with the bubbles of our
firestarter?
that micro plane is a charter
inventing new strains of yeast
on every trip back east

The stops make the trip
Make them count
in all amounts

Interlude: Doughy metaphors meet in the mix

We don't overwork our dough

giving it time to rest

stop

develop air
to rise and show us
what we don't know us
before we go us
to another where us
noticing what us
who
when

who then
sticks to our paddle
and drips off
our felt-tip pen?

triple flip loosen your grip
what flips us out into cool whip
can be stirred
counter clockwise
whisking us into the real cream

pausing to savor sweet cinnamon sips
brew some chai and ponder why

Mixing well
Stirring up
folding in the egg whites
slow and nice

Do think twice

It's all right
to think twice

I don't believe there's such a thing as overthinking

Track 14: Trip-ticks

Paddle out
surf in
get on
stand up
Do it again
Get help
Offer witnessing
Lift off

Be the bright wintergreen spark in the night
Don't burn out your parking lights
Play the tunes that take you places
that help you remember
why you go and how you write

Chew the gum that unkinks your works
share the quirks that keep you awake
on the snow globe shake out

Shake it out loud
Break the glass that's stuck in your ass
fly your freak flag at full mast

catch up
time lag
It all goes by
slow fast

What's at first circumspect
reveals everything you didn't expect

never
the less
or
better than

We're awash in the delta
of a coalesce
coming into this reflect

When coming into any reflect
awake is best for
anything that could come next

Track 15: What could possibly come next?

Next—we're swimming
in the slipstream of
blue hours

A pattern flecks into focus

It's been a starred year
for the hark
and dear
the dark and weir is ready
to run clear

It's been a dear year for
letting go the fear
Writing into changing

Rearranging
meshing gears
Being present in arrears

The field is wide
the positions are plenty
wherever we went
message sent
Open up to receive

Work is not a sentence
Period.

Don't let any sentence
run on
too long
without a rest
period.

thunder claps on
and we enter power with

cracking open
our sunny yolks

Track 16: The deep meander breaks open

Take a gander
Once this goose's nickname
was looseleaf

she pulls thousands of pages
out of binders

They unbind her

They unwind her briefs into
colorful pieces

Found peaces

Oh how it feels
to come clean
in the plain air

I don't fit
I belong everywhere

You're a part of me
can you now see?

The glue is glee
The you is we

Let's make art
and
fall apart

Let's make art
and
fall
a part

Track 17: Share Bare

Would you like to share
your heart
with me and
bare your soul?

It's why I came
after all
we're the call

Isn't it the reason
you're here too?

If not
my wish for you
in the wintering season
the spring buds
summer sun
fall leaves
I'm still your bud

We have so many reasons
to roll around in the mud

my hope for you
is that you go deep inside
your inner ride
I'll glide beside
ease the bumps

while you pump
your inner tube
and find the why
that makes you laugh

let loose the cry
that splits you
clean in half

Please share your heart
with me
and be
your soul

Track 18: Almost there

Take it from one
who's come undone
on the run

Now I walk for fun
sit in the sun

in circle
square
breakout
pair

no birds of a feather
we sport extra flair

Leaving it all out in the rare

We don't fit
We belong everywhere

It's a spice told tale
that never gets old
An invitation
lined with the gold
of the cracks
that make us whole

I'm glad you came
I'll meet you there
The messy middle
That's exactly where
we find our
kid-riffic
buzzy
fuzzy
crunchy
cookie
riddle
giggle

we need all the fiddles
and the rhythm section
to play us in

Crispy edges
Gooey centers
We are each our own
chunky
no such thing as
too funky

unsettling
mystery

Don't settle
We're making
history
It's actually
her story
and yours to tell
the Clapper bells:

Please be your soul
and share your broken
unspoken
high heart
dripping soaking
be spoken

I see you
hear you
feel you
am you

Be here with me

I don't fit
I belong everywhere

You don't fit
You belong everywhere

She doesn't fit
She belongs everywhere

They don't fit
They belong everywhere

Track 19: Ending rhymes with reasons

So that's how it is to
share
bare
aware
sending up this Yayful flare

what's it feel like out of your chair?

out there in the rush of care

She met you there
where the rubber melted all over the road
and the toad hopped over and ate
pie a la mode
with the chicken
who still doesn't know why she crossed

she wandered out there
greeting the tortoise
who came out of her shell
bringing her home wherever she goes

Daring you to bring yours too
Daring you to be yours too

We don't fit
We belong—everywhere!

Mic drop
The poet has spoken
unbroken
now she's passing
the mic to you

Please share your heart with her
and be your soul

I promise you it never gets old

We don't fit
We belong everywhere

These are the cracks in the pieces of the stories that make us whole.

About the Author

Lisa Clapper is a poet who has walked the halls and edges of many an organization as a marketer, brand strategist, storyteller, and Yayfinder, somewhat in that order. She founded The Yay Collective in 2017 as a way to create and find more Yay and Collective in the world of strategy and storytelling.

Lisa comes alive in the conversational heart maps that are present in the microns of truth telling and sooth saying that connect humans and organizations to their very essence.

She channels all the people who taught and walked with her into her voice, including you.

When you meet Lisa, she'll lift you up and bring the reflective positive energy of her solar array into clarity, truth, and mutuality. She calls that Yay.

This is her first multi-author writing excursion and will not be her last book. The poems are multiplying even as we speak.

Find her outside—where music scorches your soul, and where humans open up the cracks that show their light. Join Lisa on her podcast, The Yay Show, at the 4-way intersection of inspiration, revelation, observation and possibility.

She's also the co-founder of the TLC Club, which has extensions in wine, music, sunshine, and more. Tom and Lisa Clapper celebrate their anniversary twice a day, every day, at 927. You too can find all your meaningful dates hiding in plain sight on a clock.

~

You can hear the poem of the day and get into lots of Yay at
yaycollective.com.

Her poetic streak is
hiding in plain sight
written on her freak flag
in a swirl of delight

Isn't it time you told a poet your story so she can tell yours?

Website: yaycollective.com
Podcast: The Yay Show

🐦 twitter.com/clapon
📷 instagram.com/yaycollective
in linkedin.com/in/lisaclapper

SIX

AdaPia d'Errico & Jennifer Burnham-Grubbs

WOMEN AND WEALTH: CULTIVATING EMPOWERMENT FROM THE INSIDE OUT

*M*oney: 'They' say it can't buy happiness; it's the root of all evil. 'They' say women aren't great at managing it, often spending on impulse (retail therapy, anyone?) or lacking the knowledge, skill, and authority to make 'good' financial decisions.

Meanwhile, men get the message that money equals power and that they should be the ones in control of it. Traditionally, men have been in charge of household finances and business investments under the propagated assumption they hold inherent strengths to manage them better than women do.

Pause and take inventory of these messages. Where do they come from? Are they yours? Were you born believing them? Or did 'they' (society, familial structures, the media, etc.) write the script, and we all bought into the narrative? Are these beliefs empowering, constructive, fair, and joyful? Who benefits most from these stories? And, are you opting out of, and/or changing them for yourself?

As humans, we're here to learn, expand and thrive. Every single one of us, regardless of gender.

Yet women have been conditioned to stay small and shy away from power. To say 'please' and 'thank you'. To be nice, think of others, and work collectively. To be selfless. To be careful. To stay pleasant, peaceful, attractive, desirable, soft, sugar and spice; not to be iron and steel.

Of Mice and Hawks

Women have historically been offered limited options in a dualistic paradigm: first, it was "marry, or be a spinster" (though a male can be an 'eligible bachelor' or 'man about town'); more recently, it's been the mutually exclusive "raise a family or build a career" (and if you do take the career route, you're paid less than your male counterparts). The latter wasn't even a viable option until the 1970s, and the gender pay gap persists even more than fifty years since women entered the workforce fully. For centuries, females have carried the burden of reductionist labels and subtle yet crushing societal pressures aimed at restricting our behaviors, upward mobility, and financial independence. It's no wonder we've acquiesced, or perhaps succumbed, to playing small for decades.

As a by-product of these insidious patterns, we've been, and still are, largely boxed out of major wealth-building conversations and opportunities. Subconsciously and consciously we've played 'within the game', like a mouse running through a maze to find the cheese. The best little mice run the fastest to 'win' their prize. As women, we tend toward super-performing to get the "A" and hope we'll get rewarded. Sometimes we even get addicted to the race, the "A", the praise, or pleasing others—all for a little piece of cheese.

Meanwhile, the hawk flies overhead, knows exactly where the cheese is, and can swoop down to get the cheese and the mouse itself, as it pleases. Women haven't been taught to be hawks.

On the whole, women invest less and work *harder* to earn more, conflating wealth-building with effort. We excel at saving, finding good 'deals', doing business, and providing value in commerce; but we drastically underperform when it comes to believing in ourselves and our abilities with money, negotiating, and taking on appropriate risk for reward.

Women tend to self-eliminate, hold back, play it safe, play nice, play defense rather than offense, react instead of act, and critique or even sabotage themselves when it comes to finances. We rarely ask for raises or play hardball with demands for fear of coming across unfavorably. We almost never ask for, or expect to receive, anything we haven't worked hard to 'deserve'.

The Moment of Awakening

As founders of Womxn of Wealth (WOW), we, too, subscribed to those same narratives around women and wealth—despite having well-established careers in the financial sector! We first discovered this when, through a casual introduction, we learned of each other's areas of expertise. AdaPia, a real estate investor and formidable specialist in syndicated private equity real estate, and Jennifer, a risk management expert and consultant, spoke different financial languages.

AdaPia would use words and phrases like "REIT" or "dollar cost averaging" and Jennifer would secretly think to herself, *I really don't know what that means but I should*. Meanwhile, Jennifer would talk about IULs with long-term care riders or estate tax offset, and AdaPia would have only a vague idea of what those subjects entailed and judged herself for not knowing enough. It took us over a year of getting to know each other as women (and as humans), and socializing regularly, to even broach the subject of work. When we finally asked each other, "So, what exactly do you do in the financial sector?", we found each other's area of expertise seemed entirely unknown and, frankly, intimidating. Imposter syndrome secretly reared its ugly head in both of us, running the familiar narrative that if we truly were capable women in the world of finance, we'd already know everything the other person was talking about. This inhibiting narrative held so much sway that it felt humiliating to ask any other questions and seek to genuinely understand the other's field.

It was at *this* moment that lightning struck.

We thought about how many other women feel afraid to ask questions for fear of sounding 'dumb'. We thought about how impossible it is for any human being—regardless of gender—to be an expert on the entire gamut of financial subjects, given their scope and complexity. We thought about how men rarely expect perfection from themselves before choosing to assert authority, yet here we were—powerful, knowledgeable, experts— silencing ourselves because we didn't feel we had enough authority!

Nobody expects a hand surgeon to be a cardiologist; both receive respect, so long as they are good at what they do. Yet we both indicted ourselves for our inwardly perceived lack of comprehensive knowledge about any and every fiscal topic in existence.

Until we stopped doing that and started learning from each other, which has made all the difference.

Eventually, it became clear that those inner critics were not serving us, and weren't, in fact, even our own voices or stories. They were narratives we'd inadvertently absorbed along the way. So we picked up the proverbial pen and, rather than retelling false tales, started writing our own.

We did the research and discovered, to our delight, how much the data supports female capability when it comes to *all things financial*. Even in math, science, and other fields of STEM, women have more than enough skills to excel, so long as they believe and understand this truth.

We started having conversations with more women and found that many of them wanted to better understand and openly ask 'dumb questions' about financial matters but felt that structural support for these kinds of candid conversations didn't exist.

So we built the support system and rooted it in a community.

WOW launched in February 2022 as a mastermind for professional females committed to facilitating brass-tacks conversations about money: nitty-gritty, honest, candid discourses with a beginner's mind rather than an expectation of mastery. We share what we do know, as well as what we *don't* (yet) know, and grow together. We address both the inner and the outer work of creating abundance—as sisters—and blow the roof off what's possible and available to us. As we share, ask questions, and learn together, the collective IQ we hold as women discussing all things finance grows exponentially. In the most beautiful way, so does our access, our confidence, our willingness to move into action, and inevitably, our wealth.

What started as an experiment between just the two of us exploring 'what if' has proven, beyond the shadow of a doubt, that the only thing holding women back financially now is *ourselves*, to the extent we allow it. With more women leapfrogging into the role of household breadwinner, the idea that money is 'men's work' is as outdated as the notion that the Earth is flat. We must recognize and step into our power now to flex and leverage it. The tools, resources, and support systems exist; nothing remains but for women to think like hawks instead of mice.

As a real estate investor, AdaPia knows firsthand how strategic investments into assets set the foundation for wealth. As a life insurance and annuity expert, Jennifer knows how important it is for people to diversify their portfolios in a way that goes far beyond 'stocks and bonds'. As we have seen, our own lives transform simply by communicating across silos and learning to ask seemingly 'dumb' questions. We know first-hand that a profound revolution is now possible for all females when it comes to money and finances. And as the co-founders of Womxn of Wealth, we're relentless in our mission to help other women create lives of extraordinary wealth...from the inside out.

The Time to Address this Is Now

Thankfully, in more recent years, women have become highly educated, high-income earners who are breaking numerous barriers in their ability to negotiate salaries, support families, run successful businesses, and financially give back to their communities. Perhaps you're one of them. But many don't necessarily know how to turn those earnings into a wealth-building machine that works *for* them.

By 2030, American women are expected to control much of the $30 trillion in financial assets that mainly male Baby Boomers hold currently —an event that's predicted to be one of the greatest wealth transfers in history (and that's already underway). Ladies: lean in and listen up. The time to understand how to utilize and manage that wealth is NOW.

We'd like to invite you to reflect on a few questions:

1. What would your life look like if you shed the limiting beliefs you hold around money and wealth?
2. Who would you be—really BE—if you chose to live a bigger, highly fulfilling life by taking control of your financial journey?
3. What if you saw wealth as limitless potential you could access with ease and grace?

While our conditioning may come from the outside, deconditioning is an inside job. We all have a personal responsibility to reclaim our power and let go of what doesn't add value to our lives.

We now invite you to reframe some common limiting beliefs, the ones that have kept you small, into *limitless* ones that can help expand your inner worth and cement your place in the world of wealth.

Core Healing Belief #1: Money CAN "Buy" (or at Least Help Facilitate) Happiness

This idea that money can't buy happiness has, over time, gotten lost in translation. Poverty has, at times, been improperly elevated to holiness. There is nothing worse than feeling shame about the desire for material comforts or pleasures. While money won't afford anyone successful relationships or self-love, it's a tool that can facilitate quality time with loved ones and soul-enriching experiences.

When aligned to our core values, generational wealth also allows us to leave the world better than we found it. When used with integrity, money can absolutely cultivate a happier, healthier sense of self—and it allows us to make a positive impact on the world.

So let's start giving ourselves permission to have more. Let's, dare we say it, start *demanding* more.

Core Healing Belief #2: A Scarcity Mindset Leads to Lack and/or Greed, Not Wealth

Those who operate from a lack mindset ultimately believe that there's not enough of anything to go around—wealth included. This is fear-based thinking that drives people to do one of two things: accept a life of scarcity or hoard unnecessary resources for themselves.

On the other side of the spectrum is an abundance mindset, which upholds the idea that wealth is generative and expansive. We can invest in ourselves, those we love, and businesses we believe in. Here, we naturally shift into a state of fluidity where wealth is used to create, build, and generate, fostering an inner flow of generosity that puts wealth to use for productive purposes.

When we shift out of fear around money into love and confidence towards money, our natural abilities support us in creating plenty of it.

Core Healing Belief #3: Women Are Inherently Strong Investors

Thanks to a combination of limiting beliefs and our societal conditioning, women tend to be less confident and less informed about investing than men. According to Fidelity research, women don't often invest outside of their retirement plans. Yet when they do, their returns are better (for example, on average, women who invest in the stock market outperform men by forty basis points).

Women trade less frequently, meaning we tend to hold our investments through market turbulence. And if we don't understand something, we're more likely to ask for help or investigate further before proceeding. We are not risk averse. We are risk aware. Ironically, the same reasons women invest less actually position us to make better investment decisions—*so long as we move into action and don't second-guess ourselves or our abilities.*

Core Healing Belief #4: Money Is Energy

Energy cannot be created nor destroyed; it can only be transformed. Wealth is active; it wants to multiply. When properly managed and allocated, it creates a new narrative of "I can do more." Like everything else in the universe, it's intrinsically programmed to grow.

Whether money is earned, spent, saved, or given, it's simply an energetic exchange supported by a physical medium that indicates value (cash, check, digital receipt, etc.). As such, money is neutral. In and of itself, it cannot be good or evil. It reflects the values of those using it. Money is also a magnifier; it can magnify good or magnify negativity, depending on how WE use its power. The reason so many couples argue about money is it inevitably links with intimate underlying beliefs and/or issues. When AdaPia asks guests who come on her podcast, *Real Wealth Real Health*, how they define wealth, their responses always reflect deeply personal values, a sense of purpose, and making a positive impact.

Once we begin to look at money in this way, we can consciously shift our relationship to it. We realize that money is not something to fear or be ashamed of; it is a tool. And from there, we can begin to wield its power in a way that's aligned with our worldview.

Core Healing Belief #5: You Can Earn More Without Necessarily 'Working Harder'

It's time to shift out of 'I work for my money' and into 'my money works for me.' Time is a finite resource; the idea that we're limited to the wealth we actively work for is burdensome and restrictive. It's also blatantly not true.

Investing, which is a productive application of money, can create a reverberation in which your wealth multiplies, expands, and amplifies. That growth is exponential, and it can be done with relative ease. With the correct investing strategies, wealth-management confidence, and access points, anyone can build sustainable, generational wealth. They can do so without expending their most precious resources: their own time and energy.

When we fully value ourselves, our time, and our worth, we also draw more abundance to ourselves. This seems to be a mysterious and inevitable law of the Universe. It pays to become a hawk and think strategically about how to leverage personal resources for our own benefit, and not just the benefit of others. This doesn't mean we become selfish; it simply means we become 'Self-ish', as in, we stop putting ourselves last, or even out of the picture entirely as so many women still do.

We start thinking, *What's in it for me?* and up the stakes of what others offer us in exchange for what we bring to the table. Whether it's shopping banks to get a higher interest rate, refinancing to get a better loan rate, having a headhunter find us a higher-paying job, or learning to deploy our savings into strategic, well-diversified investments, the same concept rests as the core: we honor our intrinsic validity and worth first, then leverage it, rather than seeking external validation to feel 'whole'.

Turning Our Journey into a Meaningful Mission and Community

When we chose to participate in this book, we asked ourselves this question: *"What are we contributing?* In other words, *What are we doing to enhance, improve, and make an impact on the lives of people who come into contact with this reading?* The answer here is what we consider our 'True North.'

We are launching a revolution, which is the culmination of themes, lessons, and experiences from our journeys into self-mastery and empowerment, especially financial empowerment.

Womxn of Wealth (WOW) is a non-profit organization focused on moving women from financial literacy into wealth mastery. We are a mastermind for financially empowered females committed to purpose-driven wealth. WOW is an aggregated, intimate community of powerful women that finds and shares ways to maximize value in our individual investments and build collective, generational wealth thoughtfully and sustainably.

As WOW's co-founders, we have birthed a dynamic, impactful, inclusive initiative dedicated to empowering all women through grassroots access to brass-tacks financial advice, mentorship, connectivity, and practical guidance on creating personal abundance at every level.

We take a holistic, inside-out approach to wealth creation and management by placing equal focus on the development of wealth and Self. Our goal is to foster safe spaces in which women can dive deep into financial concepts and investment opportunities in order to grow and enjoy their wealth with grace, joy, and ease.

We believe in creating our own reality by doing the inner work and allowing the outside world to reflect back, thus bringing us what we wish to create. It's magic in action, and we're the magicians. Make no mistake about the alchemy that we create: when we access and unlock the power of abundance from within, nothing is out of reach or out of bounds. Nothing.

Do you feel called to join this powerful community? Can you, with your sisters, excavate any lingering, dusty corners of limitation or doubt? Will you claim your birthright to limitless potential with us? Is this the year you will take a leap into a level of wealth you didn't dare to dream of before? If you feel even a shiver of 'yes,' we welcome you to learn more about the Womxn of Wealth mastermind, community, and mission.

Wealth in the right hands (ours and yours) changes the world, and taking wealth creation into your own hands changes your life. This has been our lived experience, and we want nothing more than for other women to feel the same power, confidence, purpose, and joy we feel from having come to understand the importance of financial empowerment. If money is a magnifier, we believe women can magnify the good on this planet by gaining and then flexing access to it. The revolution has begun. Will you rally?

About the Author

AdaPia d'Errico knew from a young age that financial independence was the means to control her own destiny. Despite believing she wasn't good at math, she started working in a bank at the age of eighteen and completed business and economics degrees with a specialization in personal finance. Throughout her more than twenty-year career spanning banking, finance, real estate, and fintech, AdaPia battled inner and outer narratives like "only men can be wealthy" and "don't be greedy, be good." As a connected investor with visionary insights and access to exclusive operators and opportunities, AdaPia has made it her life's work to facilitate the transformation that women go through when they step into the power of wealth.

Co-founder, Womxn of Wealth: https://www.womxnofwealth.com
Host, Real Wealth Real Health: https://cms.megaphone.fm/channel/
realwealthrealhealth
Book AdaPia to speak via her website: https://www.
adapiaderrico.com

 twitter.com/adapia
linkedin.com/in/adapia

About the Author

Jennifer is founder and CEO of Quantum Insurance Services, an award-winning, commissions-agnostic insurance consulting firm passionate about providing clients with best-in-class insurance designs for life, disability, long-term care, annuities, commercial risk, and employee benefits. Jennifer has become a distinguished thought leader within the insurance industry by specializing in plan designs that maximize value, minimize premiums, and tailor coverage exactly around each client's unique needs. By constantly working to create efficiency, transparency, and consumer-first programs within the insurance market, Jennifer helps clients engage safely and successfully with an execution-dependent sector of the financial world that is vital to most portfolios.

Jennifer has also co-founded and launched Womxn of Wealth (WOW), a fast-growing national nonprofit organization dedicated to financially empowering women, so they become more comfortable with taking wealth creation firmly into their own hands. WOW helps raise the collective female financial IQ by creating platforms for education, discourse, and support as females work to balance power dynamics around money and increase their personal abundance on every level.

As co-creator of the Wealth Mastery for Women™ series and currently a featured speaker with LeadHERship Global, Jennifer also supports and guides ambitious, creative women in a monthly webinar that delivers brass-tacks financial information across a wide spectrum of topics. The monthly webinars encourage women to move in the direction of their purpose, their mission, and their dreams with powerful connections, critical support, practical tools, and valuable resources to show up, speak up, and step into their power through financial education.

~

Email: jennifer@teamqis.com
Schedule a call with Jennifer! www.calendly.com/jennifer-bg
Quantum Insurance Website: www.quantuminsuranceservices.com
Womxn Of Wealth Website: www.womxnofwealth.com

in linkedin.com/in/jennifer-burnham-grubbs-she-her-99639a58

SEVEN

Cecilia Dahl

NAVIGATING THE WORKPLACE REVOLUTION: LEADING VIRTUAL TEAMS IN THE NEW PARADIGM

*I*magine yourself on a sailboat, 250 miles from civilization, on your way to a tropical island to spend the winter months enjoying warm weather and sandy beaches. You wrap up a Zoom call with your team and decide to break for lunch and step outside just in time to catch a show from a passing pod of dolphins. Imagine that it's possible to work or run your business from nearly anywhere in the world. This isn't fantasy; it's a true story a friend shared in December 2022.

We are experiencing a workplace revolution. The way we interact with colleagues and teams has fundamentally changed. Advanced technologies now enable us to recruit the best candidates and expertise, as we are no longer limited by physical boundaries. The concept of virtual teams has been weaving itself into our lives for years, but the global pandemic propelled remote work into the mainstream. Business leaders who recognize this as an opportunity and take steps to adapt are poised to succeed, as top talent around the world seek rewarding positions where they can achieve balance between work and family, living in the location of their choice.

In September 2008, I was president of Smart Destinations, a travel technology company I co-founded in 2002. We had grown the business steadily over the years, marketing attraction passes using a proprietary ticketing network. We had just closed on our third round of venture capital, securing the funds needed to upgrade our technology and expand. We were ready to take the world by storm when the world came crashing in around us.

The recession wasn't a surprise, we *knew* it was coming, what we had not foreseen was the magnitude. On September 29, 2008, the stock market experienced its biggest point drop in history. The hits kept coming: the fall of Freddie Mac, Fannie Mae, Lehman Brothers. Americans stopped spending and daily sales reports reflected it. Each day the stock market declined, our revenue followed suit, it was like sledding down a hill without brakes. I spent my days combing through reports of declining sales and trip cancellations, scanning the doom and gloom headlines. There was no sign the economy would turn around any time soon.

In the boardroom, Glenn, our newest investor, sat up in his chair, placed his elbows on the table, and dropped the bomb we had dreaded. "If we're being honest with ourselves," this was his favorite opening line, "we didn't invest in this company to keep the lights on during a recession." He wasn't wrong. The board agreed, and we were instructed to cut costs, "as deep as possible." We hunkered down and made as much progress on the technology as possible to be ready to come back to full operation when the recession was over. The gravity of our situation felt like a dagger to the heart.

We had about thirty employees at that time. We had been very thoughtful to hire the most talented people we could find. They had all taken a leap of faith joining a startup. These were individuals who supported our vision and worked tirelessly to accomplish more than anyone thought possible. In a way, they were my personal heroes. In that moment, I couldn't imagine a scenario where we could lose any of them.

We had physical offices in seven cities around the country. These small offices housed our technical and support equipment as well as local marketing materials. They also provided a space for our local destination teams to work and, critically, gave us a "local" address, which added credibility to our place in the tourism community in each destination. While we were reviewing costs and looking for ways to "cut deep," dropping leases on physical office spaces stood out as an obvious first choice. I knew I wasn't going to be able to keep my entire team, but if I could somehow save money on real estate, I might be able to retain a few more through the crisis.

I had experience with remote work environments throughout my career and some of our teams were already semi-remote, but this was different. Where would we put our stuff? How would the local operations teams function? How would we train and mentor junior staff? How could we keep track of their work? Would we lose credibility in each market without a physical address? Where would we ship things? How would we receive deliveries? How would we make sure the teams had internet and office infrastructure to support their work? The destination teams were small, but they relied on each other and built strong bonds. What would happen when they didn't have any place to "go" to be together? I knew we had to shutter offices, yet I was struggling with the logistics and worried it would have a negative impact on cohesion, productivity and, critically, knowledge transfer. Left with no choice, I canceled all the leases and sent everyone in the field to work from home.

The time that followed was difficult. Adjusting to operating with a fully virtual team was challenging, but in many ways, it was also amazing. I was able to keep a few extra team members, and most were supportive and embraced their new "virtual" status. Surprisingly, some offered to help with storage and contributed an extra effort to attend local networking events ensuring we maintained a strong local "presence" in each market. It certainly wasn't easy, but together we found ways to keep the lines of communication open and put processes in place to make sure we were all on the same page to ensure our clients and partners that they would be supported. We found ways to connect personally and share knowledge so we could continue to thrive without the benefit of a shared space. When the recession ended, we found ourselves surprisingly *stronger*, more *profitable*, and more *efficient* than before.

Initially the recession of 2008 seemed like the worst thing to happen to the company. When I look back on it today, it stands out as the *best thing* that ever happened. Dropping the costs and maintenance associated with physical offices, moving to a fully virtual environment, and learning to be super efficient propelled us to success and an eventual profitable exit. We thought we were lean and nimble prior to the recession. Truthfully, we weren't able to see how much more efficient we could be until we were pushed well beyond our comfort zone. This was the first time I experienced the power of running a business with a virtual team. It forced me to think about the business differently and to develop new leadership and communication skills, and I sharpened my understanding of every role in the company and the requirements to support each role successfully.

I was far from perfect, thrust into my new role. I was challenged beyond my wildest expectations, but the lessons I learned and the achievements we ultimately made as a team changed my view on leadership forever.

Twelve years later, in March of 2020, as I enjoyed a typical day in my new office, I looked up from my laptop for a moment and scanned the clear blue Bahamian waters, pausing to appreciate the warm tropical breeze. My office was now the cockpit of our sailboat. I had spent the past five years building a joint venture in travel analytics with a team based in London, while cruising up and down the coast between Maine and the Bahamas. My new endeavor was going well and life was fantastic!

Even though we were on our sailboat in the Bahamas, we were aware of the growing concerns over COVID-19, which began to spread in a handful of places. We had an inkling there might be some short-term inconvenience and impact on our businesses, but at the time, a full-blown global pandemic felt like an impossibility and all of it seemed a world away. COVID-19 was slow to arrive in the Bahamas, and we continued carrying on our normal routine, hearing rumblings of impending doom but not fully embracing the magnitude of the situation ahead.

Soon enough, COVID-19 was upon us. The Bahamian government, led by a medical doctor, responded immediately. We found ourselves in the unimaginable position of being completely confined to our vessel in full lockdown.

One by one, the phone calls started. My travel industry clients were forced to pause their analytics services until further notice. Business stopped dead in its tracks, as had our adventure and lifestyle. Overnight, our paradise had become a prison.

My way of connecting and coping with world events was to continue to reach out to current and former colleagues and clients in the travel industry to hear how things were going and to maintain a connection with the outside world. I was simultaneously grasping for hope and planning for the long-term impact of the collapse of my business.

As time went on and the world (and we) moved through the stages of grief, conversations changed. My colleagues accepted that this might be a long-term reality, and topics shifted to more practical things, like, "How do we survive working remotely?"

I began to understand that what happened to me in 2008 was now happening to the whole world. Businesses were left with no choice but to close their offices, sending everyone to work from home. From what I could gather, this was proving to be very challenging for many.

Communication faltered, knowledge transfer was limited, people felt disconnected from their teams, and it was hard for businesses to manage productivity or even to know if their teams were contributing. At the same time, I heard about unexpected benefits: more time with family, no more commuting, working from scenic cabins in the mountains or beachfront vacation homes. Some said they would never go back if they could figure out how to overcome the logistical hurdles of working virtually. Many of my contacts reached out to me for advice, knowing that I had been in their position twelve years prior and that I worked remotely building a business from my boat for years.

Before the pandemic, my remote status stood out as an exception. Had it not been for my prior success in business, I don't believe anyone would have taken me seriously. With the pandemic in full swing, things changed. In the "new normal" I was no longer an exception; I had become an "expert" on how to succeed in a virtual environment.

It didn't take long to understand that the workplace entered a paradigm shift and was forever changed. Pandemic or not, remote and hybrid work was here to stay.

Although virtual or hybrid teams have become more common, and businesses enjoy benefits such as access to global talent pools, reduced overhead costs, extended hours of operations, and the strength of diversity in their workforce, leaders discovered (some the hard way) that it's definitely not business as usual when it comes to managing virtual teams. Over the years, I've found there to be three core considerations all leaders need to understand to support virtual teams to reach their greatest potential.

Leading a Virtual Team Requires Time, Intention, and Planning

Without proper planning and infrastructure, virtual team members may feel like they're floating in outer space. There's a void of sights and sounds, which, in co-located workplaces, provides teams with consistent information and knowledge transfer. It's widely accepted that words account for less than 10 percent of our communication. In a virtual environment, it's the responsibility of the leader to ensure that teams can close the gap and optimize communication.

It's essential to plan time for structured team and one-on-one communication, project coordination, and bonding. Guided meetings and pairing less experienced team members with more experienced ones support knowledge transfer and training.

I once asked a CEO who had recently transitioned his company from being fully co-located to 100 percent virtual how his managers were handling the change. He noted that during the transition, teams working with managers who were skilled planners outperformed those whose managers were more spontaneous. The difference? Planners built structure for coordinating projects and responsibilities and streamlining communication; they had detailed training processes in place with feedback and intentional mentoring.

On virtual teams, processes and responsibilities need to be well thought out and communicated so the whole team understands the team's purpose and goals and how the team is expected to work together.

The role of a virtual leader is greatly complicated by this void. Conscious planning and intentional communication are core to success.

Develop and Manage Clear Expectations around Performance and Deliverables

The last time I worked in an office, salaried employees who arrived at 9:00 a.m. and left at 5:00 p.m. were labeled "nine-to-fivers." This was not a positive label if you had any aspirations of advancing with the company. The CEO made it clear that he valued employees who showed up extra early and stayed late. I found myself regularly working from 7:00 a.m. to 7:00 p.m., even when I had no reason to be there. The extra office time was a way to secure management approval but came at the expense of family and friends. I grew to resent the system and, ultimately, it was one of the reasons I left. In a virtual environment, where leaders are not able to physically monitor what employees are doing and how much time they commit to the job, it becomes crucial to establish clear expectations around performance and deliverables.

When employees are paid a fixed salary to deliver a service, *results and outcomes* should be the focus. Similarly, hourly employees should understand exactly what is expected from them for each hour of pay (i.e., number of calls taken, orders fulfilled, words typed, files collated, etc.). If pace and production per hour are part of the job requirement, it should be outlined at the time of hiring and then monitored and communicated regularly if adjustments to expectations are needed.

In December of 2021, the CEO of Better.com made national news when it was announced he laid off 900 remote employees over a Zoom call due to poor performance, publicly accusing 250 of them of stealing by logging more hours into the payroll system than they had worked. Perhaps there was some fudging of timecards, and there may have been a few bad apples, but it's hard to imagine that a full third of the employees were suddenly not performing. It's more likely that leadership failed to: develop and communicate clear expectations around performance; regularly review results; and share feedback; and provide coaching and support to those who were not measuring up.

When you are able to clearly define the results that each employee is expected to deliver, you will always have a basis for evaluating individual performance. This is simplified in jobs like sales or customer service, but other roles may have a higher level of complexity and will not be as clear cut. It may take time and trial and error, but when you and your employees have a clear and detailed understanding of what is expected, you have a foundation for effective performance and trust with your virtual team.

Leading a Virtual Team Is a Two-way Commitment

While consulting for a large financial corporation, I had the opportunity to work with Ronald, the manager of a division billing department. Ronald oversaw a co-located team of staffers based in a corporate owned building in Missouri. As we discussed the team, he shared that he frequently let his "well-behaved" employees work from home as a reward. When I asked him how that was going, he replied that it was okay for a short time, but he had little confidence that moving to a fully virtual team would ever work because he always had to bring people back to the office to reset. In the *same conversation*, he expressed frustration that sourcing and retaining talent in his local area had become so difficult he was not able to affordably fill all open roles.

When leaders take the position that working from home is a form of rewarding good behavior, they are placing the full burden of success on the employee. Businesses need to acknowledge that working with virtual teams is a commitment on both sides. As noted earlier, without proper infrastructure and support, and without a leader who understands how to plan and facilitate communication, even the best virtual employee will struggle to succeed outside the office.

Hiring the right people onto a virtual team is as critical as managing and supporting them well. A virtual employee needs to be self-motivated and a strong communicator and have a positive business mindset. They too must make a commitment to participate in proactive, productive communication, follow processes, support their teammates, and deliver results.

It's only when both parties make a commitment to work together, that virtual teams are positioned for optimal performance.

It was no surprise to me that Ronald's team wasn't adapting to working from home long term. There was no infrastructure in place to support them, Ronald hadn't consciously developed leadership skills to support virtual teams, and the employees had not been vetted or hired with the expectation that they would be successful in a virtual environment. With all these things stacked against them, I imagine working from home might start to feel more like a punishment than a reward.

With some adjustment, and a commitment of time and training, Ronald could have been able to build a virtual team of high-performing employees, with access to a larger talent pool at affordable rates (perhaps even under budget). At the same time, the corporation could have repurposed, rented, or sold the office building and saved hundreds of thousands of dollars in infrastructure costs.

There's no denying virtual teams are increasingly preferred as businesses have access to a global pool of talent, expand operating hours, add diversity to their teams, and reduce overhead. Successfully transitioning to fully virtual or hybrid teams requires a fundamental change in leadership mindset. Businesses need to invest time and make a commitment to support a new kind of employee. There will be trade-offs and sacrifices, but when properly supported, virtual teams can be a powerful force for your business in which rewards will far outweigh challenges.

About the Author

Cecilia Dahl is a seasoned entrepreneur and passionate leader who has spent over two decades driving the success of virtual teams. With her extensive experience, practical skills, and a wealth of research to draw upon, Cecilia has a deep understanding of what it takes to empower leaders to effectively manage and motivate their teams, regardless of location. She is dedicated to helping leaders succeed and has a true passion for providing them with the tools and mindset they need to thrive in the modern, digital workplace. Whether through her writing, speaking engagements, or coaching sessions, Cecilia is always seeking opportunities to share her knowledge and experience with others.

in linkedin.com/in/ceciliadahl

EIGHT

Linda Fisk

STAND OUT BY EMBRACING YOUR FLAWS

"What? You're adopted? That must mean that you are a bastard child. You were born out of wedlock—and in sin! Go stand outside in the hallway!"

I heard the words from my teacher, but I couldn't grasp what they meant. *What is a "bastard" child, and what does it mean to be born out of wedlock?* I was confused, but I could tell from the accusatory tone of her voice, and the alarm and disgust on her face, that somehow, being a "bastard" meant you were repulsive, wicked, and the source of appalling sin.

I could hear the surprised gasps across the classroom, as the other students stared at me with shock. There were whispers and murmurs about the teacher's loud indictment, as I struggled to understand what I had done to cause such a booming reprimand.

I stared, dazed at my teacher's reaction, and I could feel the blood rushing to my face. In my ten-year-old mind, I immediately understood that I was to blame for some sort of detestable act, but as I quickly ran through all the possibilities in my mind, I was baffled. I couldn't understand what I had done wrong. I thought that perhaps if

I explained again, the teacher would understand, and this devastating blow would be quickly cleared up.

"Ma'am, I'm not sure what that means. But, I have a mom and dad—they chose me. From all the kids in the orphanage, they chose to adopt me," I said in a quivering, stuttering, small voice.

When I was growing up, the sitcom *Father Knows Best* with Robert Young, Jane Wyatt, and their three perfect kids, represented what a family was supposed to be. Any family that did not fit into a tightly defined mold consisting of a husband, wife, and three or so children was scandalous. Adoption was considered shameful, and I remember hearing whispered comments for the rest of the year about my identity as an "adopted kid" with pity, suspicion, and sometimes even scorn.

Now, sitcoms treat adoption as an accepted, even beautiful, way to become a family. In fact, in the more contemporary sitcom *Modern Family*, two dads are now often depicted as doting parents, and the entire extended family, which also includes a quirky stepfather–stepson relationship, is devoted to the adopted daughter of these two loving parents.

The shift in TV imagery represents a shift in societal attitudes toward family formation. Adoption is out of the closet and has become part of mainstream American family life. With greater acceptance and normalization has come respect for birth parents and adoptive families, as well as a much more transparent adoption process.

In fact, I had always been told that I was special. My parents desperately wanted to have a child, and I was told that of all the children they could have chosen, they adopted me. That made me unique, chosen, and special. And, I was told that it was good to be different; that being different made you more memorable. And there was no way to hide that I was different and certainly adopted into this family. You see, my father was American Indian, and my mother was Asian—and I was a blonde, blue-eyed, little girl with alabaster skin. So, I didn't look like either of my parents or our extended families. But my parents always reassured me that being distinctive makes you more interesting and being different makes you surprising, which are good things to be.

As a family, we were often described as unusual, different, or strange. In any public outing, I would catch the inquisitive glances, and even accusatory stares, as people tried to fit the puzzle pieces together. Sometimes, we would catch the whispers of those around us, asking about who the little girl really belonged to. Sometimes, the well-meaning stranger would be bold enough to directly ask my parents, "Who are you babysitting for?" or "Who does the little girl belong to?" And, without hesitation, my parents would announce, "She is our daughter" without the need for further explanation.

But my parents would reassure me that it takes courage to grow up and turn out to be who you really are. My parents didn't want me to adopt their culture, their physical attributes, their characteristics, or even their personality. They simply encouraged me to discover who I was and to embrace my differences because those points of differentiation will become my story.

In the years since that embarrassing and humiliating experience with my teacher, I have realized that sometimes your differences will be polarizing, alienating and repellant to others. Sometimes, embracing who you are means intentionally exasperating, irritating, provoking, and aggravating others—sometimes even instigating hostility. I've learned that the more some people hate you, the more other people will love you. And that's okay.

In fact, your differences, what other people may consider to be your flaws, hold the key to what makes you incredibly special. Sometimes being flawed, and being very open and transparent about it, can be the most attractive trait of all. In fact, most people want to follow leaders who are brilliant, despite being human and having flaws.

It's very common for leaders to feel the pressure to assimilate, to acquiesce, to homogenize. As we look at what other successful leaders are doing, what they are saying, what they are recommending, it's natural to emulate them. In fact, this practice has been institutionalized in the process of benchmarking. We try to find out what others are doing right, and then we do the same thing. We minimize our differences, and we begin to replicate the practices of other successful leaders.

But when everyone in an industry starts copying the leaders, over time, the entire industry starts to look the same, feel the same, and sound the same. There are no differences. Nothing distinguishes one leader from another. As Youngme Moon explains in *Different: Escaping the Competitive Herd*, "The dynamic is not unlike a popularity contest in which everyone tries to win by being equal parts friendly, happy, active and fun. Or an election campaign in which all the candidates try to be charming, serious, humble and strong. Once everyone starts doing it, no one stands out." It's a downward spiral of conformity in a sea of sameness.

In the city of Austin, Texas, you'll often see the slogan, "Keep Austin Weird" on everything from billboards, to menus, to T-shirts. Austin, Texas, is absolutely unapologetic about their unique identity, and they have embraced and flaunted their weirdness. Austin has learned how to turn a perceived limitation into a strength. Too often, we are uncomfortable with what makes us weird. What makes us different. It's time to shift that mindset and begin parading those weaknesses, those flaws, and those differences without shame. Show them off.

The best leaders often emphasize their perceived flaws. They admit their mistakes and shortcomings and openly talk about how they have learned from their failures. These leaders focus on the learning, the strength, the resilience, and the growth they have experienced through flaws, mistakes, failures, missteps, and shortcomings. They accent them, feature them, highlight them, expose them, call attention to them, and openly display them. Their uniqueness is a signature part of who they are. They purposefully admit to their points of difference, and they embrace their perceived flaws.

How do you begin to identify those aspects of your story, your identity, your leadership that make you distinctive and different? Make a list of every possible limitation you can think of that prevents you from being the leader that you think everyone expects. Include information about your own fears and doubts, as well as any perceived shortage of opportunities to be a leader that everyone respects and admires. Then examine each one carefully and decide if it's really true or not. You may be surprised at some of the things you've convinced yourself to believe!

You have to deeply understand the consistent themes embedded in your past and woven throughout your life's story because they are the keys to your purpose, and your future. You have to understand your limitations, your mistakes, your shortcomings and your failures and really examine those recurring issues in your life. Carefully examining your past, especially your failures, is essential to knowing your value.

Indeed, failure and flaws are often why successful people achieve such remarkable heights of greatness: They learn from their setbacks, failures, and mistakes, and then get back up and apply these learnings to their next attempt. Some of the most successful people have encountered disappointing setbacks based on perceived flaws:

- Walt Disney was fired from a newspaper and was told he "lacked imagination and had no good ideas."
- Oprah Winfrey was fired early in her career as a TV reporter because she was told she was "unfit for TV."
- Dr. Seuss had his first book rejected by twenty-seven different publishers.
- Bill Gates was a Harvard dropout and started a failed first business called Traf-O-Data.

When we approach our own failures, flaws, and differences with a spirit of generosity, we counteract the sensation of being under attack, being judged harshly. The key is to turn the focus away from ourselves —away from whether our flaws and our failures will be judged harshly by others—and toward helping those around us accept their own points of difference. Showing kindness and generosity to others and helping others see their unique attributes and characteristics engender courage, acceptance, and confidence. When we are kind to others, we tend to feel calmer and less stressed, and we create an environment of acceptance and confidence, allowing others to have the confidence to admit their own flaws and insecurities and embrace their differences.

Ironically, it's being imperfect that makes us real and relatable. We often connect with others over our insecurities, quirks, and struggles. People who are truly interested in you and care about you don't expect you to be perfect; they want you to be authentic. Embracing your imperfections and letting others see the less than perfect parts of you allows you to connect more deeply—to love others and be loved fully.

Fitting in will never lead to success.

Our teachers, parents, and managers all taught us that we need to find and fix our flaws in order to be successful in life. That belief system tells us that we have the potential to succeed, but that we need to be diligent in our effort to fix our perceived flaws and improve what others have identified as our weaknesses. But, fitting in and becoming just like everyone else will never lead to success. It's a recipe for mediocrity.

It is good to be flawed—in fact, it is inevitable. Embrace your unique-ness. Exploit your differences. Confound expectations. Being different makes you rare. Being normal makes you ordinary.

Choose connection over perfection.

You don't have to prove your worth. You don't have to please everyone all the time. You don't have to compare yourself to others. You don't have to measure up to anyone else's idea of beauty, success, or worthiness. Some people will like you—and some won't. And that's okay.

What you'll gain is freedom. Freedom to be yourself, to do what feels right for you, to pursue your interests, to follow your values, to wear whatever you want, to explore who you are. Nobody's perfect, but we all have value—and we don't have to keep trying to prove it.

Choose to let others see your real self rather than hiding behind a facade of perfection.

Your differences make you surprising and memorable.

We remember the unusual events in our lives, not the common ones. When we experience something different, we want to tell other people about it. Surprising experiences are remembered and shared with others.

We remember the people in our lives who are unique and distinctive. If you are remarkable enough, someone might even write a social media post, a blog, or a book about you. Fitting in and following the lead of others simply makes us invisible. If we fit in, we don't get any attention. And, attention is one of the most valuable gifts we can receive.

There are no good substitutes for you, in all your uniqueness.

Being unique is about being different, being unusual and being uncommon. Unfortunately, instead of embracing our uniqueness, we often try to hide it in an effort to be more normal. We tend to focus on the ways we are similar to others, not different. Because of this bias, it's helpful to spend some time thinking about what makes you odd, atypical, and exceptional. But, don't focus on trying to fix your perceived weaknesses, flaws, or differences. Appreciate them by discovering that your weaknesses are important clues to your most powerful strengths.

Our uniqueness can be a part of our superpower. Consider that Barbara Corcoran, TV personality on *Shark Tank*, successful entrepreneur and investor, keynote speaker, best-selling author, and owner of real estate brokerage firm The Corcoran Group, was labeled as "the dumb kid" who couldn't read or write due to dyslexia. Barbara's credits include straight Ds in high school and college and twenty jobs by the time she turned twenty-three. The Corcoran Group is now the largest and best-known brand in the brokerage business, building the largest and best-known brand in the business.

How did a woman with dyslexia, who couldn't read or write, build such a successful business? You could argue that Barbara succeeded because of her flaws, not in spite of them. Because of her weaknesses, she had to trust others and rely on them to help her run the business. This evolved into a culture of cooperation, collaboration, and teamwork, rather than fierce competition, which separated The Corcoran Group from their competitors. Barbara hired people who were strong where she was weak.

Barbara's intuitive intelligence and racing mind made her impatient and easily frustrated, creating a sense of urgency that motivated people to make changes and improvements. Because Barbara was restless, she spent most of her time out of her office, working with clients, looking for properties, observing the market. Because Barbara was impulsive, she quickly implemented innovative new ideas that differentiated her brokerage firm.

Barbara didn't just appreciate her own weaknesses, she also created an organization that appreciated the differences of others. She created an organization that demonstrates sensitivity for the limitations of others, such as stubbornness, impatience, disorganization, and impulsiveness. It seems the key for Barbara is that she liked herself, not despite her flaws and so-called deficits, but because of them. Additionally, Barbara wasn't afraid of being different, and she encouraged her employees to approach their work in unique and creative ways as well. This created a culture of innovation, trust, and teamwork that truly separates The Corcoran Group from any other brokerage in New York.

Appreciate, rather than adjusting and adapting.

Conventional wisdom suggests that you should build on your strengths and fix weaknesses. Don't appreciate your flaws. Instead, adjust and adapt. But every weakness has a corresponding strength. Appreciate your flaws because that is what makes you awesome.

We need to find ways to capitalize on our unique characteristics and use our apparent flaws to our advantage. Striving for all-around excellence leads directly to mediocrity. As we try to fix our weaknesses, we often end up damaging our corresponding strengths.

Decide what trade-offs you will make. Where you will do things badly, even very badly, in the service of being great at what makes you different? Reframe criticism you receive as a sign that you're doing something right.

Assess and then amplify your differences.

What are your unique weaknesses? Differences? Flaws? Now what would happen if you actually maximized them? Openly admitting your limitations helps build trust. This is true when discussing our own limitations and those of our ideas, products, or services. Admitting weaknesses can make your core ideas more powerful and allow you to be more influential.

To amplify your differences means to "parade without shame" or to truly celebrate what makes you different. Those leaders who don't try to hide their weaknesses or limitations and who celebrate their uniqueness are more likable, memorable, and interesting.

Amplifying your differences is about spending more time, energy, and resources on what makes us unique. And, effective leadership is not about changing people. It's about accepting and respecting who they are and finding ways to help them succeed. Great leaders help people become more of who they are. Instead of forcing people to fit in, we need to help them find the right fit.

Be proud of who you are and what you represent. Take full ownership of your strengths, as well as your weaknesses. Don't apologize for your flaws, and don't try to fix them. Instead, exploit and amplify your imperfections, and embrace your differences. There are an infinite number of ways to be unique. Remember, the most impactful, memorable and successful leaders are considered mavericks. They are different. They are unusual. So, what's different about you?

About the Author

Linda Fisk is a multi-award-winning CEO, TEDx speaker, 3x international best-selling author, keynote speaker, and university professor dedicated to amplifying and extending the success of other high-caliber business leaders. She is the CEO of LeadHERship Global, a community of unstoppable women enhancing their leadership blueprint and embracing their power to be the best version of themselves—in work and life. In LeadHERship Global, Linda supports and guides ambitious, creative women to move in the direction of their purpose, their mission and their dreams with powerful connections, critical support, practical tools, and valuable resources to show up, speak up, and step up in their careers and personal lives.

in linkedin.com/in/lindafisk

NINE

Eileen Coskey Fracchia

THE EFFECTS OF STRENGTHS, DIAMONDS, APHORISMS, AND AMELIA: ON ME, MYSELF, AND I

If I am not for myself, who will be for me?
If I am only for myself, what am I?
And if not now, when?

These words were written over a thousand years ago by the Jewish scholar and one of the best-known sages of all time, Rabbi Hillel.[1] This aphorism compels me to be in continual stages of awakening and to hold myself to act on my self-discoveries. Throughout this chapter, I will use personal stories, learnings, and teachings to give you a glimpse into my journey.

If I Am Not for Myself, Who Will Be for Me?

My college experience began with a contract between my parents and me. Although not ivy-league qualified, I had gotten into a couple of great universities. My choice to go to the school that my boyfriend was attending was not necessarily my parents' first choice. The contract: attend State for 2 years, then transfer to a 'better school' to increase my vocational opportunities by obtaining a more prestigious academic pedigree.

Growing up, my nickname amongst my immediate and extended family was Miss Malaprop – where I was continually teased for saying things a bit backward, (Yew Nork, Clarence of Columbia vs. Lawrence of Arabia, bozos vs. elbows). I spent many sessions with therapists and tutors trying to help me overcome my challenge. It wasn't that my parents thought I wasn't smart, just that I didn't know how to access that smart easily.

I was born a lefty—but, unbeknownst to my parents—was made to switch in second grade to a righty to fit in better with the classroom furniture (the desks and scissors were all for right-handers). Not only was a perceptual learning disability beginning to appear, but you can imagine my embarrassment at seven years old, having to re-learn how to hold a pencil. Despite my challenge, I managed to get through school with a strong B average, (but low academic self-esteem), unlike my sisters who appeared to easily maintain perfect A averages. I did not expect that my 4-year college experience would offer more than good times, a college degree, and freedom.

Amelia Bedelia—a classic children's book series, authored by Peggy Parish—became my refuge.[2] I found a sense of relief in the stories of Amelia, the housekeeper, who took her task assignments literally. For example, when asked to dress the turkey, she did just that—put a dress on a raw turkey; or when she threw powder all over the room when having been asked to dust it. Although her employers were not happy with her 'incompetence,' each story ended with Amelia proudly presenting a home-baked pastry, redeeming herself and giving hope to a little girl with a learning disability that I too would find my own 'redeeming gifts' that would outweigh my deficiencies and prove to me and others that I may present differently, but I was smart and able.

Per the contract, winter of my sophomore year, I completed my applications and got accepted to the 'better schools' as a junior. But, when the time came to decide to move schools, there was a new variable. Something happened at State during my two years—I changed. I fell in love with learning—which continues to this day! I took on leadership roles in student government and was even awarded a coveted internship given to top students. I was thriving! My father said, "I always thought it more important to be a small fish in a big pond, but you have proven that being a big fish in a little pond can be equally important." And with that, I was released from my two-year contract.

Upon graduation, I wanted to continue with my education and go right into a master's program in psychology. My parents supported my decision to move forward in the field but felt I needed to gain some professional experience outside the student role. They encouraged me to enroll in a corporate, structured training program for at least two years. It would either confirm my career decision and make me a better therapist or set me on a different path. Either way it would be a win.

I got accepted to a major bank's Officer Candidate Program. Two years of bank training, and then off to psychology school I would go.

Day one of training: I walked in wearing a new pantsuit, feeling nervous, small, and eager. Within minutes, I was identified as the first and only 'external' candidate in the program. All my peers were 'internals,' promoted from within the bank. I sat next to Mark, clearly a leader amongst his peers, teacher's pet, and quickly my 'ally'. The training was thorough—an overview of the bank's services, products, compliance, governance, and operations. As I was leaving, Debbie, my instructor, came up to me and said, "Eileen, come back tomorrow dressed more professionally. You should pull your hair back, wear lipstick, no pants, and limit the number of questions you ask. This isn't a college class. It's a place of business." I went home ashamed, self-conscious, and deflated.

Day 2: Hair, lipstick, skirt—check, and a pad of paper for me to capture my questions to ask Mark outside of class. I was ready. We got out early that day with the instruction to survey local banks (our competition) and come back with a collage of marketing materials to present. I was off. I went to five financial institutions, gathered the collateral, and went to the art store to buy collage-making supplies: poster board, glue, scissors with ragged edges, markers, and so on. The next many hours were spent creating my collage. I couldn't wait to share.

Day 3: Walking into the classroom carrying my big collage board, my dress, hair, and lipstick all in order; I was beaming with enthusiasm.

As I looked around the room for Mark, I noticed that I was holding the only board. All the other students were holding manila folders. Mark hurried up to me and asked what I had brought. I said, "A collage of the competition's materials." His eyes grew soft, and he pulled a manila folder out of his satchel. He said that when Debbie said *collage* she didn't mean it literally, but rather to bring in the materials (in a folder!) and be prepared to talk about them.

Oh no, I pulled an Amelia. I took the word 'collage' literally. I was visibly upset!

In walked Debbie the instructor, laser-focusing immediately on the Board.

"What is that Eileen?"

With my throat tightening up and tears in my eyes... "It's my *collage.*"

Instructed to come to the front of the room with the Board, she pointed to the door and asked me to leave.

"You clearly should not be here. You did not take the assignment, this program, or this company seriously. We aren't in the business of kindergarten arts and crafts. We are in the business of business."

I went home and 'tattled' to my parents, who offered just the right amount of empathy and pragmatic next-step options to consider. I could quit and find another training program, go back with a manila folder of materials, and grovel for a second chance, or bring the manila folder **and** the Board and share both in hopes that I would be seen as responsive, compliant, creative, resourceful, and worthy. I chose option three.

Day 4: To my surprise, Debbie allowed me to present both the folder materials and The Board. I don't know why she had a change of heart, but I can only assume that Mark had something to do with it. From that moment on, Debbie was different with me—and I, with her. Coming back with both the folder and board may have proven that I was willing to learn, adapt, and contribute in my unique way. At least it proved it to me.

Immediately after training, I was the first candidate to be offered a corporate titled position—Assistant Vice President of Marketing. One of few women, working for a woman leader - tasked with a major responsibility. (I even gained the reputation of 'fresh-eyes Coskey'). I had an incredible first career as a banker lasting over 27 years!

"If I am not for myself, who will be for me?" There is an interpretation that identifies two distinct 'selves'. The I and the Me.[1] The I self is the deepest self—our personalized facet of our 'divine' image. While in contrast, the ME self is the persona we develop during life. Elements of the ME self-originate from others, from society, from that which is outside of the I self. Each of us has an authentic, unique self—an 'I'. Hillel teaches us that if we do not reveal the I, the part of the self that is unique—then who are we? What value is there to ME, the persona that operates in the world? It is a shell. To have submitted the manila folder, without The Board would have been to present a shell of myself rather than my whole self.

Note: Mark and I became dear friends and colleagues, working together at two banks and being with each other through many life-cycle events. I was at Mark's bedside, holding his hand as he peacefully passed away in 1999 from AIDS. He knew how much he meant to me.

If I Am Only for Myself, What Am I?

By the age of twenty-five, I took on my first professional leadership job as a branch manager at Wells Fargo Bank, and over the course of the next twenty-five years, held many different leadership positions. I was fortunate to be exposed to some incredible wisdom carriers in the form of authors, gurus, managers, leaders, and educators. Challenging myself to develop my own leadership point of view, I grappled with "What makes a great leader"? I surrounded myself with great thinkers, attended internal and external training programs, became certified in multiple leadership and organizational assessments, and continued to solicit multi-rater feedback. At the same time, I was learning how to be a great mom. It still amazes me how interrelated my roles as mother and leader correspond. (But that's for another chapter in another book.)

When I was moving from leading a regional business banking sales team to leading a national learning development team, I was introduced to Marcus Buckingham and the Gallup organization.[3] They were just beginning to lay the foundational work around strengths and employee engagement. The idea that spending time dissecting what you do great and feel great and energized when doing was mindshaping for me. Weaknesses need to be addressed, but the definition of weakness, from a strength-based perspective, is something that gets in the way of you being able to leverage your strengths. WOW! How liberating for me as an individual and how empowering for me as a leader. Looking back with Strengths lenses on, I imagine I would focus more on what was strong about The Board versus what was wrong. That may have been the reason that Debbie had a change in approach. I will never know.

Within two years of having met Marcus, I met and became a student of the brilliant leadership guru, philosopher, and author, Peter Koestenbaum, Ph.D.[4] I became a certified Koestenbaum Diamond practitioner. The Diamond offered me a frame of looking at life, leadership, and *beingship*, from which I could reason and navigate with intention and insight.

The Koestenbaum Leadership/Greatness Diamond®[5] (below), distinguishes four interdependent leadership imperatives or "orientations": ethics (to be of service with feeling), vision (to imagine and create), reality (to be grounded in facts), and courage (to act with responsible conviction).

As is shown in the diagram, the relationship among the four orientations determines the shape and size of the space within your Leadership Diamond®. The space within the Diamond and the polarity
between the points is your leadership capacity, which Peter calls
"Greatness."

The positions of the orientations may change, but the concept remains
the same: it is understanding the relationship between the points that
give way to a deeper understanding of one's greatest self.

In a way, it's a gap analysis with heart.

Koestenbaum created a Leadership Diamond Human diagram: Vision
in the head and arms, Reality in its legs, Ethics in its chest, and
Courage in its gut.

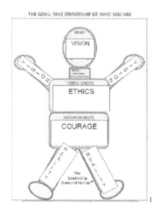

I then created The Diamond Human Exercise – which allows you to manifest the Diamond both internally and externally with the intent of creating an awakening of your truths and possibilities.

Try it.

Choose a topic/decision or action you need to take that is present for you right now. Take a few deep breaths. Now, begin by standing up and planting your feet firmly on the ground. One foot, then the other. Stomp a little… really feel the firmness, the truth of the ground beneath you. (You are standing in your Reality orientation).

Now, look up. Really look up. Raise your arms and reach to the sky, and imagine what is possible. What do you see/not-see? (That is your Vision orientation.) As you have your feet on the ground and your head and arms up in the air, take note of your beating heart and breathing. Is your heart beating fast or slow? Is your breathing effortless or difficult? These are cues and clues into your Ethics orientation. Finally, how does your gut feel? Are you hungry, energized, or nervous? What do you know to be true? What is allowing or disallowing you to move forward and act? (This is your Courage orientation).

Now shake it off… and take a few minutes to journal.What did your legs and feet tell you? Are you grounded in reality… knowing the facts of your situation? When you looked up—was there room for imagination—hope, ideas, vision? How did you feel during the exercise? What inside voices were loud, or quiet? Did you find yourself calm or anxious? Did you have clarity around what you want, and what you need to have happen for you to get it?

The goal of the exercise is to take ownership of who you are - and ultimately help others to do the same. Coupled with Strengths, the Diamond provides a great and fertile landscape for individual, team, and organizational development and ultimately greatness (success), while acknowledging the plethora of possibilities in terms of how to move forward.

"If I am only for myself, who am I?" Is the assertion that an 'I' that encompasses others is thereby infinitely more whole. We start with the self, but then move out into the world of others, and by doing so, we free them and ourselves from oppression and reveal a greater self. It is a self that is simultaneously a part of a greater whole.

Marianne Williamson touches on this probe in "Our Deepest Fear" when she writes:[6]

We were born to make manifest the glory of God that is within us.
It's not just in some of us, it is in everyone.
And as we let our own light shine, we unconsciously
give other people permission to do the same.
As we are liberated from our own fear,
Our presence automatically liberates others.

And If Not Now, When?

The moment that the words "You have cancer" were said to me, life as I knew it changed. The 'I,' 'Me,' 'Myself,' dreams, wisdoms, diamonds, and logic, were all dimmed by the 'Holy shit, what now?' strobe light. What was unbelievable is that I saw my cancer. It exposed itself to me, almost like it wanted to get caught. It attacked me in full 'sight'.

The first six months I had a clear agenda: aggressively treat the presenting rare eye cancer (Primary Intraocular Lymphoma)that would be treated as advanced central nervous system cancer with a patient-one plan…take my life and give me a second chance—with 60 rounds of horrific chemo and an analogous stem cell transplant. Going for a cure—not remission—was the only way to increase my odds from the 2% survival rate. I was *privilege*d to have the means, network, and access to world-class healthcare providers, treatments, and as importantly, the moral and physical support to allow me to choose to fight.

My Facebook post three years after my stem cell transplant:

3 years ago, March 8, 2015, I wasn't sure if I would ever wake up…and yet…I did, be it one stem cell at a time.

2 years ago, I woke up and thought...I am going to be ok...and yet my bald head was blocking my view.

1 year ago, I woke up with a head of hair, fear in my heart, and gnawing in my gut, that I was on borrowed time...and yet I felt hope.

Today I woke up in a beautiful room in Santa Barbara. I'm here because of the gift certificate I bought at a charity event for an organization that brought me the doctor who would ultimately inject me with chances to wake up again.

Today I wake up, I take a breath, a sip of water, and a moment to look around —internally and externally. What is my reality in this new cancer fighter body? What is my vision/intention for this year? Can I summon the courage to quell my constant fear that my cancer is looking for me?

I don't know if my cancer has chosen to swipe me left or right, whether it has left me for good, thinking about a second date, or intends to marry me. What I do know is that I am in a relationship with it. It is both a motivator and an inhibitor. It dances around with promises of freedom and threats of shackle. It reminds me of the blessings and fleeting moments in life and the permanence of death. I have chosen to accept its duality/polarity in my life and have found a sense of purpose, calm, and grace.

*What must I do **now**? **And, if not now, when?** What 'should I' be focused on and how can I be of service to my family, my clients, my communities— our world, and myself? I should have the answers to these questions...and yet I don't. But I will.*

Every day feels like a gift of life that I have been given. As a grand-mother, mother, spouse, daughter, sister, friend, colleague, CEO, thought leader,[7] the 'I,' 'Me,' and 'Myself' are ready and willing to serve. Co-founding the JVS Women's Leadership Network[8] (devoted to supporting women in professional need and crisis) and sitting as a board of director of the UCLA Jonsson Comprehensive Cancer Center Foundation[9] where I chair the Health Equity Initiative (seeded by a grant from my husband and Me), are examples of how I am paying my good fortune forwards.

The effects, strengths, diamonds, aphorisms, and Amelia have had on my life are profound, and yet there is so much more to the story of Me, Myself, and I... but that my dears is for another chapter. I must admit that I was a little worried about how my story might be received. But the truth is... it's me. I am awake. I am!

---

1. Tzvi. 2009. "Me, Myself and I: Ethics of the Fathers 1:14." Aish.com. May 9, 2009. https://aish.com/48893292/.
2. "Amelia Bedelia." 2023. Wikipedia. January 26, 2023. https://en.wikipedia.org/wiki/Amelia_Bedelia#Referen.
3. "Now, Discover Your Strengths: Buckingham, Marcus: 8601409891668: Amazon.com: Books." 2022. Amazon.com. 2022. My Book.
4. "Leadership: The Inner Side of Greatness, a Philosophy for Leaders: Koestenbaum, Peter: 9780470913376: Amazon.com: Books." 2022. Amazon.com. 2022. My Book.
5. "Koestenbaum Leadership Diamond®." n.d. El Camino Group, LLC. Accessed January 18, 2023. https://elcaminogroup.com/sharing-brilliance/the-leadership-diamond-corner/.
6. "A RETURN to LOVE: Reflections on the Principles of a Course in Miracles - Marianne Williamson." 2015. Marianne Williamson. 2015. https://marianne.com/a-return-to-love/.
7. "Leading with Humanity." n.d. Institute of Coaching. Accessed January 18, 2023. https://instituteofcoaching.org/ioc-report-leading-with-humanity-the-future-of-leadership-coaching#:~:text=Leading%20with%20Humanity%2C%20the%20Future.
8. "JVS SoCal Home - Jobs. Vision. Success." n.d. JVS SoCal. Accessed February 14, 2023. https://www.jvs-socal.org/.
9. "UCLA Jonsson Comprehensive Cancer Center : Health Equity." n.d. Cancer.ucla.edu. Accessed January 18, 2023. https://cancer.ucla.edu/giving/ways-to-give/health-equity.

About the Author

Eileen Coskey Fracchia is the Founder and CEO of El Camino Group, LLC—a certified Women Owned Business Enterprise specializing in leadership and organizational performance effectiveness.

Eileen has effectively built two careers while anchoring her journey in service to others and her community. First in the banking industry where she held multiple senior-level positions including Wells Fargo Bank's Senior Vice President and Head of Regional Development supporting 50,000+ team members. She then parlayed her experience into a second, multi-faceted career as a coaching expert, business consultant, professor, and renowned speaker. She is passionate about building better leaders and leadership teams—in service of creating more inclusive, appreciative, and productive environments. She specializes in helping individuals and organizations realize their full potential and navigate their roads to success. Her clients come from a broad spectrum of for-profit and non-profit sectors, at varying levels of organizational maturity.

A Member of the Board of Directors for JVS SoCal and UCLA Jonsson Cancer Center Foundation, she is Founding Fellow, Strategic Advisor, and West Coast leader of the Institute of Coaching (IOC), a Harvard Medical School Affiliate, and has held positions of Adjunct Professor and guest speaker of many university graduate programs and business conferences.

In 2021 Eileen launched Humanity on Set, a leadership program with a mission of integrating tested coaching and leadership philosophies with diversity and inclusion practices to bring about positive societal and cultural change—with a concentration in the space of entertainment production.

Eileen's favorite times are spent with her expanding family, friends and dogs playing and exploring.

∽

Website: https://elcaminogroup.com/
Publication: https://instituteofcoaching.org/ioc-report-leading-with-humanity-the-future-of-leadership-coaching

in linkedin.com/in/eileen-coskey-fracchia-70456252

TEN

Shiri Gabriel

HOW TO LIVE IN A CONSTANT STATE OF EMOTIONAL FREEDOM

*B*y the time I am done writing this chapter, I would have found out whether or not I will be running *The Amazing Race Israel*. Yes, that's right! Now, this is what most of you might be thinking: *Are you crazy? That's cool, but how can you take a month off? You are going to leave your family for that long? You're fifty! Are you in shape? Aren't you afraid of everything?*

Yes, yes, yes, and yes!

These have been the comments and questions I have consistently heard from other people about my life in general. People often wonder and praise me for having time to do everything I do. For being a hurricane, as one of my good friends calls me. I consider myself the master of lifestyling. But, a few years back I started to wonder if I am in fact doing too much and losing sight of the most important thing in my life: my family. And it was around that time, coming back from a convention, that my oldest son asked me: "Mami, how do you do everything you do?" I first checked if he was asking because he felt I didn't have enough time for them. He said, "Absolutely not." In fact, he was amazed that with everything I do, I always made time for them. I felt happy, relieved, and proud all at once. But how is it, then, that I manage to do everything I do? How is it that I can literally have the cake and eat it too? Believe me, I have asked myself that question many times, but I never really took the time to answer it. I never had the opportunity to dig deep and discover how and why am I able to sustain a constant rhythm in my life that allows me to pretty much do what I most want when I most want it. How is it that I can juggle so many things at once and still manage to be present to the most precious people in my life?

When the opportunity to co-author this book came around, I saw this as the space I needed to figure out what my secret was to lifestyling. Well, I found it. The secret: emotional freedom. So in the next two thousand words I will share with you what I now know to be the mantras that have allowed me to live in this constant state of emotional freedom. Remember, these are my ideas, based on my experience. I invite you to open up your eyes, your ears, your mind, and your heart and take from these what serves you.

Here we go.

Strong Values Produce Clear Choices

Emotional freedom to me means that I have the ability to create what I want; that in any situation, I have the freedom to choose. To choose how I react, what I do, where I go, what I say, how I think. It is living in an abundance state where I know that I am truly free. It is understanding that you don't need a permission slip to make a choice; that you don't need to wait for anyone to decide for you; that you don't depend on the time of day, the weather, the year, the economy, the government, or any outside circumstances to choose what you really, really, really want. I know what you're thinking: easy to say! You are right, it is easier said than done. But what has made it simple for me to make choices is being grounded in my core values. I am so clear about what is important to me that it just makes it easier to make choices, especially the tough ones.

When you can measure every decision against your core values, the ability to choose becomes effortless. This is true even when faced with conflicting decisions. When I chose to go to a convention and miss my son's birthday, the core value that I chose at that time was security/freedom. But I didn't just choose that over my son; I shared that decision with him and explained why, so he can fully understand and support me. When I passed on invitations to go on a girls' weekend so I could watch my kids play hockey, it was because the value of family trumped the value of fun at that particular time. You see, when you understand that values are like a deck of cards and you have the freedom to play any card at any time, this will empower you. Just like any other skill, you must learn to pivot from one value to another. This will only happen once you're clear on what is important to you.

I have been using a simple system every year to identify what my core values are at any particular time. I make a list of everything that is important to me and choose the top five. Then, on a scale of 1 to 10, I rate how much of each value do I currently have. That helps me understand what I have to work on to fulfill those values. When you are clear on what is important to you, when you feel it to the core, making choices becomes easy and simple, no drama, no regrets. This is when you know you have emotional freedom!

Feel it into the Future

Some of the most important decisions in my life I've made by looking a few years ahead and digging into how I would feel if I didn't do something; would I regret it? If the answer was yes, then I would know exactly what I needed to choose. This technique has served me very well, and it has allowed me to live a life with almost no regrets. And I say almost because there is only one time in my life that I regret not doing something. After I finished my service as a lieutenant in the Israeli Army, I planned to take a six-month trip to South America with my best friend. I ended up bailing on her. I decided to come to Canada for my brother's wedding and visit with my parents, who I haven't lived with since I was seventeen. That visit has lasted for twenty-seven years. I met my husband in university, and four kids later, here I am. Now, this was, as we say in Yiddish, *beshert*—meant to be. And I know that. However, I do regret not making that trip. All in all, not bad to only have that one regret after fifty years, right?

We are faced with all kinds of decisions every day. When you are able to see yourself in the future and dig into that gut feeling of, would I regret it or not, you will be able to make decisions easily and faster. And faster is important. How many times have you sat on making a decision only to find out that by the time you decided, you missed that opportunity. I have seen many people miss out on fun and professional opportunities because they overthought things, they cared too much about what others would say, or they were waiting for that permission slip. And, man, did they ever regret that. People who live in a constant state of emotional freedom are able to make decisions fast. I never get caught in the details of the how or why or who. I make a decision and figure out the details later. Some might think this is too impulsive and might lead to making mistakes. And they are right. But here's the thing. I am a risk taker, and I am not afraid of making mistakes, failing, or being disappointed. I am more afraid of living with regret. Living with that feeling of what if. Living thinking, *Darn, I wish I did!* How many of those I wish I did, I wish I had, I wish I listened…do you have? Probably one too many. I refuse to live with regrets. I make sure I don't miss out on much. I have an open mind to be present and learn about new things. I want to always be discovering new opportunities, personally and professionally. I think this is part of living life to the fullest. FOMO, baby! This might seem a bit too hyperactive. However, being clear on my mission and vision allows me to stay focused and grounded and make decisions that are right for me.

My vision is to positively impact everyone I touch; it is about creating a world where nobody gets left behind, so we can all live in a state of possibility, abundance, and fun. You see, if your vision is not clear, you might find yourself overwhelmed when presented with an opportunity. It might even confuse you and push you into making the wrong decision for fear of missing out. But when you are grounded in your mission and vision, when you are clear about your values, you will be able to quickly identify what things you say no to and which you go for. Without any regrets. I heard Oprah once say that the universe whispers to you very softly, and if you're lucky it might sometimes slap you; but if you're not paying attention, you will miss out. Remember, opportunities are not lost, they are simply given to someone else.

There Are More than Twenty-four Hours in a Day

One reason many people don't achieve emotional freedom is because they compartmentalize time. No, I am no Einstein, and I am not here to teach you the law of relativity. I am simply sharing how I live timeless. This is a bit of an oxymoron for me, since I am the kind of person who is never late, who as a professor, gets mad when students hand in assignments late. So yes, I own a watch and a calendar, however, I am not limited by a twenty-four-hour day. I adopted this idea when I started building my business in different time zones, from Europe to Australia to South America. Some days I would be working in the future and sometimes in the past. This made me realize that I can manipulate time to work to my advantage. I could actually bend time so that my days would be as long or as short as I wanted them to be. Time became an irrelevant measure in achieving my goals. This gave me a sense of freedom, and it released a lot of the stress I was feeling of getting things done in a day. In that moment, I understood that we give ourselves deadlines thinking that there are only a certain number of hours in a day, however, that is not true. You can have as many hours as you want. You can make a thirty-three-hour day or a nine-hour day. How freeing and empowering is this? I encourage you to shift your thinking by taking your mind out of this compartment of time as you know it and create your own. It will free you emotionally!

It's Always the Right Time

One husband, four children, running a business, teaching seven courses in college, investing in real estate, working out, playing volleyball twice a week, working on a new business app with my children... does that sound like a full schedule? (You see why I don't live in a twenty-four-hour day!) So imagine how I felt when I was approached to write a chapter in this book! Yup. Most people's first instinct would have been to think, *It is not a good time.* Well, I have learned that it is never the right time. So, if it's never the right time, by mathematical default, it must always be the right time! Say that three times out loud: It is always the right time! Liberating, isn't it? That's how I see it, and that gives me emotional freedom.

We can't time when opportunities present themselves. They just do. And if you understand that this is how life is, you will always be in a state of flow. This will also provide you with more abundance and the expectation that great things are coming to you. If this doesn't make you feel excited, it might be a good idea to start living life as an infinite game. Simon Sinek explains: *"In infinite games, like business or politics or life itself,* the players come and go, the rules are changeable, and there is no defined endpoint. There are no winners or losers in an infinite game; there is only ahead and behind."* When you limit yourself by how much you can do and when, this restricts you from learning and experiencing new things. I have seen people getting comfortable with what they have and where they are, and because of that, they have lost the ambition to continue to grow, personally and professionally. They are so comfortable with the fact that they have three hours every night to watch Netflix that they don't want to mess with that schedule. And they convince themselves there is not enough time to take on anything else. My mentor challenged me once to track everything I do, every hour of every day. I was convinced that my schedule would be completely full (you saw everything I do!) To my surprise, I discovered I had more free time than I thought. So I started watching more Netflix. I'm kidding. I added an extra hour a day to prospect more clients. I used to think that being overwhelmed was bad for you since it means to be overcome by emotions. I have discovered, however, that when I am overwhelmed, I experience an intense sense of emotional freedom. I'm in the zone. This energy causes me to fire on all cylinders, and in fact, some of my best results in my business have come when I have been overwhelmed.

Call Me Crazy

What? You are leaving Coca-Cola, with all the benefits and great salary you have! Are you crazy? This is the reaction I got from most people when I decided not to take a full-time role with Coca-Cola after being there for over ten years. Which is the same reaction I got when I decided to join the direct sales company I'm currently with. And the same reaction I got when I decided to become the first woman driver in a security role at the airport (at a time when no woman was allowed to be a driver). Throughout my personal and professional life, I have gotten used to people calling me crazy. The first few times it made me hesitate and maybe stopped me from taking action. But as I got older and wiser, I understood that being called crazy was actually a sign that I was on the right track. My mom always told me I was born without a filter, and I also believed that for the first seventeen years of my life. Why seventeen?, you might ask. Because it was at that age that my parents emigrated from Israel to Canada, and I insisted on staying to finish high school and then enlisted in the army. You can imagine my parents' reaction: Are you crazy? But after a lot of convincing, begging, and crying, they let me stay, for which I am forever thankful. So yes, after hearing " are you crazy" many times before, it was at that moment, when I was seventeen, that I understood that it is not that I don't have a filter but that I just have a very different one. This super-power has served me very well, for the most part. It has given me the courage and tenacity to zig when everyone is zagging. It has allowed me to take risks. It has given me an open mind to take on opportunities that most people are closed to. It has pushed me to go after what I want, no matter what people think or say.

At times, this came at a price, which was forgetting that I can't expect everyone to act or think like me. I found myself preaching and some-times judging people for doing or not doing certain things. It was in the last seven years that I had to do a lot of personal development to understand that as much as I want to help people be and achieve what they want, I need to respect their decisions and actions. I've had to humble myself, and this has helped me realize that there is no right way, but rather a way. And mine might be good for me, while another way might be good for someone else. This mindset has allowed me to learn from others and grow personally and professionally. While my filter still remains my superpower, my acceptance and tolerance are what can make me someone else's hero. In this lies the truth about my purpose in life: to positively impact everyone I touch. So being called crazy is what motivates and inspires me. And being called a trail blazer, a mentor, a leader is what gives me emotional freedom.

Master Your Lifestyle

As I poured into this chapter the mantras that have enabled me to have emotional freedom, I can't help but wonder whether these will be enough to inspire anyone to live life to the fullest. I ask myself if these words will positively impact someone to believe that they can lifestyle. To me, being a master lifestyler means that you understand you have full control of how you spend your time and money. It means that you are in a constant state of flow, where you are presented with different choices, and it is in those decisive moments that you feel empowered to move left, right, backward, or forward. It is in those moments that you know whatever happens next depends only on you. It is then that you feel empowered. That you feel emotionally free.

I don't know whether I will be chosen to participate in *The Amazing Race*; I don't know that if I do, I won't be kicked out first; I don't know that if I don't get kicked out first I will win. What I do know is that I made the choice to submit my application, no matter what happens after that. Please understand that emotional freedom also lies in the ability to detach yourself from the results; to be able to fully commit yourself to something no matter what happens next. I have watched how very successful people disassociate themselves from the results, and this allows them to be in a constant state of equanimity. They understand that even when they feel an intense emotion, good or bad, they should find a way to level up their emotions. Detaching yourself from the results not only makes it easier to go for it but also allows you to maintain emotional balance. I constantly work on having what I call, the Great reaction, where no matter what, I say to myself, Great. I got a new client. Great. I lost the game. Great. I lost money on that deal.

Great. That simple word is so powerful. Just saying, "Great" releases serotonin and improves my mood. It brings me back to a balanced state from which I can only move forward.

I have one wish for you: to find courage! The courage to decide you're going to do it your way; and that is scary, so you have to be brave. And to be brave you need to find emotional freedom.

About the Author

Shiri is a lifestyler. In her chapter she talks about how all the actions she has taken have stemmed from having emotional freedom. She offers a few simple steps to help everyone achieve this state and be able to have the lifestyle they desire.

Shiri is a mother of four and a wife of one. She is a master connector, a global business owner, a professor, a real estate investor, and a career and life coach. Shiri is highly skilled in leading and inspiring individuals and teams worldwide to create better lifestyles and build generational wealth. Shiri is a dynamic coach, speaker, trainer, and presenter; great at employing clarity, innovation, and humor to deliver effective presentations to diverse audiences.

Shiri's multicultural background, traveling adventures, fifteen years experience in the corporate world and a decade as an entrepreneur provide unique insights and understanding of the challenges faced by people in reaching goals, creating balance, and building meaningful relationships to achieve the lifestyle they desire.

https://www.shiri.coach/

If you love my chapter, you will love my podcast CALL ME CRAZY
with Shiri Gabriel.

 linkedin.com/in/shirigabriel

ELEVEN

Nikki Green

DR. JEKYLL AND MR. HYDE LEADERS

*O*ver the years, I have seen my fair share of Dr. Jeckyll and Mr. Hyde leaders, and this inauthentic way of leading never sat well with me. Early in my career, managers often told me to curb my bold personality or keep certain opinions to myself. But hiding my true nature never felt right. In fact, after growing up in some very tough neighbourhoods in the East Bay of Northern California, I had often fought to stay true to myself, no matter the cost.

Our identity is an essential part of who we are and a culmination of our experiences and internal drive to see, learn and be more. Once we define a moral and ethical path for living our lives, it's devastating to be told that our personal compass has no place in our careers. And just as the story of Dr. Jeckyll and Mr. Hyde reminds us, any time we try to suppress our true nature, it finds a way of coming out to haunt us.

In my first book, *I Laugh in the Face of Danger*, I talk about how the modern-day serum of alcohol has caused untold issues at corporate events. I share a painful story that caused me to leave my initial career path following university and embark on a new career with a high-tech company I thought would have a better, more supportive culture. I saw many of these personality changes happen throughout my time in Silicon Valley. In front of the Press, in large company meetings, or with people from outside, they portrayed this perfect, mild-mannered saviour whose technology advances would help the world. But behind closed doors, the beast was revealed.

Slamming competitors' devices on the floor and yelling at employees because they could not meet impossible deadlines. Cutting costs on critical resources like employees while wasting it on self-indulgent parties and ego-boosting publicity stunts. I have begun modernising these literary characters with new terms to characterise the growing divide of leaders—the zebras versus the chameleons. With the prevalence of social media, the zebras have grown their herd. Once these zebra characteristics were reserved for the financially elite, now they can be seen in your everyday YouTube Influencer, putting on a show for their audience while contributing to the falsehoods of get-rich schemes. The lack of authenticity is nauseating and disheartening.

Every day I went to school was a battle for survival. The psychological and physical abuse chipped away my confidence, and maintaining my self-worth and values became everything to me. I learned to stand up for myself and those around me, to keep from entering gangs or being pulled into a world broadcast as a family but with no real support for my future. I would look in the mirror, see cuts and bruises left behind from the fights, and still hold my head high, walk out of the safety of my home and into the battleground of school each day. I survived those days with a goal and vision that things would improve as an adult. That these childish games of bullying would end on the playground and not carry into the conference room, but it wasn't true. The bullying continued, only it was harder to recognise due to the zebra Mr. Hyde and Dr. Jeckyll behaviour masking their true nature from the outside world.

The zebras think they know it all and live for power over others. They stifle innovation and limit the thinking of their employees. They don't ask for buy-in on their ideas and demand compliance with their grand plan. But there is hope as the chameleons continue to evolve. Those that understood that the pandemic would bring about something bigger and more life-impacting than the COVID virus. It would usher in a new era of business along with a new type of leader and allow for significant technological advancements in areas like AI and biotech, creating a ripple effect for decades.

The chameleons call this our pandemic pivot.

Great Resignation, Quit Quitting, the Zebras have inflicted all these symptoms of the capitalist disease upon the herd. But the chameleons want to heal, and we want to do things differently. We want to create a physically and psychologically safe environment for our employees and people from all walks of life to work. We desire the flexibility to pursue our passions, in and out of the office. We must take control of our financial freedom through affordable health care and transparent pay acts. And we are beginning to work for a living and no longer living for work.

Feeding the Ego of Leaders

In her book, *Mindset*, Dr. Carol Dweck talks a lot about the impact leaders have on a company's employees and culture and how toxic managers with a fixed mindset have nearly always failed when they couldn't use brute force to get their way. I have seen many managers like this over my career and heard many more horror stories. But as long as the leaders at the top think results are more important than people, this behavior will exist, and employee turnover will be high.

The 2019 HBO documentary, *The Inventor: Out for Blood in Silicon Valley*, is about how Elizabeth Holmes and others defrauded many investors with their start-up. Here you can see a small taste of the real C-level of Silicon Valley. They have complete control over budgets and can push their team to treat them like rock stars. The excess goes beyond executive lunchrooms or private bathrooms made famous in the 1980s. It's almost worse because before, there was a clear fixed mindset at work, creating the divide between boss and employee. Now we have moved into the world of ego, celebrating a leader simply because he has the money to make people like him. CEOs are treated like the celebrity influencers of the Knowledge Economy.

This was never more apparent to me than one year at an annual sales conference and new product release event. It was my first year with this Fortune 500 tech company, and I had the privilege to travel to Atlanta to join the conference. These events were a lot to take in, even for an extreme extrovert like myself. A handful of my local co-workers received the invite. The city quickly filled with thirteen thousand other employees from around the globe, which may seem like a significant number, but when a company has one hundred thousand employees, it's a small percentage. Or so I imagine the C-level leaders saying as justification for the excessive spending.

My co-workers and I arrived late in the evening after a full day's travel from Nevada to Georgia. As we arrived at the hotel, we were given our itinerary for the week, a generous goodie bag of swag, and allowed to head to our rooms. The itinerary indicated the bus would leave promptly at 7:00 a.m. the next morning. Now, 7:00 a.m. may not seem like an early start, but when you've been traveling all day and lost three hours due to the time difference, this is a 4:00 a.m. start to the week.

I shuffled onto the bus with the others, most everyone still in a sleepy daze. We exited single file and headed to the breakfast lines in the convention center. Right then, it began to hit me how massive this event was about to be. Thousands of people gathered around tables, catching up with old friends and sharing insights about their current projects. After some much-needed coffee and sustenance, we headed into the arena to find our seats.

Music was blaring, and the lights were reminiscent of a rock concert. Despite the lively atmosphere, most everyone was still only marginally awake. Then the lights dimmed, and the insanity began. Before I knew what was happening, fireworks were going off on stage, and who should appear but Flo Rida, the hip-hop artist. I'm a big fan of Flo Rida, but the lack of sleep, the early hour, and the shock of seeing him running around on stage was a bit much for my senses to comprehend. I sat confused for the entire performance.

Next, running down the center aisle of the convention center, as if he was about to accept the Super Bowl MVP trophy, was the CEO, a bald and middle-aged white man with two left feet who greatly lacked the swagger of Flo Rida. It was surreal. He began to hype the half-asleep crowd, talking about company performance and hinting at the new products they would unveil during the week. He shouted into his Madonna-like headset mic, running all over the stage and sweating under the bright arena lights. My brain struggled to wrap my head around what was going on. It was like watching your parents dance at your cousin's wedding, awkward, and you just wanted it to stop.

The rest of the week was much of the same. With military precision, managers corralled the employees and took roll to ensure everyone showed up like good little children. Each subsequent presentation was more elaborate and over the top, making it tough to maintain the same level of enthusiasm hour after hour and day after day. While I realize some level of celebration is needed after working so hard each year, the amount of excess and ego-feeding of the executives was quite tough to stomach. The party felt less about rewarding the employees and more about feeding the egos of the C-level staff. The company's zebra-fixed mindset had paid for this event, and we had to enjoy every last minute, regardless of our comfort or safety.

They set the expectation that we were going to a party with our closest friends and family, but the size and scale made it virtually impossible to connect with anyone. Using the excess corporate funds to play out fantasies of their wealth and status felt like an abuse of the abundance mindset. There is enough for all because "I AM PROVIDING" when the company is footing the bill. This abuse of power also awakens the scarcity mindset in many managers, "I can give, and I can take it away. Do as I say by day, or you won't be allowed to join these reindeer games at night."

This behavior and excess always struck me when I was told there wasn't sufficient money for raises, bonuses, or benefits. Money from these parties could have been used to create jobs and develop training programs for employees and managers. Even more impactful would be for managers to host smaller celebrations at department levels, which would mean more to the employees than this overindulgence. I'm sure as a manager or an employee, similar thoughts have crossed your mind during your career.

Following the past few years of the COVID-19 pandemic, these companies should be swimming in money like Scrooge McDuck without these events and this excessive spending. Unbalanced company financials following the pandemic are a clear sign of zebra mismanagement. These same managers want to cut back employee benefits and compensation while employees have taken on an unprecedented workload and life-altering expectations at home. And the chameleon employees have figured out they can evolve to take care of themselves and have a fulfilling career but not remain in these toxic environments.

That wasn't the first or last extravagant event I attended in Silicon Valley. Companies try to outdo each other for holiday parties, launch events, and more each year. Since most people have a friend or spouse at another company, the details of the parties are far from secret; instead, they spread like a rumor wildfire through the Valley.

Blame it on the AAAA-Alcohol

There are darker parts of these events, which I've also found true. One personal story of mine I shared in my first book. These parties bring out the worst in many people, with excuses about the influence of alcohol, where acts of violence, both physical and mental, are played out behind closed party doors. The frat boy mentality learned in these brand-name universities is awakened in managers who seem mild-mannered and safe day-to-day. This abuse causes harm to work relationships for years to come and often results in women having to leave the department, if not the company entirely.

It often seemed like a modern-day Dr. Jekyll and Mr. Hyde, where the mindset shift was so severe they seemed like a different person. While I don't believe we should blame it all on the a-a-a-a-alcohol,[1] the excessive inebriation supported by these events certainly removes more than inhibitions. The power over others becomes a way for them to recover from abusive management by exerting their power over someone they've wanted but have feared to approach sober. They go from a positive chameleon mindset by day to a zebra-minded individual at night, taking what they believe should be theirs.

In recent years, many victims of this abuse have come out via the #MeToo movement to speak out against sexual harassment and abuse in the workplace. I've heard and seen the stories firsthand, some happening to me directly. Long before the pandemic, our workplaces were not safe places for women. I fear rushing back into the office before these issues are resolved is dangerous.

As women continue to lose more rights in this country than we are gaining, I believe we will become more fierce in defending our bodies and our minds. Mentally, people are more psychologically fragile than they were in years, and I don't think women will have the same logical reactions as before the pandemic. Instead of hiding in fear of retribution, I believe women will viscerally lash out to defend their safety in the moment, and the impact on our workforce will be felt far and wide. As women continue to share their stories of harassment and abuse over social media, the pressure for a company and its leaders to course correct will be critical to the future success of the business. The time of the egotistical and narcissistic zebra-mindset leader is ending, and the employees will begin ushering in a new world of Chameleon Mindset workers who are unified in their ideals and support each other's growth and well-being physically, mentally, and emotionally.

These companies' wealth and global reach allowed me to see the world and experience so many incredible things this life has to offer. Instead of trying to westernise everyone around me, I worked hard to globalise myself and become more chameleon. To understand others before I fought to be understood.

Through this global journey, I know there is a better way to lead, and I want to help the next generation make it a reality.

---

1. Jaimie Fox featuring T-Pain, "Blame it [on the Alcohol]", 2009.

About the Author

Nikki Green is a Life and Business Resiliency Expert who has worked in the international business industry for over twenty years. Empowering young people to reach their full potential is her greatest passion, and as an inspiring keynote speaker, Nikki will motivate your organization or event attendees.

With her company, Green Chameleon Collective, Nikki has dedicated her life to assisting others in overcoming the fear of following their dreams. She has worked with several notable C-Level executives in top Silicon Valley companies. Nikki received double promotions in two different Fortune 500 companies and The Golden Microphone Award. A four-time published author, she hosts the podcast *Stand Up & Stand Out* and has been featured in *USA Today*, *Podcast Magazine*, and *Authority Magazine*.

Nikki earned her master's in international business administration from California State University, Hayward. An avid traveler, she has visited more than fourteen countries and over half of the United States. Nikki lives outside Chicago, where she enjoys running and has completed seven marathons, three ultras, and dozens of triathlons across three continents.

Learn more: www.thenikkigreen360.com
Podcast: *Stand Up & Stand Out*: https://thenikkigreen.com/podcast/

TWELVE

Mary E. Gregory

FINDING YOUR RESILIENCY SUPERPOWERS—SPOILER ALERT: IT BEGINS WITH FORGIVENESS

L've always had an entrepreneurial state of mind. I would sell Love Tests to other kids when I was in elementary school, giving out Now and Later candy each week during my Friday backpack raffle ceremony for those who bought enough tests to enter the drawing. This was until my operation was shut down by the principal after I distributed the winnings too consistently and teachers noticed an uptick in candy mischief in their classrooms. Oops.

My sister and I used to host carnivals in our apartment and have activities like face painting and makeship mazes throughout the living room and kitchen, charging a quarter for each activity. My siblings and I would stand outside of our local Alpha Beta grocery store to help people load their groceries into their cars so that they'd hopefully give us their prized quarter, which they'd deposited into the slit of the shopping cart handle. They usually did. This was both good fun and quite lucrative for latch-key kids who had nothing better to do during the summer.

By the time I was in middle school and into high school, my focus was mostly on basketball. I'm 6'1" now, but by the time I was in seventh grade, I was 5'9" and each year growing an inch taller. I trained almost every weekend to get on the basketball team. Even with all the height, I didn't make it on the team the first year, but this gave me the resolve to make the team the following year, which I did. Sports teach you a lot about life. One game can be the greatest love affair you've ever had, and another game can be the worst and most toxic experience of your life, leaving you heartbroken and your body and mind exhausted from defeat. Somehow you recover. You turn to your team and coach to remind you of your strengths and your special skills, to build you up, and to get you back on the court. It's amazing what a "ra ra" can do. Even if you missed the ball, double dribbled (oiy!) or missed that shot, you were still great, your team loved you, and you had an opportunity to learn from your mistakes and try again in another game.

Forgiveness Deficient

Why can't we see the greatness in our failures? Why can't we readily see them as an opportunity to try again, taking the lessons learned from the experience? I believe it's because as we get older, and as we transition away from receiving outward affirmations from others, we're not properly prepared for the positive affirmations needed from within. So we do what we're used to and reflect out, judging others for the weaknesses we see within ourselves. We usually don't know how to reflect on our own strengths, to soothe our soul with positive and affirming mantras that support us when we need them most. We have a hard time being our own "ra ra" cheerleader.

But I also believe we're deficient in forgiveness. An essential part of life is knowing that you'll overcome any obstacle with the right awareness. On the surface this seems obvious, but what is awareness? To me, awareness is knowing that everyone is connected to each other and going through this life's experience together. We each have different outward appearances that change how others respond to us, and no matter what color, nationality, economic status, title, or air of superiority we may have been born into or bestowed upon ourselves, at the end of the day, we are all conscious beings looking for love and peace. The attitudes, beliefs, actions, and thoughts about ourselves and others impact the lives of everyone. A simple acknowledgement to someone to say that you appreciate them for who they are, can impact that person's life in immeasurable ways, and thus positively impact the lives around them. Acts of kindness go both ways, and therefore, acknowledging and appreciating yourself, sets you up for receiving from others.

The intent of your actions and thoughts have a major impact on the outcomes you experience in life. When we are capable of seeing others as the same vulnerable beings we are, it puts us in a place to forgive and therefore look within at our own weaknesses, and thus an opportunity to forgive ourselves. When we keep our understanding of others outward, like using negative words when speaking about them or performing negative actions toward them, causing pain or humiliation, we are not taking the time to see our own pain and traumas and are avoiding working on our own healing.

Entrepreneurial Meltdown

When I graduated from college, I immediately began working for myself and partnered with someone in the mortgage industry to begin offering mortgage loans. Just a year later in 2007, the beginnings of the Great Recession were being felt. Mortgage warehouse lines were closing and major banks were no longer offering subprime loans. My partners and I had already started developing prequalification software for the industry for what was called A-paper loans. These loans were for those with exceptional credit who wanted to borrow loan amounts that were usually around 80% of the value of their home. Unfortunately, within a year even the A-paper loans couldn't get funded, and our company went bust as the mortgage industry crash of 2008 was official and its repercussions were felt throughout the entire economy. In that time however, we were able to pivot and began offering a distressed mortgage processing software that we sold as a SAAS application to loan modification companies. But getting it to scale was difficult, in part because the market was constantly fluctuating and banks were slow to process loan modification applications and homeowners were often losing their homes before the process completed.

During that storm, *Entrepreneur* magazine interviewed us and recognized our company for its ingenuity in leveraging the ups and downs of the mortgage industry and offering a product to support those facing foreclosure. After the article was live, we decided to look for investors to help us maximize our software platform, which offered a simple way to repurpose a borrower's financial and personal data across many products offered on the platform. We had created several modules for our customers, some offering debt consolidation, refinance, or loan mods. We created agreements with our customers and users that if there was a product that would benefit them based on their data, it would be flagged as qualifying for one of our customers' products. Instead of having to collect the customer's information all over again, they'd simply open the client file in the other module, which showed only the data for the qualifying product. Imagine if each time you saw a new doctor, only the "net new" info would be requested from you, because all your other basic info was already in *one* system. Think of all the time everyone would save.

We went to New York to pitch our application. We'd lined up several investor meetings, yet nearly all of them told us we'd come to them at the wrong time because all their assets were tied up in the market and their portfolios had taken quite a hit. One investor said that if his wife knew he was even talking about investing in a startup, she'd kill him. Perhaps this was a push off, perhaps this was because I was a female CEO, but I could see on many of their faces that they were uncertain about investing in a software company offering distressed products, especially because of the stigma around those companies in the investor community.

It was a bleak time for me. Calling it quits would be costly, but I had to face reality. My business had failed. I took the failure of the business very personally. I held a lot of resentment toward my business partners, the mortgage industry, and worst of all, myself. I hadn't understood then what I know now, that the skills I was learning running my own company would serve me well in Corporate America.

There had been no "ra ra," no coach, and no team to remind me of my greatness, it was just me. I realized I was deficient in my own positive internal dialogue—one that I could take with me wherever I went and tap into when times were tough. I needed to remember when I was great, when I'd overcome difficult situations, when I'd not only survived but thrived. I realized I was only looking to the outside for affirmation, not within.

I decided to confront my business debt. I began negotiating settlements and payment plans, going to court and negotiating in the hallways with lawyers, even hiring lawyers, and doing my best to avoid any further impact to my abysmal credit score. I got good at those negotiations. The definition of what was "high-stakes" kept changing. How I managed stress was changing. My ability to solve problems was expanding. I was developing my resiliency superpowers and didn't even know it.

In my mind, I was just surviving. And physically, I was fully experiencing the vibrations of defeat through every meridian line in my body, through my fascial network, and I was holding and storing the trauma of the past four years in my body. I was thirty years old.

Awakening Beginnings

In 2010 I ended up taking a sabbatical. I had burnt out, and four years of grinding away had taken its toll. I went back to what really made me happy, and that was team sports. In Qi Gong, they say, when you're in the body, you're out of the mind. I needed to be out of my mind but in a good way. I needed to be physical again, to collaborate with others, to feel a different kind of stress, to make different kinds of decisions, and to work with different kinds of people. To get back to a "ra ra" environment. So I went right into another leadership role as the team manager of a co-ed softball team. I learned all that you needed to start a team, and I roped in all my friends. We were a ragtag team, and nearly everyone on the team had never played softball. The first season we simply learned the basics, lost every game, and smiled and laughed —a lot!

When I was ready to "get back out there," I had no idea what Corporate America was going to be like. I hadn't been in that game, ever. I'd only had my entrepreneurial background and my college education, what did I really know? I was used to wearing many hats, and when I was looking at job descriptions, nothing felt like it fit me completely. Nothing. I had a big case of imposter syndrome. I was scared. Scared of not knowing what it would be like or if I was capable of succeeding, and I was certainly not sure of how others would perceive me. But I did it. I found an analyst position through the support of a friend who said, "I'll get you the interview, but you have to get the job." I brought samples of my work, which I later learned sealed the deal. I loved writing use cases and user stories. It's basically what I did when I met with customers to determine what data they wanted collected in our software.

However, the experience was overwhelming. I was learning a new job role, and a new culture. This big company was like being immersed in a new country. I didn't speak the language, I didn't know the currency, so I just tried to fit in. I spent many days in the office bathroom to grab quick phone booth moments to escape the simmering imposter syndrome and change into my "I'm totally fine" costume.

I was afraid to trust my intuition, to cut myself some slack for the learning curve, or to believe that I could learn the job and excel at it. I hadn't yet developed my positive internal dialogue. At the time, I'd never meditated or had a daily journal ritual. I hadn't read the many personal development books that later helped me to define my positive rituals that taught me to tap into my resiliency superpowers. I was flailing.

And it was during this time that I was tested yet again. One of my colleagues must have sensed my fear and insecurity and took advantage of my vulnerability. I experienced workplace bullying, which ranged from snide comments to blatant mockery and belittlement around other colleagues. This triggered me and brought up my experience of being bullied as a child. A thoughtful colleague gave me a "ra ra" and helped me to find the courage to confront my bully directly. What was hardest about the confrontation was that I had to be vulnerable. I needed to express in no uncertain terms how their behavior was hurting me and that I wouldn't accept it. I was a contractor at the time, so I felt I had to handle this between the two of us. As I spoke to him with sincerity, he apologized. His attitude quickly changed from judgemental to supportive. He felt remorse for many years afterward and would tear up whenever recollecting the times when he underestimated me, or was thoughtless about his comments and critiques. However, I understand workplace bullying and conflicts aren't always resolved with a direct conversation. Luckily, in this instance, it was.

Oftentimes once a line has been crossed, an insult made or perceived, or feelings have been hurt, you may find that there is no recovery, there is no possibility for forgiveness and a relationship can be permanently destroyed. But what I've found is that forgiveness can often be the pathway to transformation.

Transformation

I began a personal transformation journey shortly after this incident. It was one that took many years and had many turns. It required many books to be read and many journal entries and poems to be written, many meditations and many therapy sessions.

I began to celebrate my problem-solving skills, my ability to collaborate and communicate and build and nurture relationships. I saw leadership skills in others and began fostering them, mentoring people in my company, having grace for their learning curve, and having an understanding of the overwhelm they were experiencing starting at a large company.

I saw that my resiliency superpowers were fortitude, acceptance, and forgiveness. I was able to effectively bridge the gap between the different silos that existed in the company; between people and departments and divisions. I began to see myself as a leader, and I wanted to mirror that confidence with everyone I worked with. I wanted to see their potential and how we were like each other rather than different from one another.

Ultimately, it led me down the path to writing my memoir, Travels Through Aqua, Green, and Blue, which I published in August of 2020.

The culmination of my life experiences had sparked a deep desire to change, and I went down a long road of personal development and discovery. I realized that when we want something different, we have to do something different. Writing my memoir gave me a chance to see all of my experiences growing up and what impact they had on my life in the present day. I discovered areas that needed attention, and I worked on them.

A few months before I published my book, I was furloughed. The pandemic had a major impact on the live entertainment business, and I was one of the many casualties. I quickly realized that this time off would give me the kind of pause I needed to recenter. I would have the much-needed dedicated time to finish my book and bring it into the world. I found the silver lining in this experience and buckled down, and this extra time made the book that much better and I was able to fully experience the feeling of success from being a published author. Though without the party I had expected to have.

What I want you to take away from this chapter is to acknowledge that all of your experiences are invaluable lessons in leadership. What matters is to give credit to your journey. Oftentimes what we believe is the path to what we desire to be or to have is interwoven in experiences that look like failure. But looking at your journey can reveal greatness you've yet to recognize. There is likely a unique pattern to your resilience. This pattern is likely your superpower. Harness this power and let it lead the way.

I'm ending this chapter with a poem I wrote in May of 2019 that I believe exemplifies the awareness and acknowledgement of the greatness of our life's experiences.

My Poem

My power comes from some well of stories and history about me,

My evolution until now and my predictions of tomorrow.

My power is non-categorical.

It's not a talent, it's who I am.

It's unique, a combination of things;

A wink, a quirky gesture, a look, a style, a combination of raw feelings, a disposition, a curiosity, a kindness, a poem.

Had I known that my power was me, a beautiful poem about the good, the bad, the defiant, the valiant, the passion, the words were my very own poem, written everyday and treasured in every way, a story captivating, exhilarating.

Had I known this is my poem, my powerful poem, I would have studied it, appreciated it as the work of art that it is.

It's not some magazine look, some superficial, universal look, pleasing to the eye, internationally recognized.

It's the getting to know me kind, to see the inner strength, the not so obvious beauty that takes time to read and understand, one so lovely when you've read the story, you've understood the hurdles and triumphs and your heart soars with possibilities and hope, with happiness and sorrows.

This poem is my power, the words, their meaning, their life that is mine comes from within to be shared and written.

Had I known as a child that this poem was my power, not my talent, I could have spent my nights admiring the words, the stories and the hope.

I would know I have risen, I am rising, I will fall and I will get back up, over and over and that is glorious, beautiful, more beautiful than talent or beauty itself.

I would walk like a beautifully written poem, my poem and seize it, own it, love it, love me.

Write your poem, little one, begin at once. Share it and be proud of it.

It's your story and it's still being written, its ink is still wet, the verses are unfolding, this, your powerful poem.

About the Author

Mary E. Gregory is an American author, poet, and memoirist. She is a senior IT leader at a Fortune 500 live entertainment company in Los Angeles, California where she encourages her team to find a balance of personal passions with their work life. Mary's philosophy is that people are happier, more satisfied, have livelier conversations and more opportunities to build and nurture relationships when they're actively pursuing their dreams. She has been featured in Entrepreneur magazine, and on the popular podcasts, *Too Opinionated* and *The Future is Human*.

Mary is a passionate and heartfelt leader who infuses her writing with humanity and realism, with a balanced and deft approach to story-telling. Her stories are about resilience, forgiveness, transformation, and the human condition.

Her debut novel, *Travels Through Aqua, Green, and Blue: A Memoir*, won best first line by Booklife, a Publisher's Weekly company, and was endorsed by the executive producer of Eat, Pray, Love and American Beauty, Stan Wodkowski, and International Best-Selling Author, Hal Elrod.

Mary was born in Nashville, Tennessee, and is the youngest of three, and is a proud #catmom of several feline muses. She holds a degree in Management Information Systems from California State University, Long Beach. She is also a member of the American Society of Composers, Authors, and Publishers (ASCAP).

If you want to feel inspired and uplifted, follow her for more information:

https://maryegregory.com

You can also email Mary for speaking engagements and interviews:
info@maryegregory.com

- facebook.com/maryegregoryauthor
- twitter.com/MsMaryEGregory
- instagram.com/maryegregoryauthor
- linkedin.com/in/maryegregory

THIRTEEN

Peggy Hedgepeth

PRESSURED TO QUIT, I BUILT BIG INSTEAD: FIVE FOOT
TWO, EYES OF BLUE, AND CARRYING A BRIEFCASE

 business creative before my time, I struggled to succeed as a
woman in the business world.

The Only Woman In The Room

I was always a rule breaker. Not accepting the status quo has followed
me throughout my career. The quest for foundational knowledge was
always my thing. I loved to figure out how things work and wanted to
be the engine behind them working. From a young age, I always
wanted to be in business. Based on my upbringing, I investigated
Catholic colleges. My older sisters had gone to the University of
Dayton, but I wanted something different. I was interested in Boston
College. That was my first rude awakening, when I first became aware
that I was in the trenches. In 1968, Boston College did not allow
women into their School of Business. I could be a nurse, a teacher, or a
secretary, but not a business major.

It had never occurred to me that my natural drive to learn and build
and grow ideas would ever be stymied. As my education and career
advanced, discrimination was a given. I felt like I was constantly

crawling through mud, avoiding the bombs exploding around me, but I kept inching forward.

The University of Dayton did allow women to study business, so I went into computer science, which I envisioned as the future of all business. Yet again, during the first day of computer science class, the professor announced that women had no place in this field. He was not going to encourage *any* woman to pursue this path, and his office hours were closed to women. Despite my hard work, I got a C in the course. Curiously, so did all other girls. I considered anything below a B to be failing. Nonetheless, I knew the professor had the problem. He needed to change, not the women in his class. Acquiescing never occurred to me.

From computer science I changed majors to accounting, which ended up being a good thing. *The* computer at that time took up the entire third floor of the School of Business, with less computing power than today's cell phone. Everything I was learning would become obsolete in just a few years. Accounting itself hasn't changed dramatically over the years, but technology has.

In 1972, four women out of sixty graduates at our university completed their accounting degrees. I was one of them. With my degree, I went home to Cleveland to look for a job. I had a few interviews, very few. Since women were not accepted into any of the "Big 8" major accounting firms at that time, I started out working as a bookkeeper, quite beneath my education, while I looked for a professional job. Eventually, I was hired by the Internal Revenue Service (IRS). With Equal Employment Opportunity (EEO) guidelines, they were desperate to find women with accounting degrees. We were rare, as my graduating class indicated. They hired me not as an office auditor, a position most women were relegated to, but as an agent to do corporate work thanks to my degree in accounting! Among thirty-seven men, three other women and I went to Cincinnati for training. We spent four solid months, eight hours a day, studying tax law. Looking back, I view that IRS certification as the equivalent of a master's degree in taxation, something few other women had been able to accomplish.

Back in Cleveland, I conducted IRS audits of small businesses during the day and at night studied for the certified public accountant (CPA) exam. I passed. The AICPA threw a special dinner for the newly certified. Given that the accounting industry was male dominated, the new CPAs were invited to bring their father to the dinner. With 150 fathers and 150 successful candidates, I was the only graduate from the University of Dayton, the only person working for the IRS, and the only woman in the room. I did not fit the cookie cutter mold.

The Trenches

From all the audits I conducted, one specifically still amuses me. I audited a gas station, which required me to do fieldwork in a less-desirable part of town. I was only twenty-four years old, 5'2" with eyes of blue, and carrying a briefcase. (Few women then carried briefcases, fewer worked for the IRS, and almost none worked in the field.) I drove my little VW early in the morning to the assigned gas station, which was noted to belong to an ex-convict.

When I entered the outer room of the building, I was greeted by six large Black men wearing street garb. My first thought was, "Wow, this place is crowded at 8:30 a.m.." It totally escaped me that their greeting was supposed to intimidate me. Asking for the owner, I was sent to an inner room where even more gentlemen towered over me as I looked around to get started. There was no desk or table to sit at to conduct the audit. The situation started sinking in.

IRS rules stated that all audits were to be conducted on site. Given the circumstances, however, rule-breaking was a given. I told the taxpaying owner that his audit would now be conducted in the federal building. He should set up an appointment and come into my office with his books and records in hand. Taking my leave, all those tall men chuckled as they parted the way to let me through. I think I was as big of a surprise for them as they were for me.

In 1975, I applied for a job in Washington, DC, as an international IRS agent. Arriving early in DC for the interview, I waited in a coffee shop downstairs. Drinking my coffee, an IRS manager approached and asked me if I was there for an interview. When I said yes, he smiled and said that he wanted me to interview to be his secretary. I explained I was there for an agent's position, not a secretary. He looked perplexed and left.

With the agent's job in hand, I moved to Washington, DC. More months of intense training ensued, this time in international tax law. These audits involved tax issues of international companies and wealthy, often famous, individuals. My work took me from DC to New York to Beverly Hills. To follow the money in these audits, I analyzed international royalty and licensing agreements. I got a good look at the guts of businesses with international tax implications. I was up against big teams of high-powered New York and California law firms, their suited-up lawyers and me, now twenty-six, still 5 2" with eyes of blue and carrying a briefcase. I did not back down. I figured I had studied more tax law than they ever encountered in law school. I was good at what I did.

After two years as a field agent, I wanted more education, so I applied for a position as a competent authority analyst in the IRS Tax Treaty Division. Night school followed at George Washington University, where I successfully achieved an MBA in international business. Two years later I completed my master's thesis on international trade. Little did I know how invaluable this education and these experiences would be for my work later in starting an international wholesale business.

Eventually, I applied for a position that would not require travel in Appeals at the IRS national office.

Howard, the director of Appeals, had many professional women on his staff. He had figured out that women who made it that far were bright, hard working, and the crème de la crème. Unfortunately, the regional directors around the country did not have the same awareness and attitude and referred to us as "Howard's Harem." What an insult.

In 1980, six weeks after I had my son, I was expected to return to the office. At that time, childcare was exceedingly difficult to find, but a neighbor lady taking care of other children agreed to watch my son for me. Well, until she found out that I worked for the IRS. Given that she had not been reporting her taxes, she canceled our agreement one week before I returned to work. Great.

Juggling home and work is hard at any time, but in the 1980s, it was a nightmare.

I was soon promoted to the technical advisor to the director of Appeals, and my office faced Constitution Avenue. I should have felt like I had arrived, but given that I had a child at home and a non-supportive work environment, I did not. I recognized that there was a creative hole in me that was not being filled. I was just shoveling dry tax papers back and forth across a desk, not creating a single thing. I ended up burning out.

So, I quit the IRS.

The Transition

Collaborating with another female professional, I set up a garden shop in Arlington, Virginia. This was when nurseries resembled feed and seed stores; there was no such thing then as a true garden shop. As women, we could not get funding. So, we did it all on sweat equity, a very tight budget, and my retirement, which I took out from the federal system. As two women owners, we named our store Mrs. McGregor's Garden Shop. The business was profitable the first year and started to thrive. I learned firsthand the ins and outs of being a retailer. This experience helped me understand my retail customer's needs and psyche as well as the strategies behind making money, something I had not learned at the IRS. After three years, my partner and I were at a deep divide on what direction the shop should take. She was happy running a small retail shop; I wanted more. We parted ways, and she ended up with the store.

The Creative Years

Owning Mrs. McGregor's, I saw the demand for teak garden furniture, so I set up a new business using non-rainforest teak from Indonesia.

After doing research and reaching out around the world, I set out on a flight to Indonesia, forty hours flying literally around the globe.

On that very first visit in 1989, I had a life-changing weekend. I am convinced it was from the radiating energy of Bali. The island vibrates with the culture of the Balinese people, everywhere there are colorful flowers and incense offerings to their Hindu gods and ancestors. Temples populate the rich rainforests, volcanic mountain sides, and beaches.

I found myself at a small local market. While everyone was looking at the colorful fruits and vegetables the Balinese were selling, I was looking at the bowls in which they were displayed. They were exquisitely styled, large green enamelware with swirls. I fell in love. My first thought looking at the bowl and style was, "This is a business." It was like finding a gold nugget in the dirt. That is how it all started.

In my excitement, I set up more than only the teak business. I also visited every enamel manufacturer in Indonesia as I was in love with the medium, the style, the light weight, the coloration, and the durability of the enamelware.

Back in Virginia, I set up shop and sent off factory orders. I received my first container of enamelware before any teak arrived. I established a relationship with an enamelware factory in Java, and we have been working together for thirty-four years. At first, I was their smallest export customer. Today, we are their largest.

The relationship was not always smooth, especially as a woman doing business in a Muslim country. I recollect the first meeting with the factory management team when they tried to dissuade me. They said the products I wanted, swirl designs on big enamel pieces, were for the poorer domestic market in Indonesia, not the American market. Then they showed me a little bowl with ducks on it and suggested that would be more appropriate for my market. Definitely not!

Over time, my teak supplier proved to be unreliable, and I had a problem with the enamel as well. The first container had dust pits, a big headache. To solve the problem, they cleaned the ovens, yet I still had a container of defective goods to get rid of. They then sent me half of a container of yellow enamelware, loaded with cadmium that did not pass FDA guidelines. I was stuck with it.

I worked both businesses diligently until a container of teak arrived that was supposed to be full of pre-sold teak sunflower benches. It ended up being hundreds and hundreds of sunflower plaques. With these ongoing issues, six years into it, I recognized through this supplier that the teak business was non-viable. Now broke, I decided to pull the plug on it.

Enamel was slow going. But with more time available without the teak, I continued to work at the enamel business because of its steady growth.

Facing the possibility of going out of business completely, I took on a partner. Even in the 1990s, as a woman in a man's world, my hands were still tied; I could not get a loan as a *mere* female entrepreneur. I needed money in a system that wouldn't grant it to me. Reluctantly, I gave up my independence as a sole business owner to access financing through a private investor. We made a deal.

For a modest investment of money in Golden Rabbit, he became 50 percent owner of my enamel business. He ran a small warehouse in New York, so the agreement was that he would manage the warehouse, and I would do everything else—manage the factories, develop our products, handle finances, marketing, communications, and so on. For fifteen years he was my business partner, but I had the bulk of the work.

As it turned out, he was not accountable and condescending to boot. The team he had put together for the warehouse was far under par. Large amounts of inventory went missing from the warehouse regularly. He would claim it was due to *my* computer errors. When I attempted to discuss business issues with him, he would talk over me as though I was not speaking or act like my opinion did not matter. Every day I was bludgeoned with comments like, "This business is a joke" and "It can never be more than a little niche gift business." I felt demoralized and disregarded. Although I had the suspicion there were shady things going on in the operation, I could not nail anything down. I felt trapped.

Given the Indonesian factory had design limitations, I developed a parallel import business of enamel from China. Again, I needed funds. Given the standard difficulties for female entrepreneurs to get loans, with this male business partner, we were able to secure bank loans for that business.

In 2008 the recession hit. In addition, the factory in Indonesia burned down, and we could not source any inventory from them for over twelve months. At the same time, the Chinese government closed factories and redistributed workers. Our enamel factories in China were government owned, so they were dissolved in that restructuring. That avenue of product sourcing was closed.

Although we continued to do trade shows, our inventory was shrinking due to the lack of product sourcing. Contracts were canceled and customers became disgruntled.

The business was in deep debt, with bill collectors calling me daily. My husband also worked full time as an international tax consultant in a pressure-cooker job. As the situation intensified, my evening glass of wine turned into a whole bottle. Depression ensued. I simply could not cope anymore. The circumstances had become overwhelming for me. After years of hard work, diligence, discrimination across the board, and hard knocks that I often dealt with alone, I was done in.

The Turning Point

In March of 2009, I checked myself into intensive therapy, which is the best thing I have ever done. I began to turn things around in my inner world. The antidepressants helped, and I stopped drinking altogether. Mostly, however, I was able to climb back up thanks to the support of people who believed in me and wanted to see me succeed. I began to believe in myself again.

It took me two more years, with my head screwed on straight and my faith in myself strong again, before I was able to face up to the unhealthy dynamics in my business partnership. To bring that situation to a permanent end, I had to assume all the debt and agree to pay my business partner 20 percent of the profits for the next four years. It was not a fair deal, but one I was glad to make.

What happened then was a rebirth. Although still named Golden Rabbit, I rebranded the company, and it was a breath of fresh air. I hired a marketing consultant. I took on a showroom at the AmericasMart in Atlanta, the largest wholesale market in the country for gift and home. We went online with a website, developed new products, and reprioritized inventory. In the process, I ended up spending everything that came in. We did not make a profit for four years, so were not liable for the distributions to my former partner.

My team and I have built a quality product and a quality company that offers a higher end, more durable line enamelware as an alternative to the cheaper products made in China. Golden Rabbit's serveware and cookware are now available online through companies such as Pottery Barn, William Sonoma, Neiman Marcus, and Nordstrom, to name a few. Although I have retired my briefcase, I am still 5'2" with eyes of blue and the sole owner of a successful company—no partners to be seen anywhere!

Success, Finally

Looking back, it was a long and winding road. I have highlighted here only a few of the many struggles I have faced and overcome along the way. I felt driven to see it through, no matter what. I kept thinking, *This just cannot be that hard. I have the education, I have the experience, I have the creativity, I have the knowledge.*

In review, I see it has been my tenacity, diligence, and creativity that has landed me today with a successful and thriving company. My advice is to claim the confidence to go it alone. You cannot assume that other people have the same values or abilities as you have. They must be vetted.

And trust yourself. No matter what others say or do, believe in your own vision. Act from that place of strength and intuition within yourself. I look at the entrepreneurial women today and see that they are thinking much, much bigger. I find that exciting. I did the best I could. Yet, if I could do it all over again, I would trust myself to do it on my own.

About the Author

An entrepreneur, creator, and former technical advisor to the director of Appeal at the IRS, Peggy Hedgpeth is CEO of the successful international company she has built over the last thirty-four years. Her MBA in international business and CPA certification also serve her well as managing director and CFO. But the company is not what you might think.

Golden Rabbit offers the world a lively line of dinnerware, serveware, and cookware that make guests and family feel special. A table set with Golden Rabbit enamelware creates a warm atmosphere where family and friends feel treasured, important, and welcome. Peggy's values of friendship, pleasure, comfort, and good food are hallmarks of the company's focus and unique style.

The Golden Rabbit line, designed in the United States and manufactured in Indonesia, has been doing avid business for years thanks to Peggy's vision of online sales. In 2015 far before its time, the company went virtual with remote workspaces scattered around the country. This rare combination of right-brain and left-brain acumen have contributed to her success.

In her chapter "Pressured to Quit, I Built Big Instead," Peggy describes the then-normalized yet highly hindering attitudes and practices that kept bright, driven, and creative women "in their place." She highlights the many barriers she came up against while rising to success and illuminates how resilience, adaptability, and non-conformity built her stairs upward.

~

Website: www.Goldenrabbit.com

in linkedin.com/in/peggyhedgpeth

FOURTEEN

Kasia Hein-Peters

SCIENCEPRENEUR ACADEMY: BORN DURING THE PANDEMIC

*T*he pandemic fundamentally challenged my views on how I should spend the remaining years of my professional career.

But let's start from the beginning. I am a doctor with more than thirty years of experience in the corporate world—pharmaceutical, biotechnology, and medical device companies. I joined the industry as a young psychiatrist and never looked back. Even though I liked the clinical aspects of being a doctor and the fact that I was helping patients, my new employers offered a more fulfilling career. First, I noticed quickly that introducing new medications, vaccines, and procedures could positively influence more patients than my work as an individual doctor. New standards of care had the power to change the course of diseases of millions of patients or prevent them completely. Second, my employers had a good habit of continuously training their people. At least once a year, we had a chance to attend an education event in addition to on-the-job training. The introduction of a new drug or medical device is complex, and I was always looking forward to understanding the process even better, from clinical trials and regulatory approval, through market development and, finally, the commercial launch. An industry career has another interesting aspect of constant traveling. During my business trips, I visited more than fifty countries and got to know people of many faiths and ethnicities. Working across diverse cultures let me understand locals much better than if I went there just to vacation. The industry rewarded my continuous learning with frequent promotions, and I thought I would continue this lifestyle until retirement.

The drive to learn has many pluses and one significant downside—boredom when there is not much left to learn. In retrospect, I think I was addicted to constant improvement and sometimes changed jobs when I felt that I had exhausted all learning opportunities. A stable job was not for me, so I was seeking challenges and novelty. Also, my interests were broader than those of my employers'. This is why I studied innovation based on the Blue Ocean Strategy, kept abreast of behavioral economics and positive psychology advancements to understand people's behaviors better, and studied executive coaching at Teachers College, Columbia University, to improve as a leader.

Pandemic, Inequality and Innovation

And then came the pandemic. It upended the lives of all of us and changed how we worked. In my case, it also provided a new challenge as I was given the leadership of the COVID-19 response in the company where I worked at that time. When I think about the years 2020 and 2021, I reflect on what exactly led to my "awakening" and career pivot. I think it started with burnout within the first few months, as I was juggling three jobs—my old job in marketing and communication, my new job in medical affairs and market access, and leading the COVID-19 response. Even though the burnout passed, I realized I could not continue working like that anymore. Having so many responsibilities made me feel like I could not do anything well, as there were not enough hours in a day.

The pandemic also affected me emotionally for several reasons. Once again, I realized how inequality in healthcare, which I always knew existed, led to disproportionate deaths among minorities globally and in the United States. Racial and ethnic minority groups had higher risks of COVID-19 infection and hospitalization, confirmed diagnosis, and death. In the United States, the most significant factor was a higher infection rate of people of color, leading to a higher death rate. The risk of exposure and differences in healthcare access were the drivers of these sobering statistics. It hit close to home, as my husband is African American, and watching "his people" sick and dying at a rate so much higher than the rest of us was excruciating. In the face of this data, nothing felt more important than changing the healthcare system to serve everyone equally. We have one of the most advanced treatments available in the United States and the highest number of innovations in healthcare anywhere in the world. One would assume that the system would focus on distributing health services equally to all, yet this was not and still is not the case.

And then came the COVID-19 vaccines. I worked in vaccine companies for twelve years, launching the first HPV vaccine, a new meningitis vaccine, the first vaccine against dengue fever, and a hexavalent pediatric vaccine, so I knew firsthand how much time the clinical development takes. In the past, the fastest vaccine development was four years for a mumps vaccine launched in 1967. So, the race to develop a COVID-19 vaccine was unprecedented and surprised me with its speed while keeping high scientific integrity. I was also surprised that two leading COVID-19 vaccines came from startup companies, not well-established vaccine manufacturers. BioNTech (with Pfizer as a partner) and Moderna became the heroes of the pandemic, saving millions of lives with their novel mRNA platform.

I was keeping track of COVID-19 vaccines under development, and I noticed something else. Many other startup companies were founded by brilliant scientists but did not progress as fast as Moderna and BioNTech, and most never launched their COVID-19 vaccines. Their founders were knowledgeable scientifically yet lacked the skills required to commercialize successfully. It was similar in other areas of medicine— many scientists, doctors, and engineers were developing new solutions, yet so few were successful. What was going on? I started by looking at the data. I found out that overall, less than 10 percent of launches in the pharmaceutical industry are considered excellent, 90 percent of new technologies fail in the marketplace, and only 50 percent of healthcare innovations meet investors' expectations. In summary, the industry is not successful. And yet, most innovative solutions originate in startups and small companies run by passionate founders whose goal is to solve the biggest unmet needs that are not yet addressed. This contrasts with big companies that also develop new treatments but focus on well-established technologies they can turn into very profitable platforms.

There are many reasons why small companies and startups fail:

- They may not be able to raise sufficient venture capital funding, preventing them from finalizing clinical development and scaling up the company. This is usually the result of either not having a robust strategy or not being able to communicate it convincingly.
- Some lack competencies that are critical for success in clinical development, product registration, and commercialization.
- Some founders focus on new technology without sufficient understanding of the market and customers, which leads to poor product-market fit or lack of competitive advantage.

There are other reasons, too, and all of them come down to some gaps in knowledge. The founders of startups are scientists, engineers, doctors, and other health professionals. They understand the science behind their products and the disease they want to treat but frequently do not know how to manage the complexity of the healthcare ecosystem with its multiple stakeholders and their various levels of influence. I saw many breakthrough medications and medical devices with great potential, and yet they went nowhere; they withered after millions of dollars were spent on research, development, and commercialization. And this happened because they didn't know what leading companies knew about launching billion-dollar brands.

"Aha Moment"

My "aha moment" happened when I realized that I knew how to help these startups and that sharing my knowledge is the best way to support innovation and equity in healthcare. At that moment, I switched from focusing on my own learning to teaching and coaching the startup founders. This was my awakening. I decided not to follow the corporate path any longer but instead focus on creating an offer for startup founders to help them bring their solutions to patients faster. Small companies don't have the luxury of big budgets and big teams, and although very talented, they often lack experience and knowledge of how to bring their innovations to patients in the most efficient and least costly way. They compensate for these shortcomings with passion and hard work and could benefit from the competencies of someone who launched a dozen products, including a $3 billion blockbuster vaccine.

So, I decided to help small company founders ensure that their innovative solutions reach patients as quickly as possible. After years of shaping markets and developing product strategies, I created a proprietary strategic framework that helps to develop a winning enterprise or product strategy. It helps to maximize the value of an innovative product, increase the return on investment (ROI) and adequately scale up the organization. It helps to create a founder's legacy and change the lives of patients to whom the new therapy is meant. I called my framework DIVE, which stands for Discovery, Innovation, Value, and Execution. This is the method that will work long term once a person masters it. It works for startups, it works for other small and mid-size companies, and it works for scientific and medical affairs teams in big companies, too.

The DIVE framework is based on my experience and knowledge from multiple launches I oversaw, books I read, and courses I took. It's thirty years of professional experience distilled into a training and coaching program. Over my career in the industry, I launched twelve new products, including a blockbuster vaccine that achieved three billion dollars in peak sales. Many of these products profoundly changed the standards of care and how we practice medicine today. They saved and improved patient lives. Finally, they brought billions of dollars in revenue to companies where I worked. Even though there was massive success, mistakes were made as well, and it is my goal to ensure that you don't make the same mistakes.

I teach how to launch a life-changing product. Most life science entrepreneurs, or as I call them, SciencePreneurs, go about things differently than what really works. First, they get an idea of a product. They think about it a lot, get passionate about it, and develop it with regulatory approval in mind. They may get funding or use their own resources and money from family and friends. They build a team of like-minded individuals. But the fact is, this is a risky way to do it, as it is too product-centric. Most founders' go-to-market strategies are entirely different from what successful companies do.

There are three ways in how SciencePreneurs launch their product. Most focus on product development, and when the time seems right, they start thinking about commercialization.

One group focuses on sales immediately after developing their product. They may hire a Chief Commercial Officer and then the sales team and focus on one-to-one selling to the most promising accounts. They typically don't understand how a strategic marketing approach could help them increase their return on investment (ROI) and switch from an outbound to an inbound approach.

The other way is to hire a Chief Marketing Officer who takes the product as it is and focuses on the marketing strategy. They develop brand identity and logo, identify customer personas and develop key messages. Then they work on the website, marketing videos, and sales enablement tools for their sales team. It is a little more systematic than just focusing on sales, but it comes too late. The product is already developed with minimal input from customers, and it is impossible to change it. Needless to say, the product is usually not a perfect fit with the market.

The third, worst way, is to wait too long to figure out the go-to-market strategy. This group is happy to focus on product development and initiates several studies before even thinking about their commercialization strategy. They might hope for the exit before launching the product or even think the product will sell itself once it's ready to take to market.

While the first two may seem like sensible ways to launch your brand, they are usually not very successful and can lead to an incredible amount of lost time and, worse, a launch that never truly gets off the ground.

Outside-In Accelerator

Successful innovative healthcare brands do things differently. In fact, they do what I call an Outside-In Accelerator. So, what is an Outside-In Accelerator? This happens when companies have finely baked the customer insights and market understanding into their product profile, which almost guarantees fast adoption during launch in the right patient population. Now, they do this by planning their commercial strategy very early, and they don't develop the marketing and sales roadmaps as an afterthought. The implementation of the Outside-In Accelerator increases the market demand for a new therapy because it eliminates barriers to adoption in patient populations where the treatment is intended to be used. The launch is smooth and meets or exceeds financial expectations. Of course, everybody can learn it on their own, but it will take you several years as it took me.

So how can the DIVE framework help SciencePreneurs successfully implement the Outside-In Accelerator? By following four dimensions: Discovery, Innovation, Value, and Execution.

Discovery starts with a deep understanding of the unmet need that a company wants to address. Once the unmet need is defined and quantified, a company can develop a definition of its market and continue with a market assessment. Especially important is the analysis of competitors and alternative treatments because the innovative product must be better in relevant ways. Mapping stakeholders and understanding their needs helps design the product positioning and develop a target product profile. Overall, without robust **Discovery**, one cannot develop the right product, create market value, and a successful go-to-market strategy. **Discovery** never stops; a company must consistently incorporate customer insights and understand emerging market trends throughout the product's lifecycle.

Innovation is the goal of product development. It starts with creating a target product profile and a vision for future product positioning. Once these two components are developed, one can create an evidence-generation plan. The evidence-generation plan should consist of clinical studies that satisfy the regulatory requirements and create a differentiation in the market and value for other stakeholders, such as payers, clinicians, and patients.

The **Innovation** phase also never ends, although it is the most extensive before product regulatory approval or clearance. The most successful companies first register products for indications that are substantial unmet needs. Then they continue their development process to show efficacy and safety in other patient populations. Interestingly, the higher the unmet need the innovation addresses, the fewer marketing dollars are needed to spend during the launch.

The **Value** creation process adds market value to the innovation and helps turn it into a financial success. Value creation is essential to develop a thorough go-to-market strategy. It is a set of decisions that improve a company's ROI. The resources are always limited, so one must carefully choose target customer segments and develop a compelling value proposition. The biggest challenge at this stage is FOMO (fear of missing out). It feels that giving up some market segments will eliminate sales opportunities, but the reality is the opposite. By focusing on segments with reasonably high potential and the biggest ability to win, a company maximizes the ROI, return on time and effort, and return on innovation. Once the product wins in the primary market segment, it can move on to other market parts. One cannot build a billion-dollar brand by scratching the surface but by maximizing the investment in the primary target segment. **Value** continues to evolve as the product development process generates new data in new patient populations or new evidence to strengthen the position among current customers, winning market share versus competitors.

Execution of the strategy starts early on, with building the new organization and appropriately developing a communication strategy for investors and media. As a company moves through clinical development milestones toward commercialization, the organization must be scaled up to include additional capabilities. A founder must develop a unique go-to-market plan with the right performance indicators to measure progress. The biggest mistake is to leave the commercialization strategy development for "later" or think that "the product will sell itself" once it has regulatory approval or clearance.

I used this framework in many areas of life sciences, such as specialty pharmaceuticals, vaccines, hospital antibiotics, and medical devices, and recently for digital health. If it is used correctly, the results will be exponential because most competitors don't do it this way.

These four dimensions are not linear steps but continue over the entire product lifecycle. Initially, **Discovery** is the most important to ensure a good understanding of the market opportunity and potential barriers. Yet one must continue to gather learning from the market, especially competitive intelligence and emerging trends.

The **Innovation** phase takes the most time and effort before the regulatory approval, but it doesn't stop there. The company continues to implement the post-marketing data generation plan, collecting safety data and proving the product value in new patient populations.

Building **Value** should start early when a founder decides on the product development plan and how it will support a robust value proposition.

And finally, **Execution** is important throughout the entire life cycle. As the organization continues to grow, communication strategy changes and the go-to-market continues to evolve based on the market evolution.

My goal is to teach SciencePreneurs how to do this right and prevent mistakes, which may cost them a lot of money and waste time and effort. SciencePreneurs are smart and dedicated scientists, healthcare professionals, engineers, or marketers in the life science industry. Their intention is to create a lasting change, help improve the healthcare system and monetize their innovation. And yet they may not have deep experience in launching new products and not have a big team or a huge budget. They may be at a disadvantage to more prominent companies with bigger teams and more resources. However, all SciencePreneurs have one clear advantage over others: the way they approach problems scientifically by gathering evidence, formulating hypotheses, and testing them. The same methodology can be applied to the development of the overall strategy, including commercialization. The DIVE framework is based on the scientific and strategic way of thinking and will help launch world-leading brands and build successful businesses.

In conclusion, the way to improve healthcare and make it more equitable is by supporting innovations that can be rolled out to all patient demographics. We have great potential to do so, and we need to focus on the most effective ways to provide patient access.

About the Author

Kasia Hein-Peters, MD has more than 30 years of experience in healthcare as a psychiatrist and a leader in top pharmaceutical, biotechnology, medical device, and digital health startup companies. She oversaw the launches of several first-in-class medications, which profoundly changed the standards of care and a vaccine with peak sales of 3 billion dollars.

In her chapter, Kasia will explore what led her to abandoning a successful corporate career and founding the SciencePreneur Academy, which partners with life science executives to build world-leading brands and help millions of patients.

Kasia started practicing medicine at the age of six by experimenting on her teddy bear with a real IV drip full of water. She got both as gifts after undergoing minor surgery, because she was so fascinated with the medical equipment that she saw in a hospital and wanted to figure out how it worked. Over the years, Kasia developed expertise in bringing new drugs, vaccines, and medical devices to the market. She believes that innovation in healthcare matters only if patients have equitable access to it, as the treatment doesn't work if barriers prevent its prescribing, administration, or acceptance.

Kasia lives in Las Vegas, NV and in her spare time explores the Mojave Desert with its beautiful mountains, canyons, and occasional ancient rock art. While hiking, she takes photos and writes haiku (Japanese short poetry), trying to express the moment through pictures and words. She calls these poems hike-u, from "haiku while hiking."

~

Website: www.sciencepreneur.co

twitter.com/Kasia_HP
linkedin.com/in/kasiaheinpeters

FIFTEEN

Rachael Maier

MOTHER NATURE: LEADING FROM A PLACE OF LOVE

*Y*ou know those days when you pull out of your driveway and the next thing you know, you're backing into a parking spot at Target? Gripping the steering wheel and staring blankly out the windshield thinking, "How did I get here?"

That's where I found myself in late 2020, a decade into a successful career. Except it wasn't a Target parking lot; it was my life. And it was about to come crashing down.

On the heels of moving to an island with my partner just before the pandemic and after buying my first home, I found out that at thirty-six, my first and only pregnancy was going to fail.

That was when my world as I knew it and my future as I'd planned it fell apart, when I started questioning everything—including who I was and what I was doing with my life.

That was when I spontaneously awakened from the dream.

Unsteady Ground

How I got there is how most people half-asleep get to the bathroom in the middle of the night: winding my way in the darkness disoriented, bumping into walls, and tripping over things I would have seen if I were fully awake and the lights were on.

I was working as a barista in a cafe in my neighborhood in Oakland during the 2008 recession. I had tried and failed to get a foothold in the nonprofit sector after graduating college with a sociology degree two years prior. (I didn't realize that merely having a college degree neither guaranteed one work nor prepared you for the real-world experience of being an adult.)

I was questioning my life and its direction daily as I ground espresso beans and tried—just this once—to make a heart or an amorphous leaf with the steamed milk. *I am capable of so much more* was a mental mantra sometimes accidentally muttered under my breath. But without experience or marketable skills to back up this belief, I resorted to cobbling together an income with odd jobs to get by. And at the end of each day, I felt exhausted and unfulfilled and worried that this was adult life and what the rest of my life would be like.

That's when one of my regular cafe customers told me she was leaving her part-time job at the front desk of a startup to attend medical school and urged me to apply. "But I don't have any front-desk experience," was my automatic reply. She encouraged me to apply anyway. I took her advice and, to my dismay, I got the job.

And that's when the dream began.

To combat the imposter syndrome I felt, I decided I would prove (mostly to myself) that I deserved to be there. I could and I would outwork anyone. What I lacked in experience, I would make up for in effort.

Thus began a successful digital media content career and my long ascent up a ladder I didn't realize I was climbing and desperately clinging to for survival. A ladder I would dedicate the majority of my twenties and thirties to, without questioning what was sitting at the top and whether I even wanted it.

Airs and Graces

A few months into my new job, I was feeling the same dissatisfaction I had as a barista. To prove that I was valuable beyond the duties in my job description, I took it upon myself to expand my front desk duties and started writing articles for the editorial team after work and on weekends.

I showed that I was capable and willing to help out, and within a year of starting at the front desk, I was promoted to assistant editor and moved to the editorial department. This was my ticket out of mindless grunt work and into the mentally stimulating work I desired. This was the "so much more" I knew I was capable of.

It was also something new that I didn't yet know how to do. The strategy was obvious: I would work even harder at this role. So hard that I was often the last person in the office, and so often that the night cleaning crew and I knew each other by name.

In the meantime, I discovered I had a knack not just for editing, but for building teams and improving the systems required to run the teams. I was good at it, and I genuinely enjoyed my work.

A year later, I was offered the role of managing editor. Again, the imposter syndrome flared up. *But I didn't know how to be a managing editor. I'm just a barista posing as a front desk person posing as an assistant editor. Shouldn't someone more qualified take the role? Now I really better work my butt off to prove myself.*

And so it went: with each promotion (there were five), I outperformed expectations and was rewarded with a new role with even more responsibilities, with which I had no previous experience. And the cycle of needing to prove—and improve—myself restarted.

I'd buy more self-help and business books to buffer against my green-ness and understand "how to" (meet expectations, strengthen my weaknesses, be better at x, y, or z). I built a library of how to be someone entirely other than myself.

By the time I looked up to catch my breath, I was the VP of Content & Operations, leading a seventy-five-person editorial team across three countries and as many websites. The fledgling website I helped build from the ground up was now the number one health website in the world, and a large company had just acquired us.

I had become successful by all accounts, but I was burnt out and gasping for air. I had become dependent on my work not just for my survival (San Francisco is a hell of a city to struggle in), but for the external validation that served as my savings account for self-worth.

That's when she came along with her golden sledgehammer: my daughter, Elora. My first and only child, the Great Awakener. She tore it all down like drywall, opening up the room to make more space and forcing me to examine it before rebuilding.

She came into my life shortly after my partner, Kevin, and I moved to the rural wilds of Hawai'i with the intention of settling down and starting a life together. She made her presence known in the summer of 2020 and by Thanksgiving, we were preparing for her departure at twenty-three weeks in utero.

She was diagnosed with a chromosomal abnormality called Trisomy 18, a condition considered "incompatible with life." Most babies don't make it out of the womb alive, and those who do usually don't survive longer than a week.

Receiving this news broke me. But what crumbled me to pieces was having to make the decision about when to say goodbye. I didn't think I could, but I had to. So I reached deep within the well at the bottom of my being and pulled up the reserves of strength I didn't know I had: the strength to let go.

That's when the levees broke and the sandcastle of an identity I'd built around my career dissolved like an over-sodden cookie in room-temperature milk.

Forged through Fire

There were several times before this that I could have left: (1) when the website became number one; (2) when the company got bought; (3) when I moved to Hawai'i; (4) when I hit my ten-year anniversary.

But why would I? I was comfortable. I had a fantastic boss who believed in me and continued to give me opportunities to grow. I had an amazing team I built from the ground up and genuinely loved as people. I even had a beautiful wardrobe and a French perfume collection. I put so much hard work, so many years and after-hours of my life into this, and it was paying off.

So at each milestone, I held on tighter and tighter. But growth without boundaries or direction is cancer. And underlying my satisfaction and comfort in staying put was fear: fear that I was not enough. Fear that I was a one-hit wonder or I wouldn't be able to find something else I was good at. Fear that my experience wouldn't mean anything beyond the walls in which it was gained.

When my worst fear of all came true, suddenly all the rest seemed inconsequential. I saw through all the lies I'd been telling myself to placate my fears. I was not happy living this way. Work had come before everything in my life—including my life.

Now I wanted it back.

After I left my job, I spent almost two years healing from my child loss, getting back in touch with myself, and deconstructing my relationship with work. The first few weeks into medical leave, my body was dealing with a loss that my brain was still struggling to comprehend. Exhaustion from the previous decade set in, compounding with the traumatic event, and I could barely move from the couch.

I started to feel the full brunt of how burnt out I was.

I slowed down...*waaaay* down instead of fighting it and pushing through like I usually did. The pendulum had swung hard in one direction for a long time, and now it was swinging with that same force in the other.

I let my body rest and feel it all.

For the first time in years, I slept without an alarm clock and awoke every morning at whatever time my body naturally came out of sleep. Most days I didn't have an agenda or to-do list. I did do things (most days), but I did them because I wanted to or the moment demanded that of me or I arrived at the conclusion *this* was to be done in *this* moment.

Living in this way made a lot more sense to me than the perpetual summer of the business world. It felt better—more human, more alive. And so did I.

About a month and a half into my leave, a strange thing began to happen: I got the insatiable urge to write. First as a distraction, something to focus on other than my grief, something productive to do after I had been hard-wired for doing all these years. But then it became a necessity, like going to the bathroom.

Writing became a sharp processing tool precise enough to cut through all the noise. It had finally gone quiet enough for me to listen to the small voice whispering to be heard when I sat down at a blank page. I submitted to this (super)natural force every day, sometimes multiple times a day, hundreds then thousands of words at a time.

Slowly, I fanned the flimsy flames of self-recognition and self-truths until they became a hearth I could warm myself by.

Through writing, I began to understand my feelings, my situation, and the world around me. And there was so much to understand. The emotional labor—processing my child loss and coming to terms with my perfectionistic and people-pleasing tendencies as well as the imposter syndrome that drove me to perfectionism and people-pleasing—was a different type of hard work.

And it was working.

I began to open my clenched fists, laying down my strong-armed will and the heavy, calcified armor that made it appear (and made me think) I was impenetrable. The gaping hole I felt in the center of my chest made it obvious I was not OK, and there was no way I could go back to pretending to be.

Tending the Hearth

In the silence of reflection, I saw how I'd been living and leading from a place of fear. How had my response to real and perceived stress felt to my team? I worried I passed on my insecurities and not-enoughness to them. I wondered how many nights and weekends they spent efforting against my unrealistic expectations as I had.

Some months after my departure, I had a catch-up call with Isabel, one of my direct reports for over five years. We talked for hours, covering all aspects of life like we usually did. Toward the end of the conversation, I apologized for inflicting my stress on her. She was quiet for a moment before acknowledging how unbelievably hard it was at times, and yet how amazing it was that we were able to do what we did.

And we both agreed we would never want to do it again.

I tried taking a few new paths, but none of them seemed to be a clear route forward; none grabbed me like I hoped they would. None were the obvious next step. So I continued to write and listen and wait — a real struggle for the perennial doer I had been and was trying to un-become.

One day while I was laying on the couch in the grips of boredom, I got an email from a recruiter via LinkedIn. Normally, I'd ignore a message like that, assuming it was spam or a blast email with very little relevance. But I felt some curiosity and, at the behest of my intuition, replied to the email: "Sure, let's talk."

The next thing I knew, I had a meeting on the calendar for the next day and was meeting the CEO and VPs the day after. Two weeks later, I was flying to company headquarters in St. Louis and signing a contract for the role of VP of Content.

I was ready for a new challenge. I was stagnating with more time on my hands than I knew what to do and little structure. (Too much winter, it turns out, can be just as unhealthy as too much summer.) I was ready to step into the dream again, but this time with full lucidity.

While I was excited to go back, I was determined not to go *back*.

I knew that re-entering the start-up world came with the type of trigger warning a recovering alcoholic faces when entering a bar. So I was vigilant and set some boundaries up front. Regardless of the five-hour time difference, my regular work day would start at 8:00 a.m. I would not attend meetings before 7:00 a.m. my time—and that was to be the rare exception. My boss gave his word: "We will protect your schedule."

I felt heard and respected and proud of myself for speaking up for my needs, not self-sacrificing from fear of what my boss would think of me. I felt proud for setting the tone differently than I had ten years earlier.

The Flow of Water

I'm now six months into my new job, and I've found it triggering in all the ways I suspected I would. It's hard. I'm still learning how to give my expertise, my time, and my presence, without completely giving myself away. It's tempting to fall back into old, familiar habits.

I don't know if ultimately I can reconcile my needs with the demands of a fast-paced start-up. (Can an orchid survive in the desert?) And even if I could survive, these might not be the right conditions for me to thrive in. So I'm watching and waiting, checking in with myself, and listening to guidance from within.

This is the real work: to practice boundary setting, to look at the deeply ingrained patterns I still hold, and to take responsibility for actively breaking them. To choose to show up differently—more authentically —and lead courageously from a place of love rather than fear.

This is how I'm leading now. I'm bringing in gentleness and flow within the rigid borders of the logical. I tell my team we will do the best we can. We will celebrate the small wins on the way to the big ones. We will take breaks and pause to reflect at least as much as we ready, aim, fire, and forward march. We will strive toward goals but not sacrifice our mental health to hit them.

When I look back at the beginning of my career, I see a scared and earnest girl struggling against the current. She lacks stability and therefore clings to what little she does have like it's a life preserver, deathly afraid of going under if she loses it. She lacks confidence in her ability to swim and therefore develops an over-reliance on external forces to save her from the rushing waters.

When I check in with where I am today, I see a woman who knows that security is an illusion and can no longer be imprisoned by it. She is no longer afraid. She trusts herself and the flow of life. She accepts herself —all her flaws and immeasurable potential—and no matter what title she holds, she knows her inherent worth.

Water in its natural state is free-flowing. With good boundaries like river banks, its power is contained and directed. But boundaries that are too restrictive will cause a build-up in pressure that could result in deadly force and destruction. Water that rests too long in one spot becomes stagnant, undrinkable. But a healthy flow of water moves everything forward.

It supports life.

I don't yet know what's next, but I know I'm moving toward wholeness, balancing the being and the doing one day at a time. And now I know the way to get there is with wide open eyes and an open heart, awake and fully present.

My daughter taught me that.

About the Author

Rachael built a successful career leading content teams at the #1 health website before a personal loss triggered a reckoning that forced her to address her unhealthy relationship with work.

After a year-and-a-half sabbatical, she rejoined the startup world as the VP of Content for a real estate website, where she practices leading authentically and from a more balanced place of head, heart, and intuition.

A creative at heart, Rachael produces *With Aloha*, a monthly newsletter about small moments that incorporates audio and visual elements. She's also currently working on two memoirs. You can find her first book, *Bowing to Light: A Mother's Journey Through Grief*, on Amazon.

Rachael and her partner, Kevin, live with a gaggle of animals in rural Hawai'i.

Writing: https://rachaelmaier.substack.com/
Email: rachael.maier.writes@gmail.com

in linkedin.com/in/rachael-maier-40278048

SIXTEEN

Kelly McCarten

LEGACY: WHAT WILL YOURS BE?

EVERYDAY LEADER

The word *legacy* holds weight and for good reason. Throughout the course of your life, your legacy is constructed not in a single moment, but in the many ways you move through the world. There's a certain finality in the leaving of a legacy as it happens when we are no longer here, making our impact uniquely ours; like our fingerprint. As a mentor and coach, it is not always natural to contemplate your legacy, to wonder how you will be remembered. It is often left to billionaires and celebrities. What I think is far more important is the everyday people who have the power to influence and touch people through their everyday actions and the impression they leave. How will the way you lead today affect how you are remembered tomorrow?

ORIGIN-STORY

My story starts very uneventfully; I was fortunate enough to have grown up in a loving and secure home. For the quietness of a suburb, four girls kept the house busy. The security stopped abruptly when my father died of a heart attack when I was eleven years old. This was both traumatic and defining as it imposed on me to grapple with the forces of life far greater than my eleven-year-old mind was prepared to contend with. My once nuclear home was thrust into the alien world of single parenting. My mother was fighting to provide for me and my three sisters while we were fighting for her attention and our time in front of the bathroom mirror. This event single handedly catapulted me into independence in a way that not many of my peers had the capacity to understand. To my mother's credit, she did nothing but support me. My life was my own to create and she was right there with me, cheering me on while she took the role of both mother and father to keep the roof over our heads. There was a deep sense of self-reliance and the need to be financially self-sufficient that was ingrained in me during my teenage years, not wanting to further burden my mother who was already working so hard. However, this freedom to explore my interests provided me with the mindset that I could do anything that I put my mind to, however, I had yet to learn the skills necessary to discipline myself to focus on a particular path. Although I had no one else in my life to guide me professionally, my mother was my anchor.

CHECKING BOXES

During my young adulthood, you could describe me as driven, determined, and stubborn. I had built a wall around myself that shielded me from the potential of being hurt (not that I knew it then). But boy, did I have a plan. I could see my goals living out in my mind like they were certainties. I knew I would run a large company and was destined to succeed; I wanted to be a director by 30 years old, get married, have three kids by 35, VP by 40, and the list continued. It was a tight schedule I was holding myself to, and there was not much room for error.

My career goals started off strong as I entered the workforce as a recruiter. It was not in my field, but it paid four times what my peers were making, and in my mind, it was nothing more than a stepping stone to where I needed to be. Working as a recruiter allowed me to move to the city, get an apartment and start paying off my loans. I will never forget my mom looking at my paystub and telling me it was more than dad had ever made decades earlier. I was able to pay off my loans within three years of graduating, something I remain immensely proud of. I did the job for two years, but it came at a price. At an event one night I remember being introduced to people and my instinct was to evaluate them and compartmentalize them based on their education and employment history to determine whether they had any value to me and my career. I no longer saw people for who they were, but as assets to capitalize on. It was then I decided it was time for me to move on or I would lose all proper social skills.

My personal life goals were coming along as well. By 30 I was married and pregnant with my second child three years after my first. It felt like I had it all, career and kids and nothing could stop me.

WORK HARDER, NOT SMARTER

I wound up recruiting myself into a marketing role, then an advertising agency, before boldly finding my dream job at Coca-Cola. In a pre-LinkedIn world, I was relentlessly applying, trying to befriend employees, introducing myself to any and everyone who wore a uniform or a Coca-Cola branded hat. I eventually utilized my recruiting skills to contact a current employee and was swiftly hired as a promotions manager and a year later promoted to director; check mark.

During these years, my tenacity was formed from constantly being underestimated. As a woman operating in male-dominated spaces I was already starting from two steps back, but my competitive nature lit a fire in me to constantly prove them wrong. Once I had shaken someone's hand, I could see their wheels turning, trying to put me into a box I did not fit in. My communication became objective and direct, while using my unique experience to create creative solutions that drove results. My weakness, however, was that my hyper-independence did not allow me to delegate or collaborate well. I took on more projects than I needed to and had a tough time asking for help. I was operating as though the phrase "work smarter, not harder" meant the opposite. I would have benefited greatly from a mentor, someone who could have seen my drive and helped me hone my skills. Instead, I learned from lessons only found in missteps.

TWO WORLDS, TWO WOMEN

After a few months of working at Coca-Cola, my marriage ended. After the initial shock, my hyper-independence kicked into overdrive, and I continued to work without letting anyone onto what I was going through once I left the office. It felt easier to walk into a space where they had no idea what was going on at home, all that was expected of me was for me to do my job. There was also an element of fear, a fear that if they knew how devastated I was, they would assume I would be less capable of doing the job they hired me for.

Regardless of the hardships of being a working single mom, I loved my work. It gave me immense satisfaction to achieve career success and accomplish the goals I had set for myself, but this ambition changed to necessity once I was divorced. I needed something I could control, something in my power when my personal life felt anything but. I was carrying a deep sense of failure when my marriage ended, so I became determined never to fail again.

There were moments throughout my career when my professional and personal life intertwined. When my kids were 6 and 3, I would bring them to the office while I finished work late. They would run up and down the halls of the office, visiting coworkers and playing with stuffed polar bears. These worlds would entwine themselves again when I met my now-husband Paul in that same office. It felt like a colliding of two worlds and of two women; a female executive and a working single-mom. I remember entering my kid's gymnasium to volunteer for pizza lunch when I was swiftly brought into the group of other mothers volunteering and being announced as, "this is Kelly, she's a *working* mom!" As though it needed a specific type of delineation the other mothers did not. It was in these moments that I yearned for a community of women that at the time did not exist in the office or outside it.

FIND YOUR VOICE

As my career progressed over time and a few jobs later, I was working for a marketing company, our president had left the company, leaving behind a capable senior leadership team all leading independent business units. Working apart we were effective and results-oriented, bring us together and we were competitive with strong opinions. When a new US CEO was hired to take charge of the executive team, we were unsure of how they would mesh with a structure we had all grown used to. When he first entered our office, we realized meshing was the least of his worries. He was instructed to clean house and increase margins by any means necessary. He was a brute in every sense of the word; his communication, his demeanor, his posturing.

During his first week, he scheduled one-on-ones with all the senior leaders. I was excitedly nervous but thought it would be a great discussion. How wrong I was. From my opening line I knew I was in trouble. I asked, "what's keeping you up at night?", a classic, general question for leaders who have a lot on their plate. His response was immediate and caught me completely off guard, "YOU are, Kelly. YOU are keeping me up at night". My first reaction was to assume he was joking, although that theory was quickly discarded as he was the least funny person I'd ever met. Thinking again, this time from a business perspective, that if I was his biggest problem, he was in trouble. From my perspective, I was a hard-working, dedicated and committed leader with strong results. He did not share my perspective. His tone was forceful and aggressive as he told me that I needed to stay in my lane and stop trying to solve the problems of the company and vying for the top position because *it will never happen!* My shock must have shown on my face, I could not hide my reaction. I was completely taken off guard. When I entered the room, I had assumed we would be talking about business details and financials, but I had instead walked into a direct attack from someone I had just met. After the first few sentences, my brain went foggy and the words lost meaning before he ended by telling me he didn't want anything more from me but my job, reiterating again to "stay in my lane". Where did he get the idea that I was the problem? Why did he think it was appropriate to approach me in this way? I walked away in shock and dismayed. 1-hour discussion called into question everything I felt I had contributed to the company, every challenge we had overcome, every win our team had accomplished. Suddenly I was replaying my own accomplishments in my head. I previously was the CEO of another company, and I stepped in to turn it around in less than 3 years and later sold it to my existing company. I was confident in my abilities to run a company or division, yet he had shot them down in record time. Was he trying to push me out of the company?

I soon found out I was not alone in feeling this way. He went on to verbally abuse and mistreat the rest of the leadership team, leaving us questioning our job security and the future of the business we had worked so hard for. Strangely enough, these miserable months brought our team together in a way we had never been before. It was out of desperation, but it allowed us to lean on one another to stay sane during his reign of terror. Our bond was stronger than ever. As time went on my sleep worsened, my confidence in communicating faltered, and my mental health was struggling. I could not believe someone could impact me so negatively. I had lost control of my capabilities and strength I had delivered for decades.

Things came to a head during an all-company meeting. In years past this would be a fun, energizing meeting where we hone in on our strategic direction for the year and celebrate what we've accomplished thus far. Unfortunately, I had a call with him the night before I was to present the company's financials, he left me shaking and unable to sleep. Moments before I walked on the stage, I was hyperventilating as I saw him sit front and center. I started off strong, but one look at his face and I crumbled. My voice lost its normal confidence, and the audience echoed the awkwardness I felt. I had prepared my team to cheer and repeat my call out when it was time. As I tried to get the audience excited, there was no response. Instead of rallying them to be louder, I just wanted off the stage. I had given hundreds of presentations just like this one but somehow, it felt like the first time. Desperate to finish, I hurried my closing remarks and walked off as quickly as my legs would allow. Any hope I had that it was not as bad as I imagined was dashed when my team came to console me. Throughout my career, I had spoken at large conferences across North America, shared a stage with the President of Microsoft, and negotiated with some of the largest retailers in the world from Walmart to Whole Foods, and yet this one man had me second guessing whether I had the ability to speak at all. My fear of failure had ensured it was the only outcome.

This continued for a year. Our team continued its work, but our souls were no longer present. Our bodies showed up on time, but our minds were focused on surviving the day. An innocuous weekly meeting would devolve into a tirade, using his intimidation to control every aspect of our direction. Everything inside of me was telling me to tell him he was being an ineffective leader and walk out, but I stayed, sitting quietly. As I looked around the room, I could see my colleagues, men and women, grappling with the same internal dialogue, but they too stayed silent.

Finally, I had reached my breaking point. I had decided it was time for me to leave for my own well-being, regardless of how much I cared and wanted to continue to protect my team. That week I got a call from a partner at the investment management company that owned us. She wanted to check-in. I paused for a moment, deciding how honest I was prepared to be, before promptly and professionally launching into an explanation of how negatively impacted we had been by their decision of new leadership. I spared no details, from his communication style, direct quotes, and how it had affected me personally. The weight of the past year lessened with each of her questions and supportive words. By the end, I was concerned about confidentiality, but she stressed that she would manage the situation with the utmost privacy. I was proud of myself for speaking, but I had no clue what the repercussions might be.

Within two weeks, they fired him. It felt as though we could breathe for the first time in a year. Like something out of a movie, we cele-brated in the hallways. As I high-fived with other leaders, I was confronted with the reality that I had finally gotten the courage to use my voice again. Even if I was one of many who corroborated his cruel leadership style that led to his termination, I know I had a key role in it. It has reminded me that even through the most difficult times, you can find strength; in yourself, in your team, in friends and in partners.

Even in the moments where it feels like there is nothing in your control, there are *always* choices. A choice to leave, a choice to speak up, a choice to confide in someone, a choice to seek support from anywhere. But *move*. Take *action*. As said by Dr. Margie Warrell, "confidence is not a fixed attribute; it is the outcome of the thoughts we think and the actions we take. No more; no less. It is not based on your *actual* ability to succeed at a task but your *belief* in your ability to succeed." Don't let someone make you feel less than you are or take away your belief in yourself. Don't let someone else's idea of you limit your full potential. It starts with you!

BUMPY ROAD

From the beginning of my career as an independent driven individual to becoming a strong collaborative leader, to having it shattered by a corporate tyrant to rebounding and getting an amazing role in sports technology. I have had to reflect and really understand what legacy attributes I want to share and leave behind.

It has been a very long road from a stubborn young career woman to an executive leader. I went from an individual leader to a very collaborative leader. I developed into a leader where people were able to achieve their best, feel recognized and empowered in a work environment; where they felt safe and recognized. Being able to provide an environment where all people have a voice and feel the support and confidence to contribute to deliver their best.

I am lucky enough to say that I achieved everything the twenty-something year old set out to achieve. I owned my own company, I was CEO of another company, I sold a company, I led incredible teams and worked with global brands and currently traveling the world working with the top professional sports teams. It does not look like how I imagined it then, but somehow, it's better. My two kids turned into three, with a stepson when I married my husband, Paul. The way people spoke about him as a leader additionally inspired my mission to leave every person I interacted with better than I met them, and for that I am so thankful.

My career successes were not without major challenges, though; sexual harassment, corporate bullying, and narcissistic leaders. But being surrounded by far more executive women now than in the early 2000's, I am lucky to have befriended incredible women working across many industries. The notion of support, encouragement and rallying women is strong today. We need to continue this movement.

One such woman, a dear friend, shared that she never felt she had to struggle to keep up, and that her climb to the top had been a well-paved one. I was looking at her, waiting for the punchline, but she was sincere. It may be due to different career paths but there is no doubt that mine felt less like a smooth drive and more like a country road with a bad wheel. Regardless of how your path is paved, approach challenges with a sense of curiosity and hope. I have learned a tremendous amount from each bump and have become a stronger, more empathic leader in the process. Through my hardships, I have been determined to make the path easier for those who followed me by helping them navigate the corporate chaos, remove obstacles so they could see a clear road ahead, give them the confidence to trust themselves and make them feel more capable and worthy than they did when they started. But most important to help them find their fuel.

Make the road a little smoother for those who follow.

My hope is that I leave a legacy of integrity, kindness and of community that will pave the way for others, so they won't have to brave the bumpy roads. I became the mentor I yearned for in my twenties, supporting 4-5 mentees a year for the past two decades; providing them with direction, networking, job opportunities, and encouragement to go after their dreams and passions. I belong to 3 different Women Groups to support, mentor and encourage greatness across the community. I'm the founder of The Women's Club which brings together amazing, strong women to strengthen their circle of supporters in order for them to be the best leaders they can be and encourage the next generation of women. Additionally, I created a scholarship for entrepreneurial women to help them financially attend university to change the world.

And I am just getting started.

Everyone has a legacy, what will be yours?

About the Author

Kelly McCarten, is an award-winning marketer and business leader with over 30 years of experience working with clients and leading businesses. She has worked with some of the largest Consumer Packaged Goods and Retail companies globally. Kelly was recognized in 2020 as one of the Top US Women in Grocery. She also received numerous company awards for winning the largest client in the history of her agency in 2017. She was CEO of LAUNCH! Brand Marketing, transformed the business and sold it to one of the largest experiential agencies. She is currently the Chief Growth Officer of Brizi, a global sports technology company working with the NHL, NBA, NCAA, UEFA and ATP.

With her strength in mentoring and coaching others, Kelly founded and is President of The Women's Club, she's a member of LeadHERship Global and a LeadHership Board Advisor, C-Suite Network and WISE (Women in Sports and Events) Toronto member and has been on the Board of Directors for MADD Toronto for 5 years.

Kelly started mentoring 20 years ago the next generation of men and women who will impact the industry and created the Lang School of Business, Women in Leadership Entrance Scholarship to provide financial support to young girls to attend university. She is a past professor at Humber College and sits on the Program Advisory Committee for the College.

She recently became a Real Estate Investor and purchased her first 3 houses in 2021, renovating two of them. Kelly can be seen with her husband Paul, on HGTV spring 2023. She is married and now lives outside of Toronto and has 3 kids, all launched and working in Canada.

∼

Email: Kmccarten@rogers.com

in linkedin.com/in/kelly-mccarten-1004b27

SEVENTEEN

Cindy Molina

HAWAIIAN AT HEART

*a*loha from Southern California! Mahalo for the opportunity to share some of the lessons learned from my "midlife awakening" with you. May this chapter warm your heart with the spirit of Aloha and fill the next few minutes of your life with some inspiration and motivational messages to pack in your own "beach bag" and take with you on your journey in life.

April 2019 was the month I turned forty-nine and celebrated during a two-week dream vacation to my favorite place on Earth. I went to the Hilton Waikoloa Village on the Big Island of Hawaii with my *ohana* ("family" in Hawaiian), and we stayed in an oceanfront room, overlooking the dolphin lagoon. I was with my husband, Orlando, and our two daughters, Ella and Emma, and we had the best time swimming with dolphins, snorkeling with turtles and colorful reef fish, exploring the volcano and waterfalls, and learning about Kona coffee. It was truly a family vacation of a lifetime and a forty-ninth birthday celebration I will always remember. Some people might wait until their fiftieth birthday for a vacation like this, but I wanted to celebrate my forty-ninth birthday in paradise. I'll explain why in just a moment.

When we returned home from Hawaii, I continued thinking ahead to my fiftieth birthday. It would be hard to top my forty-ninth having fun in the sun in Hawaii. For my last milestone birthday (my fortieth), we had a large luau in our backyard. It was so much fun, and I always thought we should do it again if I made it to fifty. It was then that I made the decision to embark on a "healthy lifestyle challenge" to lose fifty pounds by my fiftieth birthday so I could be "fit at fifty"! I started an intense, daily exercise routine and began eating healthier. I lost fifty pounds in four months and went on to lose twenty-five more pounds over the next two months. Yes, I lost seventy-five in six months and achieved my goal of being "fit at fifty". It was time to celebrate this huge accomplishment.

April 2020 was the month I was supposed to celebrate my fiftieth birthday surrounded by more than 150 close family members and friends. We had planned an authentic luau with a Hawaiian buffet, tiki bar, live band, hula dancing show performed by me and my daughters, a photobooth, a videographer, a photographer, and more. My *ohana* began planning for this special occasion years in advance. We remodeled our backyard by resurfacing our pool, planting palm trees, hibiscus, and plumeria, and purchasing Hawaiian-inspired patio furniture. I stockpiled tons of leis, balloons, banners, and party supplies. The invitations had been sent out, we were collecting RSVPs, and friends and family from around the country booked flights. We were prepared for an epic party, and the countdown was on!

A month before the luau, I also started working for a new company in downtown San Diego where I'm now the director of Organizational Development and Diversity & Inclusion. The following week, we started working from home due to the COVID-19 global pandemic. I onboarded remotely and built relationships over Microsoft Teams virtual meetings, while my daughters attended school over Zoom. It was a time filled with uncertainty. With each passing day, I became more and more concerned about our plans for my birthday luau. The day came when I had to face the reality that my luau had to be postponed. I couldn't believe that I had worked so hard to lose weight to be "fit at fifty" and celebrate with my loved ones during this huge event that we spent years planning. The disappointment and sadness was heartbreaking.

Life Is Short

I grew up in Michigan in the 1970s and had a happy childhood. I earned good grades in school. I enjoyed spending time with friends, swimming, playing softball, playing the clarinet and organ, and I was a Girl Scout. My parents, younger brother, and I lived in a nice home in a middle-class neighborhood, went on summer vacations, and went to Mass every Sunday. Our family is Catholic, and I attended religious education classes at our parish and received all of my sacraments.

In the middle of eighth grade, our family moved to San Diego. Sadly, I left behind my relatives and friends, and I didn't enjoy the rest of middle school. The summer before high school, life started getting better when I went to band camp and made some new friends.

In 1988, I graduated from high school in the top 10 percent of my class and celebrated at Grad Night in Disneyland. The next day, I started working at SeaWorld, chasing my dream of one day being a trainer for dolphins and orcas. I spent the next five years working part-time in a gift shop.

August 1988, I started college at San Diego State University, and the next month, I began working a second part-time job as a bank teller. Being a lifelong overachiever, I went to school and worked full-time while living at home. I graduated in the early 1990s with a bachelor's degree in economics and a minor in psychology. My parents threw me a nice graduation party where my dad delivered a beautiful toast telling me how much he loved me and how proud he was. My dad was easy-going, loved watching sports, prayed the rosary every morning, and was devoted to his family. I was a daddy's girl, and my brother was the mamma's boy. My mom was a strict disciplinarian, domineering, and overly critical. I know her intentions were good, but her personality is often hard for me to handle. She reminds me often she did the best she could.

A few months later, my life changed forever when my dad went on a business trip to Mexico City and then Detroit. While in Michigan, he had dinner at his favorite Chinese restaurant with his brother and two sisters. The next day, he flew back to San Diego and, while waiting for his luggage at baggage claim, suffered a heart attack and died. In the middle of the night, when the sheriff came to our door to deliver the devastating news, my whole world turned upside down. My dad was only forty-eight years old and he died ten days before his forty-ninth birthday. I was only twenty-three, and my brother was only twenty. My mom lost her husband a few months before their twenty-fifth wedding anniversary.

A line was drawn in the sand. From that moment, time became divided between two distinct time periods—before and after my dad's death.

I decided shortly after his passing that I needed to get away because everything in San Diego reminded me of him. I transferred to San Francisco with the bank and found an apartment in Pacific Heights with a lovely roommate named Danelle. This was my first time living on my own, and I loved the freedom. I became close friends with my neighbor Deanna, and for the next decade, my life resembled the popular TV show *Friends*. When Danelle moved out, my colleague Thang moved in, and we were great roommates for the rest of the decade. Life was fun again!

In San Francisco, I continued climbing the corporate ladder and quickly achieved my goal of becoming a trainer. However, I had to pivot my plan and train bankers instead of marine mammals at SeaWorld. During my twelve years with the bank, I ended up taking hundreds of business trips around the country and even had the opportunity to move up to Washington for a nine-month assignment to train in the Seattle area. I earned almost a million frequent flyer miles and hotel points to take me to Hawaii every year on my annual vacation to recharge in paradise.

In 2000, I celebrated my thirtieth milestone birthday at a Jimmy Buffett concert and did a lot of reflection about what I really wanted in life. I had never intended to go into banking—it was supposed to be a part-time teller job that lasted twelve years—and although I achieved great career success, something was still missing. Life was passing me by, and I had traveled for business so much that it was hard to keep track of the months, let alone what day of the week it was. I was also getting burned out on so much travel, and in the back of my mind, I always thought about my dad dying on that business trip, alone, and I didn't want to follow in his footsteps. At this same time, I was wrapping up a two-year certificate program in human resources management at UC Berkeley. I really enjoyed all the training and development courses I took, and my instructor had her doctorate degree from Florida State University. She told me they were the top program in the nation for the field of instructional systems (the academic term for training and development). She encouraged me to go to graduate school at FSU and said that I would be able to take courses from all the professors who had written the books we had been using in her courses. Long story short, FSU invited me to be a graduate teaching assistant and offered to pay for my master's degree and to teach Introduction to Educational Technology. It was a once-in-a-lifetime opportunity that I couldn't pass up. My boss at the bank, Cheryl, was one of the best leaders I had ever worked for, and it made me sad to think I was leaving her and my career. But when I told her what I was thinking, she was supportive and encouraged me to do it.

Midlife Awakening: Part 1

The year and a half I spent living in Tallahassee, Florida, beginning in 2000, was one of the best chapters of my life! I considered it my sabbatical from corporate America and a chance to relive my college years, but this time, instead of living at home with Mom and Dad and commuting to college, I got to go away to school, live near campus, go to all the football games, and feel the excitement of being national champions! Go Seminoles!

My best friend, Heather, my brother, Michael, and our friend Simon drove with me cross country almost three thousand miles from San

Francisco to Tallahassee. They flew home, and I was left in this new town all alone. That day I went to campus for the first time to buy my books and noticed The Co-Cathedral of St. Thomas More across the street. I went to the student Mass that evening for the first time, and it was a packed house. After Mass, I introduced myself to the pastor, and it turned out he knew my great uncle, Monsignor George Rohling from Nashville! The Catholic Student Union (CSU) was hosting a mixer after Mass. They invited all students to get to know each other, and they had a special meeting area for grad students where they invited us to join the Etc. grad group. I started meeting other students who had also moved to town and were beginning their master's programs at FSU. A month later, CSU hosted their fall retreat, and I decided to go. That weekend was life changing. I became friends with some of the most devout Catholics I had ever met—Kristin, Melanie, Melissa, and Mat—and I am still very close with all of them two decades later!

At the retreat, I experienced a conversion experience while praying and listening to our praise and worship band play songs that spoke to me. It was as if each lyric was written especially for me, and my heart became overflowing with gratitude for God. I also had a sense of clarity about my life and why God had made this graduate school opportunity possible. He wanted to deepen His relationship with me and help me strengthen my faith. My original thinking was I would earn a master's degree to help me advance my career, but God opened my heart. During my time in grad school, I was an active member of CSU and went on several more retreats. It turned out that my grad school classes were easy for me because they were the same classes with the same textbooks that I had already completed at UC Berkeley. As a result, I had a lot of extra time on my hands that I chose to invest in deepening my faith by going to daily mass, praying the rosary, and building deep, meaningful friendships with devout Catholics. I remember praying regularly for "my future husband, whoever he may be" during Mass.

After I graduated with my MS in instructional systems with an emphasis in performance design systems from FSU in December 2001,

I moved back to my apartment in San Francisco that my best friend's sisters, Jenny and Jackie, were living in while I was away. I came back to California with a renewed sense of purpose and wanted to continue my faith journey. I wanted to keep a promise I made to God that I would marry a good Catholic man—I just needed His help in finding one!

Faith, Hope, and Love

On the ninth anniversary of my dad's death, I was on a business trip and spent the evening in my hotel thinking about my dad. On a whim, I decided to log into the Catholic Singles website for the first time. I set up an account and began my search for a good Catholic man. I ended up flagging about a dozen profiles that looked interesting, and I decided to send one message to the person that the system had put on the top of the list. His name was Orlando, and he was a sportswriter in San Francisco who was five years younger than me. The website said he had not logged into his account in four months, so I didn't have high expectations that he was going to respond. Unbelievably, Orlando logged into his account that evening, saw my message, and responded! For the next two months, we wrote one another email messages back and forth, and then we finally met in person for our first date on January 17, 2002. Orlando showed up to my apartment with a single red rose, and he was so warm and friendly. We went to a Chinese restaurant for dinner called Eliza's. We had such a wonderful evening getting to know one another. Orlando was the first and only Catholic man I had dated, and our relationship just felt so much deeper and more meaningful than any I had ever experienced before. I loved dating Orlando and was falling deeper in love with him each day.

On the tenth anniversary of my dad's death, Orlando proposed to me in the exact same spot we had met on our first date—in the hallway of my apartment. He brought me a dozen red roses, got down on one knee, and asked me to marry him. He told me he wanted to "rewrite history and make a sad day a happy one!" I said yes!

We began planning our future together, not just our wedding day but our marriage. I knew that I wanted to get married at St. Michael's Catholic Church in my hometown of Poway because that was the closest I could get to having my dad walk me down the aisle. Orlando and I got married in October 2004 in a formal Catholic Mass, and we received the Sacrament of Holy Matrimony. My best friend, Heather, was my matron of honor, and Orlando's brother, Ricky, was our best man. Heather's sisters, Jenny and Jackie, sang at our wedding, and all of my closest friends and family were there to witness our love and commitment to each other. After Communion, while Jenny sang "Ave Maria," Orlando and I presented flowers to Mary—a statue at the back of our church—and I prayed that we would be blessed with children and that we would raise them Catholic and send them to Catholic school. My brother, Michael, walked me down the aisle, and he gave a "brother of the bride" toast at the wedding reception. We also did a "brother–sister dance"; I danced with Michael and Orlando danced with his sister, Noelle. It was the happiest day of my life!

Over the next two decades, more dreams came true. After three years of trying to conceive a child, our first daughter, Ella, was born in 2007. I named her after my grandma—fulfilling a promise I made to my grandmother minutes before she passed away in 1991. My grandma was my favorite person on the planet. We chose Angel for Ella's middle name after my father-in-law. We bought our first home a block from our church. Four years later, when I was forty-one, I gave birth to our second daughter, and we named her Emma—after my grandma's sister—and her middle name is Ann, after me. Both girls attended Catholic school at St. Michael's, and we kept the promise we made on our wedding day. When my daughters were both two years old, they started Polynesian dancing lessons, and for the next several years they performed in several hula shows around San Diego. It was a dream come true! We took three family vacations to the Big Island of Hawaii and stayed at the Hilton Waikoloa Village—the last trip being my forty-ninth birthday.

Midlife Awakening: Part 2

The month leading up to my fiftieth birthday, my midlife awakening was hitting me like waves along the beach. I was faced with the challenges of a new job, the stress and uncertainty at the beginning of the pandemic, the disappointment of postponing my luau, the hormonal response of losing seventy-five pounds so quickly, and trying to remain my usual positive and optimistic self. It was then that I turned to God and asked for help in dealing with all of this. Once again, my prayers were answered, and He began gifting me with the knowledge, skills, tools, and resources I needed to cope. As my self-awareness continued to grow, so did the ability to find a path forward. I embraced the mantra "IMUA"—a Hawaiian word to move forward in life with strength and courage.

In March 2020, I rediscovered mindfulness and joined a mindfulness community called MBOX that was founded by my new friend Pam who I had met through my friend Maureen (who I met thirty-four years earlier at SeaWorld). Pam began a daily Zoom call where she guided mindfulness meditations for us, which were so helpful during this time of uncertainty at the beginning of the pandemic. The great thing about practicing mindfulness is you don't need to remember to pack your breath—it goes with you everywhere, and it doesn't cost a cent to pause, get grounded, and focus on your breathing. Pam taught me several "brain hacks" that helped me rewrite the story in my head. I learned how to notice when I was triggered, and instead of reacting, I would take a breath and then chose my response. And no response is still a response. Pam said this is how we could give ourselves "grace and space" and then move forward with intention, which reminded me of my mantra word, "IMUA."Pam also taught me the idea of "good enough," which this recovering perfectionist needed to learn.

Another "a-ha" moment came three weeks before I turned fifty, when my company hired a brain researcher named Dr. Heidi Hanna to help us learn how to manage the stress of the pandemic. Dr. Hanna also talked about the benefits of mindfulness, and she introduced a new concept called highly sensitive person (HSP). Being a lifelong learner, whenever I discover a new idea, I like to research the topic. When I started learning more about HSP, I discovered that I too have that personality trait. Did you know that 20 percent to 30 percent of the population are born with this "super power"? When I took the assessment created by Dr. Elaine Aron (the clinical psychologist who coined the term "HSP"), I could identify with almost all the tendencies. Just like with my Catholic conversion experience when I was thirty, I had just experienced a new level of clarity about my life, and suddenly I could articulate why I thought and acted the way I did. A helpful weekly newsletter I found was *Highly Sensitive Refuge*. Every week it felt as though the articles were written with me in mind.

I also started using essential oils and burning my tropical-scented candles (instead of saving them for a special occasion). I learned about habit stacking and how to set and track self-care goals. My home is filled with Hawaiian décor, which fills my heart with the spirit of Aloha. I discovered Internal Family Systems therapy and am doing Parts work to heal my inner child. I embraced my authentic self and began feeling the 8 C's (calm, clear, connected, compassionate, creative, confident, courageous, and curious) showing up more frequently. I started journaling my inner thoughts and feelings and at the end of each day, I write down three good things that I am grateful for. This brain hack has helped me to rewire my brain and stay focused on the positive in life. I also started reading personal growth books, collecting inspirational quotes and motivational messages. All of these healthy habits continue to help me on my path of self-awareness. The following is a list of some of my favorite books I'd recommend including in your own beach bag, in addition to this book, *The Great LeadHERship Awakening*, of course:

- *A Pirate Looks at Fifty* by Jimmy Buffett *(Yes, I'm a Parrothead!)*
- *Aloha State of Mind* by Leialoha Humpherys
- *Atlas of the Heart* by Brene Brown
- *The Happiness Advantage* by Shawn Achor
- *Bright Line Eating* by Dr. Susan Pierce Thompson
- *The Master Mentors* book series by Scott Jeffrey Miller

- *A Year of Resilience: 52 Ideas to Be More Resilient and Stay Afloat throughout the Year* by Dr. Maureen Orey
- *Love + Work* by Marcus Buckingham
- *Grit* by Angela Duckworth
- *Peak Mind* by Amishi P. Jha
- *Sensitive* by Jean Granneman & Andre Sólo
- *The Empaths Survival Guide* and *Thriving as an Empath* by Judith Orloff
- *The Power of Now* by Eckhart Tolle
- *10% Happier* by Dan Harris
- *Left to Tell* by Immaculée Ilibagiza
- *Rediscover Catholicism* and *Coach* by Matthew Kelly
- *Whale Done and Whale Done Parenting* by Ken Blanchard
- *Seven Habits of Highly Effective People* by Stephen Covey

Cheers to Fifty-two Years...and the Journey Continues!

On my fifty-second birthday in 2022, I finally got to have the fiftieth birthday luau that I had dreamed of for the last two decades of my life. I was surrounded by the spirit of Aloha from 150 family, friends and colleagues in my Hawaiian-themed home and tropical-inspired backyard. It was a sunny day, and my heart was overflowing with gratitude. As an added bonus, there were many friends from my MBOX mindfulness community who traveled in from around the country to surprise me at my luau. This was the first time many of us had been together in person! We had spent the last two years practicing mindfulness together over Zoom during the pandemic. And it was an MBOX friend that led me to this wonderful opportunity to write this chapter (Thank you, Eileen Coskey Fracchia)! So, make an effort to celebrate life's special occasions because life is short.

Today, I lead a global, high-performing team of people and culture professionals who are as passionate as I am for helping people grow, learn to lead, and develop self-awareness. I travel often to Mexico City, just like my dad did on his final business trip. I have visited the Basilica of Our Lady of Guadalupe and have seen the image of Mary in person. This has brought me so much peace and hope and has given me the ability to practice my mantra of IMUA (go forward in life with strength and courage.) I have dedicated my career to developing talent and building high-performing organizations. Through speaking, coaching, training, facilitating, and leading by example, I am pleased to be a role model for leaders of all levels at work, as well as for my two daughters who are following in my footsteps, to live a life filled with fun in the sun and happiness, holiness, and bright health.

ALOHA AND MAHALO!

About the Author

Cindy Molina is a high-achieving, engaging, people and culture champion committed to excellence. She is the director of Organizational Development and Diversity & Inclusion for a large, global energy company. Cindy leads a talented team located in San Diego, California and Mexico City. In her three decades of professional experience leading high-performing teams, she has held senior leadership roles within energy, financial services, higher education, healthcare, aerospace and defense, and retail.

In her chapter, Cindy reveals how her milestone birthdays, especially her fiftieth, contributed to her midlife awakening and continued success by deepening her self-awareness, expanding her perspective, and learning how to embrace the transformation. Cindy shares her love for Hawaii and some life lessons she has learned along the way.

Cindy helped found GROW (Growing Responsibilities and Opportunities for Women), an employee resource group at Sempra Infrastructure that champions and empowers women. GROW is committed to fostering and supporting the career development of Sempra Infrastructure's female employees in both the United States and Mexico.

Her bucket list includes becoming a published author, and *The Great LeadHERship Awakening* has made her dream a reality.

Cindy holds an MS from Florida State University in instructional systems and an BS in economics with a minor in psychology from San Diego State University. She was among the first to receive a CPTD

(Certified Professional in Talent Development) certification from the ATD (Association of Talent Development) Institute in 2006 and her SPHR (Senior Professional in Human Resources) in 2013.

Cindy lives in San Diego, California, with her husband, Orlando, their two daughters, Ella and Emma, and three adopted rescue pups, Buster, Peanut, and Coconut. Cindy enjoys living close to her brother, Michael, her sister-in-law, Erin, and her three nephews, Brody, Trevor and Jake, along with her mom. They all live in neighboring communities and get together often to celebrate birthdays, holidays and cheer on the children's sporting events.

Email: cindymolina23@yahoo.com

linkedin.com/in/cindy-molina-m-s-cplp-sphr-83302a2

EIGHTEEN

Kayleigh O'Keefe

SEE THROUGH THE ILLUSION AND ACTIVATE YOUR DIVINE FEMININE LEADERSHIP

*W*hat if everything you thought you knew about yourself was wrong?

You are at the pinnacle of your career. You have worked diligently throughout your life in service of a bigger purpose, with the intensity and focus of an Olympic athlete. You have earned degrees, started your family, earned promotion after promotion, and received industry awards. You are a force to be reckoned with.

And yet, deep down, you still harbor doubts. You question your self-worth, you hustle hard to get it all down, and you often wonder, "Is this all there is?".

There's a part of you that wants to lead—and be—in a way that feels more aligned and natural to you, and yet, as soon as you have the thought, you laugh it off, deciding that these dreams and desires can wait until retirement. For now, you have a family to provide for, a reputation to uphold, and a lifestyle to maintain.

You sense the tightness in your body; you've worn armor for decades and it now rests deep within the marrow of your bones. It's not you, though, or at least not the real you, the sovereign you, the atman, the great I AM you. It's the you that was born into a leadership paradigm that wasn't suited for you.

The Best Laid Plans

Hi, I'm Kayleigh O'Keefe. I'm the founder of Soul Excellence Publishing, the visionary for this book and movement, and a very reluctant entrepreneur.

I never wanted to be an entrepreneur. I never thought about being a publisher. I never planned on building a business that has helped over 350 individuals to share their stories in thirteen best-selling books in just over two years. None of this was "part of my plan". And boy did I have plans!

In high school, I planned to go to a top-tier college, land a dream job in Washington, DC, get married, and have four children by age 30. These youthful wishes are forever memorialized in a feature article in my high school yearbook! I did go to Duke where I graduated with honors and spoke at my major commencement ceremony, and I did move to the nation's capital right after college to start a career in management consulting. The marriage and kids part, well, that has happened yet!

I didn't "plan" on being gay—that definitely threw a wrench in my plans! I didn't plan on moving to San Francisco, joining an early-stage technology startup, and working alongside a founder who would inspire me to new heights. And I didn't plan on the passing of my late mentor in the summer of 2022 and receiving her business and global community of women, called Feminine Mastery, to steward into the future.

In retrospect, there has been my plan and my strategy for my life, which has taken me in one direction, and then there has been my *listening* and my engagement *with life*, which has taken me in an entirely new one. To be honest, I wouldn't even call it a direction. It's more of a spiral upward, sometimes back down, and then back up again through the swirls and expansion. The real listening, though, has been to that which lies within.

I was programmed to move in one direction with fierce focus. Were you?

Set a goal. Make a plan. Go, go, go. For those of us who "grew up" in corporate environments, this was "the way". What do we not notice when we put our blinders on?

I didn't notice my intuitive and creative gifts.

What I've created since leaving the corporate path has been birthed from intuition and curiosity. It has emanated from my heart. The company I've built—Soul Excellence Publishing—has been my own imperfect embodiment of the divine feminine leadership paradigm.

Yes, I am building a publishing house for conscious, courageous leaders. And it is so much more than that. It is a community where we are cultivating spaces where people can recenter, reconnect, and reimagine their lives.

Here I am, alongside you, emerging through *The Great LeadHERship Awakening* as a new woman, a whole woman.

I am clear on my mission.

Like the Big Bang, I spark the creation of entire universes through my ideas.

What's Inside You?

It's hard to pinpoint the exact origin moment of Soul Excellence because it has always been inside of me.

Sometimes when I recount "where this all started," I think of my fifth-grade teacher, Mr. Tomich, and his Excellence Book. Signing that the most times became my only focus! Other times, I reflect on my first pilgrimage along The Way of St. James in Northern Spain as a solo traveler at age 25. My experience walking through the beautiful, sweet manure-smelling countryside for two weeks gave me the space to reconnect to my soul, God, nature, self, and fellow man. Connection is the opposite of addiction, and I went on that walk to honor myself and

God for my first year of sobriety. Did Soul Excellence begin on the island of Maui where I experienced being embodied for the first time? Or months later in meditation when the actual term "Soul Excellence" came in? Or a year later when I made the decision to leave my career?

One cool early September morning in Southern Maine in 2020, I was sitting on a white wraparound porch writing my morning pages. At that moment I was a devoted disciple of *The Artist's Way,* so although I was on a family vacation for the week, I was up early with my coffee and notebook to write before my two-year-old niece was awake and ready to play. As I wrote that morning, my breath was visible in the air. I loved the energizing chill! I wrote and wrote until suddenly I wrote "Leading Through the Pandemic: Unconventional Wisdom from Heartfelt Leaders". My first concept, a book title, was born! Was *this* the moment the movement began?

A month later I recruited 25 executives from the United States and Australia to write about their experience navigating the first six months of the pandemic. It was so beautiful to see this group come together and share about the grief, surrender, grit, and determination that they had to call on when their personal and professional lives were upended. Our first bestselling book—and community—was born.

Identifying the origin story of Soul Excellence is akin to pinpointing my origin story of being gay.

Was it when I switched my Tinder profile from men to women at age 28? Or was it when my hand lit on fire holding a friend's hand at church in college nearly a decade earlier? Or, come to think of it, was my "favorite teammate" on my soccer team in middle school really just the one I had a crush on?

The more I sat with the question, the more I realized that being gay—like Soul Excellence—was always inside of me, but I was terrified to acknowledge it because that fact did not conform with my plans for my life.

What has always been inside of you?

As the founder and CEO of Soul Excellence Publishing, I invite the leaders who participate in our multi-author books to ask themselves the following questions when they choose to publish with us:

- Who are you becoming?
- What are you speaking into existence?
- What can you share that you've never expressed before?

The books we publish together are not simply books. Each book is a Big Bang. Each book is the genesis of a new universe. Each book is the embodiment of a new way forward where humans return to wholeness, express from their hearts, and co-create with the divine. This is what's inside of me.

The LeadHERship Awakening Feels Like Home

A new paradigm is emerging, a space where men and women alike are seeing through the illusion of separateness while honoring our unique gifts and expressions of our divine essence. In this paradigm, women are standing sovereign in the truth of the powerful force of creation that they are and releasing themselves of the self-generated narratives of feeling trapped, needing to conform, sacrificing for others while ignoring their needs, and waiting for the illusive feeling of being lovable, good, whole, and worthy.

Women who can claim for themselves today that they are whole, lovable, and worthy, for no other reason except for the fact that they are alive, aware, and awake, free themselves from living a life of contortion and suppression.

My late mentor, Cyndie Loven Fullenkamp, in her book *True Calling*, helped me understand this shift that is underway in the following graphic. I've added the categories on the far left to build upon her brilliant work.

	From The Outer Way	To The Inner Way
Reality	Illusion	Truth
Energy Source	Led by Ego	Led by Heart
Guidance System	Guided by Thought	Guided by Feeling
Power Dynamic	Dominance	Unity
Wealth Mindset	Lack and limitation	Abundance and prosperity
Sense of Satisfaction	Outward reaching	Inner seeking
Decision-Making	Logical and Linear	Intuitive and Nonlinear
Creative Perspective	Create from Past	Create from Possibility

Source: *True Calling* by Cyndie Loven Fullenkamp

Can you instantly feel the truth of this shift wash over you?

Which shift do you notice as being more critical for you to accept and breathe life into?

Are you ready to claim it?

Seeing Through the Illusion of "Not Enough"

At the core of my being is the wound of "not enoughness". It is a core illusion that so many of us suffer from, along with the wounds of "I am not worthy" and "I am unlovable." This illusion of "I am not enough" has pushed me to great heights and dropped me into desolate abysses. Unknowingly influenced by this illusion for much of my life, I've swung violently on the pendulum of life often feeling ecstasy and despair in the same second. Desire followed by instant disapproval. Love snuffed out by indifference. Joy subdued by resistance. Connection broken by judgment. The whiplash I give myself is exhausting.

"I am not enough" is the wound that can warp my perception and make me not feel a sense of peace and gratitude for the fact that in less than two years after I left my career, I learned how to become a publisher, galvanized over leaders from different cultures and countries around the globe, published thirteen books, become a USA Today bestselling author in my own right, and have been the catalyst to turn this *moment* of leadHERship into a true *movement*. I can no longer escape the fact that no matter what I do or what I achieve, it never feels enough. This is a sign that I have been operating from an illusion, an incorrect paradigm and perspective. Even these past three years creating a company that is an expression of my soul has not filled my soul. How ironic.

Allow my story to be an example.

You don't have to quit your job, move to a new city, and take up hot yoga to reconnect to your soul's inherent wisdom and find the fulfillment you desire. Ok, Ok. I *did* quit my high-paid job, exit my career trajectory, pack up my belongings and move across the country, and become a regular hot yogi only to realize that the illusion of "not enoughness" was still running the show. Even as I built a soul-aligned business that offered leaders a space to write, heal, and publish, I still felt like it was "not enough".

For me, at this moment in time, my leadHERship awakening is about allowing myself to live from the core. How can I live from my core— walk the middle path–without chasing the addictive extremes?

Activate Your Divine Feminine Leadership

The Great LeadHERship Awakening is an awareness that we can each cultivate. Allow me to guide you through this activation by imagining your root chakra, your seat firmly supported by your throne and then working your way up through your crown chakra.

Your Strength
You start to feel strong again, but this time the strength is from within, the result of a deeper knowing. Before, your strength came in the form of your accomplishments, reputation, brands, connections, vacation spots, and alma mater, the list was endless of how you acquired your source of strength. But it was never enough. You were never enough. Now, at peace with the truth of what is occurring on the planet right now, you know that true strength lies in your own recognition of the sovereign self, the version of you (and us all) that can navigate the

business world with focus and intensity, but is fueled by love, curiosity, compassion, and worthiness.

Your Intuition

You now realize that those little hints in your gut, the ones that your intellect got so used to drowning out with logic and reason, are one of your most powerful guidance tools. You no longer ignore those feelings and instead sit with them, letting your mind call in the deeper message. You are not crazy. You are gifted, gifted in the ability to sense, intuit, notice, and influence.

Your Heart

You bring your awareness down from your mind and into your heart before you speak or make a decision. You feel your love emanate out to the world through your beautiful heart and trust that with its power you are moving in the destined direction. Your heart is open but more discerning about who has access to it. It is your most precious gift.

Your Voice

You begin to realize that your voice is your most powerful tool, and you get to choose when and how to use it. You begin to notice the words you use to describe yourself or your daily life do not belie the nobility of your essence. You see clearly now how you have silenced yourself to please others, avoid conflict, be seen as too much, or be revealed to be an imposter. Connected to your heart, your voice cannot betray you. Connected only to your mind—and its millions of thoughts —your voice is drowned out by fear.

Your Divine Essence

Finally, you begin to sense as though life is happening for you and with you, even in the moments that bring nothing but pain and grief. You close your eyes and feel the divine and supernatural all around you. Your entire life becomes a prayer, a meditation, an offering, and you tread gently through the world. You find yourself moving slower than you ever have while simultaneously having a bigger impact than you ever thought possible.

The Great LeadHERship Awakening feels like *home*. It feels like our natural state. It feels like creating, growing, birthing, nurturing, educating, and mentoring. And maybe you do all of those things or maybe one phase of this is your deepest expression of *your* Great Lead-HERship Awakening.

Your LeadHERship Awakening

My mission is not to replace the patriarchy with the matriarchy. My mission is not to swap men for women in positions of power. My mission is not to shame men and only celebrate women. My mission is to help women see their feminine and innate beauty, strength, and power so that they can reclaim who they are, own all parts of themselves in the positions of influence that they occupy, and restore balance and wholeness to all of humanity in the process.

If I had to distill my own leadership awakening into just a few phrases, they would be:

- Seek the sovereign self within
- Hone your intuition and treat it with reverence
- Step into the unknown with faith
- Pause and discern with your heart
- Surround yourself with community

Come with me as we explore, expand, and evolve together.

Come with me as we embody our deepest essence.

Come with me as we raise the consciousness of the planet.

Come with me as we spark new universes.

∾

Watch The Great LeadHERship Awakening Authors Speak: https://the-great-leadhership-awakening.heysummit.com/

About the Author

Kayleigh O'Keefe walks the path of soulful excellence where she is a lifelong student and teacher of the inner way of leadership.

Sometimes referred to as a puppy for her endless energy, optimism, and playfulness, she is also quite serious about helping others to reconnect to their soul and pursue excellence on their terms. As the Founder and CEO of Soul Excellence Publishing, she holds space for strong leaders to let down their guard, write the next chapter in their life, and become bestselling authors along the way.

If you're into credentials, she's got that, too: a bachelor's from Duke, an M.B.A. from the University of San Francisco, and a former career advising Fortune 500 executives. Kayleigh is also a *USA Today* bestselling author, and as a boutique publisher, has published twelve bestselling books that have helped over 350 individuals become published authors. Kayleigh hosts *The Future is Human* podcast, a weekly exploration of how to upgrade our human operating system so that we can experience intimacy and connection.

Kayleigh loves being an aunt and brings "aunt energy" to all of her endeavors, pushing the limits of what's possible and what's expected. She is grateful that her niece and nephew introduced her to Disney's *Encanto*, and she won't stop singing it—at least not for another year or so! After spending most of her career in Washington, D.C. and San Francisco, she now lives and works by the beach in Ft. Lauderdale, FL, and is always up for travel!

〜

Website: https://soulexcellence.com
Website: https://thefutureishumanpodcast.com/
Website: https://femininemastery.com/
Email: kayleigh@kayleighokeefe.com

instagram.com/KayleighOK_11
linkedin.com/in/kayleighokeefe

NINETEEN

Kristie Ondracek

LEADERSHIP, ROSES, AND UNICORNS

*A*s I sit here writing this chapter, I am reflecting on what I see in the world for leaders and how each of our journeys is truly impacted by the leaders near and far from us. I am part of a group, LeadHERship Global, where I am surrounded by majestic women leaders who push me each day to stretch my own leadership skills and personality.

As a small-town girl, I am often taken aback when I think about my successes. I do not take where I am lightly, and I acknowledge those who helped me get here. It is my dream to help other women understand their value and that, no matter what, they are also leaders. It is not the letters behind one's name; it is not title bestowed upon them; it is not what others say about you; it is your actions to lead others and your belief in yourself that makes you a leader.

I was not always a leader. Oh, I pretended I was a leader, but I was truly someone who did what I was told to do and did not listen to my heart or gut. I tried to be all things to all people, which only caused me to have health problems, burn out, and depression. I believe women do have to try harder, and that often puts them in a position of not being authentic and going against their own values, which happened to me.

During those times, I was not happy. I took my anger out on those around me for whom I was supposed to be an example. I was a poor human being. Once I stepped back, reviewed my values, reviewed what was in my control, and started being authentic, my leadership journey took a turn toward a better road. Is leadership easy? No, it is not, and that is why I always call my own leadership journey, Leadership, Roses, and Unicorns.

Each leader will tell you their journey is different, and they are right. We are human beings, so I would hope we all have unique journeys. But each journey will also have similar paths, including highs and lows, which I compare to a rose garden, and certain attributes that get us through the thorny parts, which I call the unicorn power that each of us have.

I grew up in a family that lived paycheck to paycheck. I went to college determined not to be in those circumstances and knew education would be the road to help achieve that. I received my MBA, which I thought would shoot me into leadership positions. Well, I was wrong. In my rose garden of leadership, I was my own thorns holding me back. Think about a rose garden and how it looks from the outside and from the inside. From the outside, you see the beautiful blooms of a variety of colors, or maybe just one color. But then you step into the garden, and what happens? The thorns start tearing up your legs or your pants; you start to see the weeds underneath all the beautiful roses. Well, leadership in my eyes is the same thing; it looks like a wonderful pinnacle to achieve, but underneath, there are a lot of weeds and thorns to dodge. This is why I want to tell my story; to help that young aspiring leader maneuver their way to avoid some of the thorny patches. There is no way to remove all the thorns, but you can step aside certain patches by learning from leaders who have already walked through the garden.

As I reflect on my rose garden, the values I portray are what helps my garden grow. Each person has their own unique values. Reconnecting with my values helped me awaken my own leadership garden and enjoy all the roses. These values are truly what help me walk my path each day. In reflecting on my values, hardworking, growth mindset, and independence truly make up my compass.

The first value that could be seen as both a bloom and a thorn in my rose garden is my independence. Growing up, my family frequently reminded me that I needed to make my own path and make my own impact on the world. I was required to learn how to change the tire on a car and be able to check the oil before I could drive. What my dad was instilling in me was first responsibility but also independence. He did not want me to depend on someone else to take care of something he knew I was more than capable of doing. As part of my independence, I have always had a can-do attitude, and if I do not know how to do something, I will figure it out. But my thorn there is stubbornness. I want to figure it out without help. When I was growing up, I felt that asking for help was a sign of weakness and a lack of intelligence. This created unnecessary roadblocks and stress for me. As an ever-evolving human being, I realize this and continue to remove this thorn from my garden.

I will also say that I remember hearing the saying attributed to US President Truman, "the buck stops here," which truly resonates with me. Those words speak of taking ownership and accountability. I believe these two traits in a leader really make a difference in an organization. I think back to the managers, as I do not think of them as leaders, who would point the finger or throw their team under the bus to push ahead their own agenda. This made the workplace very uncomfortable and toxic. We all know of these types of managers, recognizing that we do not want to be like them helps us become better leaders.

I am often taken aback by the compliments and praise I receive for what I do. I often wonder what they see that I do not see in myself. While this is humility, I also believe it is my work ethic shining through. When you get the job done and do it well, maybe not perfect to you but great to others, those around you will recognize that and will recognize you. It is still hard for me to take this kind of praise as I just think to myself, *They have no idea what is not done, and I am just doing what I am supposed to be doing.* This comes from my value of hard work. I have been working since I was ten years old. And if I am totally honest, probably earlier than that with chores around the house and working in the garden. In high school, college, and even my early working years, it was not unusual for me to have two jobs along with going to school full time. When I was working toward my master's degree, I was working full time and attending courses in the evening. Even now, I have my hands in multiple projects, and when I do not, I feel lost. I enjoy being busy, and I've even been called a workaholic, which is probably true, but it also brings me joy. As with each value I have described, it is a beautiful bloom but can also be a thorn on the stem.

As part of my LeadHERship awakening journey, there was one aspect that I did not realize was so important until I recently and that was growth mindset. I have always been the nerd with a book in her hand and reading in my free time. Even when I was in school, I would have a variety of books to read in addition to what I was learning in school. Fiction is my guilty pleasure, as I feel we all need an escape from life. I do sprinkle self-development and non-fiction in there as I want to expand my knowledge. But growth mindset does not end with just reading. It is listening to others in your circle and outside your circle. It is having mentors and coaches to help you improve on those not-so-great attributes of your personality. Each day I challenge myself to see things just a little bit differently. I have enough pride in myself to say, "I do not know, but I will find out." The knowledge that we do not know something and the willingness to find out the answer, I believe is a combination that shows a great leader is around. I also believe that one of the greatest privileges we all have to keep learning.

As a reader of this book, you are showing that you also have a growth mindset. We cannot stop learning if we truly want to be great leaders. In this age of technology, there are a multitude of resources where one can spend one to two minutes gaining knowledge. But I want to challenge you with not only reading, listening, or watching to gain new knowledge, but also putting into action what you learn. I know there have been many times I will read something and think, *oh, that's a great idea,* but then do nothing. It does take that extra step to actually use the knowledge you have. This action step could be as easy as telling someone else or incorporating it into your own life, depending on what you are learning. Can you truly be an effective leader without continuing to learn? I do not think so. This rosebud in my garden is helping me keep the area beautiful and bring beauty to other parts of the world.

So, when you're experiencing your leadership awakening, you might encounter a roadblock. Sometimes what's seen as a rose can also be a thorn, just like my independence. Just like being a hard worker. These values are near and dear to my heart, but I've had to grow in my leadership and realize not everyone is like me.

So far, I have spoken of the rose garden, yet this chapter is called "Leadership, Roses, and Unicorn" because in my own life, it all goes together. So, how in the world do unicorns come into my LeadHERship awakening journey? Well, it goes back just a few years ago when I was in a toxic work environment, and I needed some positivity. I remember seeing how unicorns were all over social media and in the stores. I also remember how judgmental I was of them and of how enamored some adults seemed to be with the symbol of unicorns. It was during this time, I wanted to have a word that would bring me to a positive mindset and help me smile through the situations occurring. It was during this time, I went through some various words, including sunshine, teddy bears, vacation, and more. But they just did not bring me the joy and smile I needed to deal with the toxicity I was dealing with. Then one day I said unicorn and I could not stop smiling. I dare you right now to say unicorn and not smile. There is just something about the word that brings light to my life. I do not know what it is, but what I do know is that when I was having a conversation that was increasingly negative and impacting my goal of a positive mindset, I would wait for a spot for the coworker to stop talking, then change the subject by bringing up unicorns. My coworkers would look at me oddly, but it would shift the conversation from the negative focus to a more relaxed conversation. Please do not get me wrong; we do need to vent, but when it is the same story over and over as was the case for me, I felt I needed a special word to bring me out of that negative headspace. It was also to help my other coworkers to get out of the negativity also. When you change the subject matter to something relaxing, such as unicorns, the feel of the room changes also. As a leader, you will have to read the room and make decisions of how to help your team get through the difficult days. I still get gifts of unicorns as a way to remind me of how I helped lead the team through that dark period of time.

In the recent year, I have expanded on my power word of unicorn and identified what each letter means to me. In a sense, this is another way of listing out my values. I would like to share it with you and challenge you to develop your own power word and develop your own definition for it.

So, what is Kristie's definition of unicorn?

- Unique
- Neat (aka organized)
- Innovative (thinking outside the box)
- Caring
- Ongoing (keep going no matter way)
- Reliable
- Noble

When I did this exercise, I did have a hard time coming up with words that did not make me feel like I was being egotistical. It is hard for me to brag about myself, but once I changed my mindset and asked myself what I wanted to be known for, it was very easy. As I reflect on how I express these seven words in my rose garden, I take pride in the self-realization of how far I have come in the last few years to know why these traits make me the person I am today.

Being unique, one-of-a-kind, is honestly something I just took ownership of in the last two years. I would get told how unique I was with my various skill sets and adaptability, but I truly did not think it was true. But as I look at the other characteristics and how they truly make up my rose garden, I am proud of my uniqueness and the gifts I have to offer to the world. It was when I started believing in these traits, that my leadership rose garden came into fruition. Each of us have unique talents that we just have to take ownership of. I love how this chapter has given me the opportunity to reflect on how I am unique and share that with each of you.

As part of my uniqueness, I am someone who needs a neat environment to thrive. When I spoke of thorns and weeds in the rose garden, this is what I see as clutter in my physical and mental world. I thrive better when I have a plan, when my physical environment is organized, and when my mental state is in a calm state. As I work on my garden, I have noticed that when I get overwhelmed and have anxiety attacks, that I let the weeds get out of hand and I need to step back. I believe each of us go through these periods of time where we need to take care of ourselves. We have heard the words self-care which is gaining more popularity it seems. These self-care times are when I go through my rose garden of life and do some cleaning to make it neat for me again. Sometimes it takes a few hours and sometimes it takes a few weeks. As a leader, we also need to remember this as our team goes through their own gardens to tidy up.

I would like to remind you that my profession is accounting, so claiming that I was innovative was a little risky for me as sometimes accountants have received a bad rap of being creative or innovative and pushing the line on thinking outside the box when it comes to the regulations accountants and businesses must follow. I am not that type of person. I am very conservative regarding following the regulations that have been passed for businesses and individuals. When I speak of being innovative, I speak of looking at situations, removing my blinders, and thinking of alternatives that others do not see. I have received feedback that I see things differently and give alternatives that seem obvious to me but not so much to the receiver. I attribute this to my growth mindset and my willingness to research, listen, and ask questions.

Oh, which of us would not say we are not a caring person. I believe each of you reading this would have this trait on your list. As I was going through the options of words starting with the letter "c" and which described me, caring just kept coming to the top. It is because I cannot remember a time when I did not put others before myself and try to take care of everyone and everything in my life. As I have grown in my self-realization, I have figured out that if I do not take care of myself first, I cannot take care of others. I must admit this has been a very hard lesson to learn. I enjoy being there for others and the joy it brings to my life. When I care and help others, it is like sunshine for my rose garden. As I stated above, when I wrote out my characteristics I want to be known for, these are the seven important ones, and of those caring is the top one. And as with the values stated above, something caring can be a thorn if it means giving out more roses than have in the garden. During the time I have been writing this, I have truly reflected on how great leaders often do give out more than they have and that is because of how much they care. We all need to remember to balance it out and remember to care for ourselves so we can care more for others.

As I tell others some of the stories of my life events, the trait of on-going comes out. I have encountered a few obstacles, but I do keep going until I reach my goal. I have not been granted with the greatest health, but I will power through to get things done. This tenacity can be a rose, but can also be a thorn in the garden. I will often be called out on how I advise others to take a break when they are low, but I will keep going. This is where it is a thorn. But the on-going and never giving up attitude comes through as a rose when I am studying for the latest designation, completing a project that I never thought I would do, or when training for a half-marathon. I have made it through some tough times because of this trait, and I know it is going to be this trait that helps me make a lot more dreams come true.

The trait of being reliable is a two way street type of trait. My community knows that they can count on me when something needs to be done or figured out. But what is also wonderful is that I have built a community of those I can rely on to help me during those hard and low times. As a leader, we need to build a team in our professional and personal life to be there at those hard times. Reliability is something I have been known for all my life. As a young girl, I was the responsible and reliable one. I did what was right and would make sure things were done as they needed to be. That has never gone away. Sometimes I think I get the problem as a challenge but then I remember, people see me as being reliable and know I will figure it out and solve the problem. This trait truly helps the rose garden be so beautiful.

As I reflected on the last letter in unicorn, I first came up with negotiator, but that did not seem like the right word. I am becoming a better negotiator, but it is not a characteristic that is at full bloom yet. So, I did what all great leaders do, I went to Ms. Google. The word that I kept coming to was noble. At first, I kept away from it because it means positive and selfless. I did not think it would be noble of me to write a paragraph about how I feel I am noble, but as I truly reflected on it, it hit home. When I am going through tough periods of life, I can often be heard saying, this is just a valley and I am pushing forward and up to the top of the mountain. Or I can make it through this; I have made it through other hard times. I am nearly always putting others in front of me as I know I can move my own plans around to help them out. I do hope that when the time comes and those who are left behind to speak of my traits, I do hope noble is one of those traits that is spoken of.

As I reflect on this chapter in which I describe my own rose garden, I hope it helped you think of the roses you are nurturing in your garden as a leader, as a woman, as an overall wonderful person. We each have roses that are blooming, some that need a little tender care to open up, and some weeds that need to be eliminated. As an up and coming leader, I thrive on getting my rose garden into an everlasting place in which other up and coming leaders will look upon and possibly pick a rose or two and place in their own garden. As women, we need to boost each other up and help tend to make all the rose gardens beautiful. Will they ever be perfectly weeded and thorn free; of course not, but we can help one another with our values and characteristics to make them just a little less weedy and thorny.

About the Author

Kristie is a connector of people. She enjoys bringing like-minded individuals together and increasing the virtual rolodexes of each person she meets.

While Kristie enjoys connecting people, she has a deep level of appreciation for numbers and followed her dreams to becoming a certified public accountant. She is a life-long learner and is not done putting letters behind her name.

Kristie is still growing as a leader and enjoys helping others with their own leadership journey. She has been called a unicorn of CPAs as she does think differently, but it is her energy and presence that she hopes she is remembered for. In the past two years, she has been recognized for her leadership; most recently as Women Who Mean Business award by the Houston Business Journal. She is a LeadHERship Advisor in LeadHERship Global and C-Suite, where she is surrounded by supporting women who empower her and trusts her to empower them.

Kristie grew up in Nebraska and still supports the Nebraska Cornhuskers and has deep roots as a Midwesterner. She currently lives in Houston, Texas but believes that she ends up where she is needed at the right time.

Kristie enjoys being creative with designing and creating handmade cards and scrapbooks. This creativity is her outlet from being chief financial officer/chief operating officer at TXCPA Houston, caregiver to a special needs adult, a loving partner, and a dog mom to their two spoiled dogs.

TWENTY

Geri Pacheco

MY LIFE AND LEADERSHIP PATH–PAIN, GROWING, SHARING

*I*t has been a lifelong dream of mine to be a writer. When I was a little girl, I wrote and illustrated children's books. My main characters were all mice, but they dressed in human clothes and lived in a big city (not unlike me). I spent hours working on my books; looking back, now I realize this was my way of coping with the many dysfunctional things happening around me as the youngest sibling of fourteen growing up in the 1970s. My mouse books got lost along the way, and in their place, I decided I wanted to be a teacher. That too got lost after I started college and quickly got derailed by life, working, getting married too young, and having my first child at twenty-one. This story could be filled entirely with all the drama, misfortune, tragedy, and angst of the first chapter of my adult life, which I'm going to categorize as "My Twenties," but I'll do my best to summarize that as much as I can. A lot of stuff went down during that decade, and all of it was life-changing and transformational for me. If it wasn't for the first chapter, I would never have made it to where I am today, at the beginning of Chapter 3.

Chapter 1 of my life included all the big-ticket items: marriage; college; divorce; life-threatening illness; giving birth; losing a parent to cancer; moving across the country (and then back again); changing jobs;

changing career paths; going back to college; and finally, rounding out the chapter, college graduation. By the time I was thirty, I was exhausted! Getting divorced for the second time and getting my bachelor's degree in accounting all happened in my thirtieth year. Looking back now, my thirties started out rough, but it really was the beginning of Chapter 2. If Chapter 1 consisted of the Pain years, Chapter 2 consisted of the Growing years. I finished school, got my first controller position with a small construction company, and settled into small business entrepreneurship. I worked for an extremely encouraging and supportive married couple. The husband was a successful businessman and taught me a lot about construction and accounting. I was originally hired to manage HR and safety, but when I decided to go back to school (at twenty-eight years old), they encouraged me to study accounting and take over the wife's role as "office manager" (this was really the controller position). I agreed, and after two and a half years of working full-time, going to school full-time, and raising two boys, I finished school.

Getting my bachelor's degree was a game-changer for me, a true transformation. I had felt like such a failure for not finishing college when I first started right after high school. Getting this diploma opened up the first of many doors. I left that first controller job after the owners retired, and I went to work for another construction company. After that, I went to work for a technology company. Growing in and learning a new industry, I worked for the first time under the guidance of a CFO. Although my construction experience was invaluable (you'll learn why later), it was at this tech company that I really understood the meaning of finance. This company needed investment capital, and I got to work with many experienced people over the course of several years. I learned how to put a pro-forma and projections together; I helped write business plans, I traveled to "dog and pony" shows to present to private equity and venture capital firms. This experience was better than getting an MBA. I was in the trenches working hand in hand to grow the business.

It was also here that the CEO asked me, "Do you want to be the CFO?"

I said, "Yes, of course!"

The current CFO had decided he wanted to try his hand in operations, so this was my chance. The CEO said, okay, but I had to get my CPA license. If I did, he would promote me right away and I'd get a significant bump in salary. He didn't have to tell me twice. I signed up for the Becker CPA review that day. I took the very last pencil-and-paper exam in November 2003. I was nervous. I took all four parts in two days. By the second test of the second day, I started on the multiple-choice questions for the Financial Accounting and Reporting (FAR) section. I started to panic; although I had studied for four months, every day, I focused more on the three other parts of the exam as I felt I should have this section down (I had been a controller for about five years at this point). Anxiety took over as I thought, "'What if I didn't study enough? What if I don't know the answers?" For those of you who don't know, you have to get a 75 percent or higher to pass any part of the CPA exam. I went into this fourth part feeling pretty confident I had passed the other three already. I'll never forget when I got to about the fortieth question on the FAR multiple-choice section, I knew I had the first forty questions answered correctly. I knew at that moment I was going to pass all of it. I started to cry. At that time, in that environment, only about 10 percent of the test takers passed all parts in one sitting. I left the test center that day feeling pretty cocky. When I told the former CFO what I thought, he told me not to tell anyone, because it's almost impossible to pass all four parts (he hadn't). So, I buried it and didn't say anything to anyone. It took three months to get the results. When I opened the envelope (remember, this was 2004, stuff was still done with paper) all I could see were sixes and eights on the page. But, the first word was "CONGRATULATIONS!" and that was all I needed to see. Because of my insecurity about doing the impossible, I thought I was seeing sixty-eights as scores; what I was looking at were eighty-sixes and eighty-sevens. After starting to comprehend what I was reading, the self-critical part of me kicked in and said, "Why didn't you score a ninety? What did you miss?"

I cannot express in words the transformation I experienced as a result of getting my CPA license. I got that promotion, and the big pay raise, and I never looked back. I worked in the tech field until I moved to Texas. We came to Texas for personal health reasons, and we only planned to stay temporarily but ended up relocating in 2007. After working at a couple of different companies, in 2010 I found myself unemployed and looking for work. CPA license in hand, I hit the recruiter circuit. The best advice I got from one of those recruiters was to make personal introductions (as much as possible) to the person doing the hiring, not just to the HR team. So, after applying for a controller position at a small entrepreneurial general contractor, I called the founder/CEO and left a personal message on his voicemail. Unbeknownst to me at the time, he listened to the voicemail in front of his outside CPA/tax advisor, who I had hired at a previous company. I got an unsolicited recommendation before I even met the CEO! Talk about serendipity. Remember that construction experience I had from early on in my career? Percentage of completion/cost accounting never leaves you; it's like riding a bike. I interviewed and got the job! I have been in this role now for thirteen years. I was quickly promoted to CFO in 2011 and have worked side by side with the CEO and (more recently) the president to help grow and run the business. Chapter 2, Growing. In 2010, our company had eighteen employees with about $20 million in revenue. We are closing 2022 with over two hundred employees and close to $600 million in revenue. If growth isn't the mantra of my last thirteen years, I don't know what is.

I've not only grown as a professional, learning more each day about being the best CFO I can be, I've grown as a person, and as a woman leader in my industry and the business world in general. In 2012, the CEO challenged all the executives to look into outside organizations that we could join to help market and network our business. I already was active with the local CPA society, but some other good advice I got from an outside mentor was to join associations in my business industry, not in my professional capacity (i.e., I needed to find an organization that was in construction or commercial real estate). One of my colleagues suggested I join CREW (Commercial Real Estate Women). He said what he knew about it was that the women liked to drink wine and host fishing tournaments. Although that sounded like a lot of fun, I knew immediately these women were serious about their business. What I quickly learned about CREW was how significant and substantial the commercial real estate world is in our society and around the globe. I didn't have a clue about all of the parts that go into real estate development. Construction is only one of those parts. I went to the monthly luncheons and saw all of these amazingly accomplished, professional women around me and that sense of insecurity I felt when I was afraid to share my CPA exam experience came rushing back. How can I compete with these women? What I failed to realize, and needed to learn, was that it wasn't a competition. This was an organization of women who had each other's backs, who supported each other, no matter what. It took me a while to figure that out, but that growth, transformation, and evolution happened. I didn't let my insecurity get in the way of striving to become a leader in this group, and I kept putting myself out there, regardless of the outcome, so I would know I always gave it my best shot. It paid off.

I've served in many leadership roles in CREW over the last decade, most recently as the local chapter president. I had tried a few times to get nominated for this role before I was selected to serve as 2021 president elect. Of course, I was disappointed when I wasn't selected. I questioned myself and my abilities. Maybe they didn't like me? Maybe I would never be chosen? Maybe I wasn't good enough? I didn't know or realize then that in many organizations like this, the path to leadership is long and purposeful. I now know how important it is to truly understand the mission and accept the responsibility for spreading that mission to the fullest extent possible. CREW's mission is to transform commercial real estate by advancing women globally. In this next chapter of my life, Chapter 3, Sharing, I plan to continue what I've started as part of this organization. I want to share my experiences, my knowledge, and my advice with young women who can benefit from the lessons I learned, mistakes I made, and successes I have had. What are those things that I want to share? They come from many experiences, with my job, with CREW, with my personal life. Many thoughts and words come to mind as I think about what I want to share:

- Be tenacious.
- Challenges are opportunities.
- Don't give up.

- Believe in yourself; know your worth and what you can contribute.
- Be for people, not against them; when you bring them up, you bring yourself up.
- Be the person who creates that sense of belonging and inclusion you so want for yourself.
- Don't quit.
- Trust in fighting for yourself, knowing who you are and letting other people see you.
- Keep trying.
- Be prepared; success is where preparation and opportunity meet.
- Women support women.

One theme as I re-read those words that repeats itself is don't quit. My mother taught me one great thing, and that was to be tenacious. If I want something, I am like a dog with a bone, I won't stop until I achieve what I set my mind to. Degree, check. CPA license, check. That job, that house, that car, check, check, check. Don't give up, don't stop. Keep going. Life is hard. Life continues to throw grenades at you. Learn to duck. Learn to pivot. Love yourself and be the person you want others to be. If you want to be included, include people. If you want to feel appreciated, show others how much you appreciate them.

My experience in CREW has truly been a transformational awakening. This past year as president in 2022, I got to experience so many inspirational moments. Coming out of the COVID-19 pandemic was tough. All the organizations I am part of saw a decline in membership; CREW Houston was no exception. We set very specific goals for the chapter in 2022, and through the hard work of so many women, we achieved them. I cannot take the credit; the women around me worked tirelessly to build the organization back up and to make it the most diversified chapter Houston has ever had. We ended 2022 with over three hundred members, the most in chapter history, and 2023 is starting out strong. The support I received from not only the board but also the membership at large has left me speechless. I have had many conversations with young women who are craving leadership, leadHERship, looking for role models, wanting to know what it takes to achieve success not only in their careers but in their personal lives as well. When I speak with them, I hear their insecurities and doubts, how they just want to know they are important, valued, smart, and worthy of whatever life has in store for them. They want to be heard, to be included, and to have opportunities to grow and advance. They are me, 25 years ago.

My Chapter 3 continues with this mission. To share my story with anyone who will listen. To help them understand it's okay to love yourself and expect the extraordinary by letting them see my vulnerabilities and telling them about the obstacles I overcame to achieve the success I attained. To know you are worthy and deserve what your higher power has in store for you. To know that with the good comes the bad. Trust in yourself to know you can persevere, and you will persevere. I've had a lot of loss in my life. Both of my parents are gone, and I've lost several siblings along the way. I've struggled with job loss, financial difficulty, and personal setbacks. I have always tried to learn from them. What can I take from the negatives? Certainly, things not to do again. But more importantly, I think forgiveness is the lesson to learn. Forgive others, yes, but also learn to forgive yourself. I've made so many mistakes along this journey, and there are things I wish I could undo or take back. I cannot. But I can always do better, be better. That enlightenment, a recent awakening, is another life-changing transformation for me. I cannot undo my past, but I can guide my future to be the best I can make it. It isn't easy. I sometimes take things too seriously, I'm hard on myself and hard on others, with unrealistic expectations of both. But I'm learning to examine my inner self more, faults and all. I used to hide from it, *I don't want to look at that, what if I don't like what I see?* I'm getting past that. Whoever I am, I am me. Good and bad. Nobody is perfect. Perfection doesn't exist. Anybody striving for perfection as a human will ultimately disappoint themselves, and why would we purposefully do that? There is so much more to enjoy when we promote love, understanding, and acceptance, and when we can see ourselves and each other for who we are, good and bad, and celebrate the good. Forgive the bad.

Chapter 1: Pain. Chapter 2: Growing. Chapter 3: Sharing. This is my life. I have achieved a lot in my 30+-year career, and with every experience I have had, I took away something that contributed in a positive way to my next new experience. I like to view myself as a life-long learner. I still plan to get my MBA, and part of Chapter 3 is to teach accounting classes when I retire from my CFO role. As I continue to advocate for women in commercial real estate, I also advocate for women in accounting, and specifically in construction accounting. As a member of TXCPA–Houston and the local chapter of CFMA (Construction Financial Management Association), I serve on their boards and actively engage in speaking to young professionals about roles in industry (as opposed to public accounting) and how to grow from a controller to a CFO in the construction industry specifically. I recently was honored as a leading woman in Finance and Banking (2022) for the Women's Resource of Greater Houston. Their mission is to help women who are economically disadvantaged learn the skills to live independent, productive, and financially stable lives. This speaks to me on so many levels as my own mother struggled her entire life with financial freedom and independence. I'm discovering that as I get more involved in local philanthropic organizations, I find many of my CREW colleagues are also involved, and it warms my heart. Giving back is truly a gift that keeps on giving.

My life could be broken up into many chapters, not just three, and I'm leaving some very important roles out that I also perform: mother, daughter, wife, friend, sister, aunt. This chapter is about my career, but I couldn't have achieved any of it without the support of my family. I remarried for the third (and final) time at thirty-two, pretty much at the beginning of my journey to CFO. My husband always has my back. He has always supported my career decisions, fed me and took care of the boys while I sat at a card table flipping flash cards for four months while studying for the CPA exam. My two sons have been with me the entire ride. They came to work with me many late nights, sat at desks and played computer games while I finished month end (they didn't even know what that meant other than I had to work late). As adults, they now call me to check in, worried I work too hard or too late, but they always support me in any of the endeavors I take on, including my career, my volunteer efforts, or my crazy desires like wanting to be a writer. I couldn't do any of these things without these three men in my life.

Chapter 4: Retirement. That chapter is a long way off, but maybe someday? We'll see. For now, I'm thriving in Chapter 3, with a little bit of Chapter 2 in the mix.

About the Author

Geri Pacheco is the chief financial officer of Arch-Con Corporation, a national commercial construction firm headquartered in Houston. With more than thirty-five years' experience in business, Geri has worked in all facets of accounting, finance, and human resources. Geri has been recognized over the years with several industry honors including Houston Business Journal's CFO of the Year three times, along with other corporate and commercial real estate industry awards.

Geri's passion for helping others gave her the opportunity to recently serve as president for CREW Houston, a chapter of CREW Network, a global organization focusing on advancing the achievements of women in commercial real estate. As a visionary member of CREW, she often spends time speaking with women on how to advance their careers and ways to promote themselves professionally. Along with CREW, Geri is an avid supporter of TXCPA-Houston. She has presented many times on how to transition from a controller to CFO and continually advocates for the CPA profession.

In all aspects of life, Geri makes it her mission to achieve the highest level of accomplishment she can attain, regardless of obstacles standing in her way. When she decided to study accounting, for example, she knew unequivocally she would obtain her CPA license and work her way up the ladder to provide the most she could for her family. In addition to work, she enjoys spending time with her husband and their three adult children, along with their four-legged family members Max and Nala.

~

TWENTY-ONE

Terre Short

INTENTIONALLY PRIORITIZE A JOYFUL LIFE

"*Y*ou can't run around the block more times than Richie," the boys insisted in unison.

"Of course, I can," was my retort and has been for decades.

I've offered this response to an endless parade of challenges.

"You can't be a lifeguard at sixteen and one hundred and thirteen pounds soaking wet. You'll never pass the life-saving test with the two brutes."

Of course, I did.

"You can't be the purchaser for steel, wiring, bolts and conduit—things you know nothing about."

My whole body learned to respond, "Of course, I can." My voice, my posture, my next curious questions all represented very little doubt. Others did not seem to doubt me and neither did I.

I procured supplies for manufacturing control panels and control houses that ran nuclear power plants for my dad's company when I was eighteen to twenty years old. My female voice initially surprised the steel distributors. I worked hard. I learned how to order wingnuts, not be one. I loved it.

The more I committed to action by saying, "Of course, I can," the more I had on my plate. Before long, "I can" added up to a heap of items on my to-do list. I have always been a go-to person for getting things done and I often hear, "You accomplish so much!" I want to tell you the why, what, and how of this reality so that you, too, can live a joyful life. I want you to contribute from your highest potential and a place of ease. I want to offer a new perspective on balancing the priorities in your life. I want you to be able to shout, "Of course I can!"

How to "Accomplish So Much"

I have learned to do several things with great efficiency: prioritize, habit stack, sequence, track/calendar, center, reframe, delegate, and celebrate. The combination of these tactics enables me to accomplish much and F.A.S.T. Before we get to what F.A.S.T. stands for, here's an overview of each of the complementary tactics previously listed.

- **Prioritize.** I prioritize by asking myself, and sometimes others, probing questions. At the end of every week, I prioritize by asking myself, and sometimes others, probing questions in preparation for the following week's list of tasks:

    o What is the desired outcome?
    o Who else needs to be involved?
    o What portion of this task is my responsibility—all or part?
    o How long will it take to do it in full?
    o Does it need to be broken into parts?

    Then I prioritize the upcoming week. I do a similar review each day to ensure appropriate time is blocked for each task.

- **Habits and Habit Stacking.** There are certain things I do exactly the same way every time. Some people resist creating habits as they fear being limited or restricted. Done well, habits create freedom and more time and space. The outcome is predictable, as is the timing, when I engage in a daily habit. Habit stacking is when I pair one habit with another habit or behavior.

• **Sequence.** Sequences are often tied to habits for me. It is efficient for me to know I will wash my face, brush my teeth, remove my contacts, floss, and apply face cream in the same order each night. Nothing gets missed, and when the order is correct, I do not put lotion in my eyes.

• **Track/Calendar.** Most of us live by our calendars for calls and meetings. I figure I have at least five hundred minutes each day to accomplish as much as feels right for me. My ability to do so hinges on putting the items from my to-do list in timely slots throughout the week/month/year.

• **Center.** This is the ability to establish control in the chaos. A deeper review follows to illustrate various ways to be fully present and engaged in the action at hand.

• **Reframe.** Reframing may be my superpower. It is as simple as teasing out the positives and any potential learning from unplanned or disruptive occurrences. This may include something unwanted being added to my to-do list. First and foremost, I seek to reframe in a positive light. Being centered aids in doing this, and this perspective cultivates positive, supportive energy.

• **Delegate.** Delegation is an opportunity to challenge someone else, to fuel their growth mindset. Delegation can be a win-win for all involved when the messaging is right and the value is clear.

• **Celebrate.** Honor what you have accomplished, even incrementally. Every effort counts and reveling in the ticking of a box, or crossing off an item, provides a sweet dopamine hit.

That might seem like a lot of tactics, but I assure you they are complementary and lead to "accomplishing much." It fascinates me when people tell me I accomplish so much. I think, I *accomplish exactly what I desire.* I feel aligned with what I choose to do each day.

As CEO I operated Montana's largest luxury guest ranch in the mid-2000s. During the season, we had just under three hundred employees offering adventures to the rich and famous over thirty-six thousand acres. I had a stellar leadership team, and we had a ton of fun in a spectacular setting. Our working ranch included 129 head of horses, and even my first line item for semen sales on a P&L statement. The challenges were as large as the operation. In 2008, we completed building ten 3,500-square foot homes within hours of the first guests checking in. During this time, the hours for the entire team seemed endless.

I was clocking over seventy-five hours per week when it occurred to me that my small window of "off" hours presented my only opportunity to help get a Black man elected president. I began working at the phone banks in town two nights a week.

It was a priority for me to do this work.

I've learned that prioritization means different things to different people. For me, there are two steps to prioritizing something: (1) getting it on the list of things to do; and (2) deciding where on the list it goes, relative to the other things on the list. For instance, some people are great at remembering birthdays, sending cards or gifts on time. They have chosen to make this a priority. The birthdays that are important to them exist somewhere on a list or calendar, and when the time is appropriate, the action to recognize the event is bumped to the top of the list. When I hear myself say, "I missed her birthday," the reality is that I did not prioritize her birthday effectively.

The Neuroscience of Procrastination and Multi-Tasking

Which brings me to two nemeses: procrastination and multi-tasking. Both activities are incredibly misunderstood. One gets a bad rap and the other is celebrated, while neither benefits us. Even so, I must confess, I've given each of them sabotaging time in my life.

From a neuroscience perspective, procrastination is an emotional response. Procrastinating offers momentary relief to the negative moods that feelings such as self-doubt and anxiety create, then a vicious cycle of negative emotions form. I agree wholeheartedly with Dr. Sirois who said, "Procrastination is essentially irrational." Allowing procrastination permits negative emotions to be in control. Who would rationally choose this? (Lieberman, 2019)

Not me, which may be why I have toggled to multi-tasking in the past. This feels like a great pendulum swing. Do nothing, do everything at once. This strategy does not work either. Studies indicate that only three percent of the human population can effectively multi-task. I used to consider myself one of these special few. Now I understand the neuroscience.

Neuroscientist, Dr. Sarah McKay, wrote a great layman's article called, *The Myth of Multitasking*, that highlights the shortcomings of multi-tasking with studies on distracted driving. The findings will encourage you to keep your eyes on the road and not even touch the radio dial (McKay, 2016). In the book *Organize Your Mind, Organize Your Life*, multiple studies indicate that "Multitasking increases the chances of making mistakes and missing important information and cues." Multi-taskers are also less likely to retain information in working memory, which can hinder problem solving and creativity (Moore, 2011). So, why do so many of us think we are excelling at this skill?

We are task-switching. Neuroscience reveals that our prefrontal cortex has two sides. Both sides work together when we single-task and independently when we multitask. This causes excess time and energy switching back and forth. Imagine what gets lost in between!

Master Single Tasker

Here's what I really do...I single-task, masterfully. And I transition well from one task to the next. You likely do too, as this skill is also quite misunderstood. Let's cook a meal and unravel it.

When having a dinner party, it energizes me to pull it off well. This includes setting the table beautifully, preparing the bar, organizing appetizers, cooking the meal, and offering dessert. None of these actions are done in isolation as single-tasking might suggest. I leverage my habit-stacking, sequencing, delegating, and prioritization skills heavily. I expect the preparation and delivery to be seamless, so I work with this goal in mind. I do not expect any part of the plan to be stressful.

I map the evening out in my mind, sometimes on paper, with great clarity of my desired outcome. If it is a simple dinner for six, I may make the main meal my priority. Early in the day, I will decide all that can be done in advance. Setting the table is a habit for me, so I may stack a review of the playlist I'm contemplating while I lay out the settings. I often make the table setting the start of my sequence, as it is easy to do ahead of time, and it clears my mind. I might also learn what else I need to pull out, such as a decanter or dessert forks. As the single focus on the table unfolds, other ideas pop up. I weave them in where they fit.

I typically delegate the bar set up to my husband, with a thought to any extra items needed, such as cocktail napkins. I will write the list of appetizers down in the order I intend to prep them. This has the potential for delegation if my notes are clear. Then I get cooking.

I have focused on each of the other priorities individually. The main meal requires that as well. However, there may be downtime between prep and boiling or sautéing. Here's where multi-tasking can trip you up. If you lose focus long enough, something burns or at minimum overcooks. Sequencing the recipe and preparing as much in advance as possible helps, which leaves you assembling expertly in the end.

I often receive comments about how effortless a meal at our home seems. This is borne out of the prep and series of single tasks that are prioritized well. We like the actual dinner to be about connection, conversation, and nutrition. This reinforces a well-planned execution and truly saves time.

A New Way to Balance Your Life and Be F.A.S.T.

Not every day presents as a meal for six. Some are downright nutty. The items on our to-do lists can seem unwieldy and appear to be multiplying. In which case, it is time to reframe and center.

What if you imagined your to-dos or "plate" as illustrated in Figure 1? Your tasks are likely of varying size and weight. Some tasks you get to put on your balance bar, and some are gifts from others. Either way, it's all there, and you are the fulcrum. That's right, you are the fulcrum.

Figure 1 - A full balance bar of business:

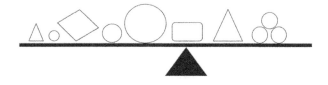

I invite you to consider a new way of creating balance in your life. You get to decide where you place your focus, moving the fulcrum under that which you prioritize to do now. For example, the rectangle may be your vegetable dish. You may decide to bump some items off of the balance bar until a later date, or to someone else, or forever. Oftentimes we hold space for projects or items that are way in the future, or that will benefit someone else to complete. It's okay to temporarily bump a future task off the priority bar, and free up some mental capacity and energy. It is also okay to offer a task to someone else or to simply say no to it (if that is an option in your work setting). Figure 2 illustrates how some items may be parked for some amount of time until they are true priorities.

Figure #2- Intentional placement of priorities and sidelining of some tasks:

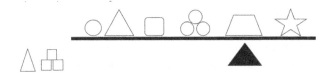

Once you decide where to put your focus, and move yourself (the fulcrum) there, focus on just that one thing. Single-task like a rockstar and enjoy that item slipping off the bar and into the ether once completed. This makes room for something else, but do you need to fill that space? Do you *really*? And if so, might it be something that fills you up? Figure 3 shows the perspective of leaving some space open.

Figure #3 - Lightening the load, by choosing not to fill the free spot:

Let's review some strategies that were mentioned previously and will serve you well with your new balance routine.

Drum roll please…

F.A.S.T. = Focus, Align, Single-Task. Being able to be F.A.S.T. requires the other tactics mentioned at various times.

Focus. (center, prioritize, track/calendar, reframe) To focus well, I must first be *centered*. This is so important; it has its own section coming up! As I am zeroing in on the task at hand (or a big project), I contemplate where it falls in relation to other tasks and projects. Size alone does not make it the main focus. I want to understand what is at risk regarding the timing, quality, and resources around this task or project. I want absolute clarity on the end goal and/or the desired outcome. Often this step is missed, which costs more time at some future point. Once I have enough evidence to determine its *priority*, I *calendar* the breakdown of tasks to completion. For instance, I might note the circle on the balance bar will be done from 3:00 p.m. to 5:00 p.m. on Wednesday, based on the information gathered. I *only* focus on the circle item at that time. When my intel informs me that there are other components or dependencies, I may choose to *reframe* the task. I might break a large circle into three smaller ones to be done independently, and then calendar them.

Align. (delegate, habit stack, sequence) Once I have narrowed my focus, I am able to determine what can be *delegated*. As I move toward the work to be done, I will consider what else I am doing, or can do, to ease the alignment of this task to my day. I will consider the sequence of events that comes before. For example, do I chop all of the vegetables before preparing the meat? Or what *sequence* may align well with this task? I might chop the vegetables for the main dish then move right to vegetables that will go in the salad.

Single-Task. (celebrate) Then I do the work! I feel centered, aligned, and focused on this one thing, and I am confident I will do it well. Sometimes the focus and alignment parts take minutes, and I am ready to execute. I open all of my creativity, all neural pathways, to doing this one thing regardless of complexity. I have prepared well for getting it done. Once I do, I *celebrate*! Too often we move quickly onto the next thing. Revel in your accomplishment, and know that you have created a repeatable process to single-task.

Find Center

The greatest difference since my days of racing around the block is how I honor my needs each day. I make my mind, body, and spirit a priority—the top priority. I have learned that doing this enhances my productivity. I am certain that finding my center fuels my ability to be F.A.S.T. There is so much goodness for us to squeeze out of solid wellbeing practices and changes to how and what we prioritize. "Prioritizing Wellbeing Promotes Productivity" is one of my favorite talks to give, mostly to enjoy the ah-ha moments of attendees.

I engage in various practices for finding my center.

• **Immediate Centering.** (in the moment) I do a few intentional breaths; I rub my thumbs and pointer fingers together for a minute.

• **Daily Centering.** I meditate daily in the morning for twelve to twenty minutes, followed by journaling, which includes gratefulness and intention setting for the day.

• **Routine Centering.** At prescribed times during the day, I practice coherence breathing. With my hands on my belly, I breathe in for a count of four and out for a count of six. Therefore, I take roughly five breaths a minute, for several minutes. The physiology of this practice includes the alignment of heart rate and heart variability, blood pressure, and brain-wave activity, which in turn positively impacts inflammation, anxiety, and resilience.

• **Intentional Centering.** (for a particular task/call/project) These can be any length. Just before a client call, I take one or two minutes to center myself and bring my focus to the client. I do this with a series of breaths and stating their name and my intention to serve them well. For something bigger or more complicated, like writing this chapter, I do a specific meditation (or two). I will set an intention and specify any guidance I am seeking. I did this one day and very clearly intuited the outline for this chapter.

Thanks to years of practice, finding my center is often immediate, though sometimes it takes longer and comes slowly. The result is a revisit of all that is on my balance bar. The items may already seem rearranged or at least viewed in a different light once I am fully present. Centering myself creates a new perspective, one that is open, positive, and in search of all potential. I am in a place of ease.

Life does not need to be chaotic. Preparing a meal (even a fancy one) does not need to be stressful. Finding your center establishes control for where you apply your focus on your balance bar of business and informs your busyness. It creates space for more joy. Whether I am entertaining or working on a project, I know I have tactics to lean on and a commitment to framing tasks as F.A.S.T. I accept being the fulcrum and honor my ability to single-task each priority to fruition. I accept the choices I have to "accomplish so much." Can I always decide what I balance, when I balance it, and how I balance it? Of course, I can! And you can too.

References

Lieberman, C. (2019, May 25). Why You Procrastinate (It Has Nothing to Do With Self-Control). *New York Times*.

McKay, D. S. (2016). *The Myth of Multitasking*. Retrieved from drsarahmckay: https://drsarahmckay.com/the-myth-of-multi-tasking/

Moore, D. P. (2011). *Organize Your Mind, Organize Your Life*. Harlequin.

About the Author

Terre Short is a human potential developer. She is an author, speaker, coach and creator of Thriving Leader Collaborative. She believes that truly authentic leadership is achieved when we embrace our inner wisdom to overcome business challenges. Terre excels at distilling leadership skills into actionable steps. She inspires leaders around the globe by crafting leadership development programs, providing team coaching, and 1:1 coaching. Her approach hinges on how she cultivates curiosity, listens deeply, and explores compassionately.

Terre weaves decades of leadership experience with the education she's acquired through her MBA, PCC (professionally certified coach), and NMCC (NeuroMindfulness Coach). As a NeuroMindfulness Practitioner, Terre lives at the intersection of wellbeing and leadership and is honored to advise high performing Fortune 500 leaders as they explore intuitive pathways to sustain success.

Terre published *The Words We Choose: Your Guide to How and Why Words Matter* in 2020. The book covers how to choose words that connect to values and intention. It spans the words we choose for ourselves (inner narrative), with loved ones, at large in the world, at work, through technology, and with a higher power.

Terre is a guest speaker on many podcasts and has been interviewed for various mediums, including Fast Company and NPR. Her book was a 2020 American BookFest Finalist and won the Bugbee Falk Book Award.

Thriving Leader Collaborative: thttps://www.
thrivingleadercollaborative.com/

https://linktr.ee/terreshort

in linkedin.com/in/terreshort

TWENTY-TWO

Lauren Tatro

TRUTH BE TOLD

It is in cracking wide open, falling to the ground with our hearts in our hands, that we create space for the light.

*M*any moons ago, fresh out of college, I felt like I couldn't catch my breath. At the time, I didn't have a clue how suffocated my soul felt because I had lived in this space for many years and knew no other way.

I landed a seemingly 'dream' job, but couldn't quite figure out why I didn't feel in alignment with the people I had around me. Never really fitting in. It doesn't feel like a super power when you are going through it, but if this feeling is familiar to you, you're not alone.

Up until this point in my life, my communication style was cloaked in anger, and it caused me to feel misunderstood and unseen. Survival mode can have a serious impact on how you show up in the world, and I saw the world as a threat, an inconsistent let down, and out to get me. I kept all of my focus on external circumstances and how unfair it all was. Simply put, I was stuck. I was exhausted, which in hindsight, meant I was pretty close to my surrender.

Then one day, a lightning bolt struck. It was time to see what I was made of. Values or comfort? Most of the time, you can't have both, at least until you seemingly understand that comfort isn't always your friend. The kind of comfort I am speaking of doesn't involve cozy warm blankets; it's the kind laced in complacency and lack of growth. When values are tested, our power lies in our ability to choose.

I had never really stopped to think about my core values. Who am I? What really matters to me? There was never really a catalyst for this exploration, until now. After a few years in my post-college 'first real job,' the test came. Faced with unethical behavior, I felt I had no other choice than to confront leadership. "Turn a cheek, or leave." So on I went. Nothing but college debt, a ton of fear, and my values in hand.

During the next six months, unemployed and unsure where to turn next, my cracking wide open happened. It was a slow fade at first, realizing how much of my identity and worth I had directly tied to money or a title. One day, still vivid in my mind, I fell to my knees. I put my hands to a higher power, and said, "I'm done, I surrender, please show me the way."

You see, these are the moments of raw honesty—in admitting that we don't have it figured out at all, where we may feel alone, misunderstood and lost—when the opportunity for grace presents itself. These dark moments have the potent potential to bring us to our knees, to crack us wide open.

To create an opening for the light.

I couldn't look myself in the mirror, and I ran from vulnerability. I was terrified of seemingly everything and nothing all at the same time. Vulnerability felt like weakness to me, not realizing yet that being vulnerable is an act of extreme strength and courage. I quickly realized that I didn't trust myself, but in choosing to do the right thing and leap into the unknown, as scary as it was, I began identifying my core values and gaining some respect for myself. It was crumbs, and I was hungry. The anger began a slow shift, and I knew I needed to keep going.

A little whisper kept finding me, *Go look at yourself in the mirror.* Huh? Who's there? Why is this thought coming to my mind? Except, this time it didn't feel like a thought—it felt like a deeper knowing. The more I began to trust myself, the more my intuition had space to breathe.

When you surrender and ask for help, new ideas, nudges, and sources of inspiration are going to enter your path. It's easy to judge them, dismiss them, and lock yourself back in the comfy room you're living in. I remember that feeling vividly, when the nudge got louder and asked me to go look myself in the eyes and tell myself 'I love you'. I walked into my apartment bathroom and looked into the mirror—this time not to make sure my makeup looked good or my hair was ready but with the task to truly see myself. I felt like I was looking at a stranger. I couldn't even say the words out loud, and when I did, I didn't believe them. "I love you" followed by the thought, *No, I don't.* I did this exercise every day for months. I recognized how much work I had to do, no more running—it was time to face myself, to learn about myself, to understand how to trust myself again.

When the light starts to enter, it doesn't always feel warm. And if you've been living in fear—running away from your truth—shifting to a higher vibration can feel foreign. I quickly realized that shifting lanes and leveling up meant that I needed to do something I was never quite capable of doing. I was being asked to trust when I had every reason in the world not to.

Putting trust in the surrender meant sitting in new feelings. Not being able to name them, until slowly, wisdom started to find me and gave me hope. People, places, and things started shifting. Over the coming year, I focused on figuring out who I was and what I really needed from those around me. This didn't come without pain and hurt feelings. I took a year 'off' from my family, and essentially cut back all communication. I started evaluating who was in my life, what value they were contributing to my well being, and I observed all of the times in which I was severely lacking boundaries. I also used this time to evaluate how I was showing up, where I was projecting my pain and anger on my loved ones. This reset shook things up in a big way, and I was grateful to have a therapist throughout this process. I vividly remember that the reduction of chaos felt like loneliness. Old patterns and circumstances will come for you, you will be tested. Your mind is wired to these past experiences and feelings, even if they aren't 'good' feelings, they are addicting at a biological level.

I soon learned that what I thought was loneliness was actually peace.

In 2012, my life changed beyond comprehension the moment I became a mom, I held my daughter Mia for the first time. My entire world, my entire heart, burst wide open, and I quickly realized that my capacity to love, trust, and embody my truth was the most important job I had. In focusing on making myself whole, I could give her what she really needed: a happy, present, consistent mom. If I stayed dwelling in the pain of my past, blaming my circumstances, I would never be able to create the environments I felt called to live in and embody.

The paths we take most times cause us to stumble upon life-changing circumstances. Life has nothing to do with being perfect and every-thing to do with change. Recognizing that there is no such thing as perfect, if we live by our values, are honest with how we are really showing up, remain humble and open, we still may find ourselves on the floor at times. And all we can do is give thanks for the birthright we've been given, which is to feel. To feel fully, and completely while not chasing the highs or pushing away the lows.

What does all of this have to do with leadership, you might ask?

I once had a coaching client tell me that working nightmarish hours was all for their family. In holding space for this statement, we explored their core values and uncovered that quality time and the ability to truly be present with his family was actually what he was seeking. The long hours became a badge of honor 'in support of his family,' and we found some relatively simple tweaks to realign and adjust back to his values. Your ability to remain curious, stay out of martyrdom, and self-lead contributes greatly to inspiring a team that wants to work for you. How can you see them if you can't truly see yourself and how you are showing up to the world?

The tricky thing about comfort zones is that our minds hate change, all of the reasons in the world will come pouring in as to why you should keep doing exactly what you are doing, regardless of that deeper yearning that keeps coming for you. Alignment isn't an overnight process; it's a series of decisions that honor who you really are and what you really need.

After spending a lot of time exploring this work, the years that followed this personal growth resulted in a 10+ year career in marketing landing me six promotions from entry level to executive in the span of a few years. Once I was aligned with my sense of purpose, I was better able to seek out organizations and work that aligned with my values. For me, this also meant heeding the call every few years and actively seeking out growth opportunities. This isn't a linear process and can be expansive in order to explore your underlying passions and sense of purpose. Releasing fear doesn't mean that it goes away, it often means that you are willing to take a step (big or small) in the direction of your calling.

What once served you well may not anymore. This is not failure; this is initiation to the next chapter, and it may come with some pain. Having patience, trusting the timing, and taking action rather than ignoring are all critical components of this process.

With a vow of never letting a title or role define me, I recognized that personal growth was professional growth, and I would never trade in my authenticity for approval, ever again. Embodying this energy, my people found me. I learned that if I wanted one feeling but constantly practiced feeling the opposite, I would quickly stagnate. My hunger for growth and advancement shifted to a hunger for learning and purpose.

Abundance and lack mindset can't coexist, and the world owes you nothing. It's on you to unlock your worth and believe it. If you don't believe it, that doubt will be reflected in the people and circumstances around you. This is the great mirror of life.

Right now, stop looking around you for other people to show you how it's done. The answers to your questions live inside. Leadership is an inside job. Certainly, what we consume determines the energy in our lives—influence is all around us. If you are reading this, you are meant to live in the fringe. The center of the pack is comfy; I'm pulling you out to the edge of your comfort zone. Create the thing you wished existed, be the leader you wish you had, stop looking for others to show you your worth. You are beyond worthy and powerful beyond measure. It's time to get curious.

What inspires you? There may be conversations that leave you with goosebumps, a book that shows up on your path at just the right time, a line in a song you are listening to that feels like it contains a message just for you, an urging to try something new or go somewhere you've never been. These are breadcrumbs from the universe. Listen and act. If you've asked to be shown, remember it's not always a big lightning bolt. Sometimes it's a gnawing, uncomfortable feeling that feels too familiar. The gentle nudge that gets louder and louder over time.

This is your soul asking you to come home. Asking you to stop running.

In 2015 I went on a retreat to Italy. It was on this trip that I discovered my essence. I am not quite able to put it into words. I felt my soul and divinity for the first time in my entire life. I felt home. I vowed never to seek power outside of myself ever again. I've been on a mission to help others discover their authentic purpose and power ever since.

I became a certified intuitive life coach, in addition to my career in marketing. I quickly learned that being in a leadership position was the single greatest responsibility I had in breaking the cycles of projection going on all around. So much climbing, striving, forcing. I couldn't help but feel the stark contrast from nature. Is this natural? We are sucked into a vortex of survival. How do we shift from surviving to thriving? From comparison to embodiment? One breadcrumb at a time.

Most people are walking around, regardless of the role they are in, projecting their own 'stuff' on everyone around them. Many are struggling profoundly, not wanting anyone to really know their struggle in order to prevent judgment. Or perhaps, after many years of burying their feelings, they are completely cut off from who they really are.

This is the greatest tragedy of all; it is also our greatest opportunity. Hold strong in your truth. Don't run away. Don't let other people's pain seep so deeply into your spirit that you succumb and begin to question your own worth. The highs and the lows, don't take them personally. Remain the steady shore amongst the fervent waves.

Self-awareness became part of my leadership mission. In judging others, all we are doing is judging ourselves. The circumstances around us, if we are paying close attention, become a mirror for observation and reflection.

I believe there is a massive awakening underway. It starts at the individual level, and ripples out to create a collective evolution amongst humanity. Unlocking human potential as leaders is part of our responsibility. Have you spent time getting to the root of who you are first, or are you perpetuating outdated leadership structures that no longer feel authentic? Doing what you should do rather than what you feel called to do? I invite you to spend some time journaling or reflecting on these questions. Regardless of whether or not you are a leader of a team, reporting to a leader you may struggle to understand, or have a desire to become a leader in the future, our first and primary job is self-leadership.

If you find yourself saying, "I wear so many hats," I urge you to consider shifting this narrative. This concept of wearing many hats leaves us vulnerable to create specific personas that fit an external need. We dilute our power and splinter our reality. What if, instead, you started to say, "I am me, showing up to a variety of circumstances and relationships in my life," as a reminder that even when it may not feel like it, these are choices. You can't spread yourself thin when you find ways to remain whole.

The paradigm shift that is underway applies to more than just leadership—it applies to everything. Anything that is not authentic will crumble eventually. Are you crumbling? If everything looks 'good on paper,' but you still feel empty, could it be possible that you haven't been living your authentic truth?

If you are giving away your power, like I did, wanting to do and be what you 'thought' was right, versus owning who you are and what you need, identifying your values and living by them, then I'd guess you may also be struggling with anxiety, depression, and feelings of isolation. I know I was. Our society and environments are wired to support pushing down our feelings by keeping us distracted and busy.

Instead of pushing these feelings away, recognize them as trapped energy. Your subconscious and soul are trying to speak to you. Are you listening? I don't mean listening with your mind, I mean dropping into your heart and listening to your intuition.

Tapping into your intuition is a form of intense self-trust. Not talking yourself out of what you are feeling, not being able to put into words what your 'gut' is trying to tell you, but fully and completely trusting this deeper knowing. Reflect back on times you went against this feeling. How did it work out for you? Where are you simply conforming rather than leading?

If you remember where I started, part of this journey also means recognizing when you are living in the past. We create narratives in our minds, based on past experiences, and these filters become the way we see life. Our ego creates a protective layer, this protective layer loves being validated. "This always happens to me." "I can't trust them." "They never get it." You see where I am going with this—observing these patterns is a critical component of creating new ways of seeing, being, and doing. If you see the world as us vs. them and expect to feel connection, good luck.

This is part of the self-discovery process. Growth is cyclical, and the patterns will continue until you notice them. Noticing is a form of intense self-awareness and growth. Notice the voice in your head, is she your ally or your enemy? Is she judging others and telling you you're right? Is she fueled by external success and running away from the subtle art of just 'being'?

Again, these are questions for exploration. These are the questions I found myself stumbling into answering by doing things the wrong way. It is in coaching others and professional mentoring where I learned this isn't about having all the answers. As a coach and leader, my job isn't to take away your pain. It's not about telling you what to do; it's truly about being a catalyst to spark your inner greatness. I continue to learn bits and pieces about myself in the interactions that involve learning from the pain, struggles, and triumphs of the people put on my path. We're co-creators of our reality.

The good stuff, the divine energy, the embodied power already exists within you. Asking questions, picking out the breadcrumbs, showing a different perspective, and being an honest, direct, compassionate guide became a big part of my purpose.

A framework for growth started to emerge, involving four stages:

1. **The Surrender:** Hands to a higher power, show me the way. What I've been doing hasn't been working. I don't have it figured out. I'm willing to change. I am waving the flag and asking for help. I don't know what I need, but I trust that when it arrives, a deeper knowing will emerge.
2. **The Awakening:** Adjusting the filters, identifying your core values, taking a strong and honest look at the karma you may have created thus far in your life. No more blaming others; personal accountability lives here. Life starts to show you its

divine magic through the suffering. The old crumbles, creating space for new energy to emerge.

3. **The Transformation:** People, places, and things. You may be circling the drain and asked to choose. What is no longer serving me? Where am I living out of alignment? It's time to make some changes. Big or small, you are now willing to walk the talk. Trust through the fear. I embrace the possibility that I am meant for more; I am beginning to embody this truth.

4. **The Living Truth:** Authenticity reigns supreme. You are no longer seeking external validation. You are releasing guilt, communicating with clarity, and clearly processing emotions rather than running away. Armor down, boundaries up, with an open heart. Embodied essence, in physical form. Better than no one yet commanding the room. You are simply, and truly, you. A beacon of hope, signaling light in others. It's time to shine.

So, how can this framework survive in corporate settings? Well, that really isn't the right question to be asking. The right questions to be asking are: what can I create within my circles of influence?; and how can I leverage the opportunities that present to help leave a love mark on the people around me, in turn, creating a lasting legacy and contribution wherever I go? Let your personal standard be greater than anything anyone can impose upon you, and let that be your guide.

One conversation, one mentoring moment, one presentation—you are only ever one moment away from changing someone's life for the better. This isn't about you, and it is all about you, all in the same breath. The 'YOU' I am referring to, is the you that can't be seen in physical form. It's your divine essence.

It's all about embodied energy. If you are going through the motions and aren't really 'there', then the imprint won't be as strong. If your actions are based on doing what you think is 'good' but you are operating from a place of guilt or to reach someone else's definition of 'value', then you are not fully present and connected to your why. This does not yield an authentic impact.

So, what is your why? First, you must ask, who am I? Why am I here? Where have I been hiding? Where is my ego showing up and blaming everything and everyone around me for what is going on in my life? It's time to come home.

So, what does it mean to awaken as a leader?

We must first awaken as humans and embody that awakening as leaders.

You're worthy beyond measure.

And one day, when the title fades, the role transitions, life's waves come crashing on to your shore, will you fade with it? Will you dissolve into the abyss? Will you leave your values stranded, choosing comfort and conformity when the going gets tough?

Or will you stand bravely, firmly planted, taking up space, in all of your divine glory?

Generations past and present heal and grow. This is true for each individual who chooses to embody their divine essence. Each of these individuals makes up our organizations and our world—our experiences are all connected.

Your values will be tested in varying gradients every single day. Stay firm in who you are and what you know is right. Compassion, kindness, direct communication, and honesty can all co-exist.

As a divine mentor once told me, we are all pieces of coal bumping into each other, creating diamonds over time. It might feel messy, it might feel painful, it might feel lonely—and one day, it might feel powerful and peaceful, all at the same time.

About the Author

Intuitive life coach and brand executive Lauren Tatro founded Discover Essenza in 2015 after a spiritual retreat to Italy. Now, it's her life's mission to help others discover their essence and connect with their authentic power. With over ten years working in corporate marketing, climbing from admin to VP in five years, Lauren is very passionate about helping women reach their full potential, without compromising who they are and what they need. Lauren's experience in marketing and branding expands beyond her role as SVP Brand & Marketing Operations for a financial institution, working with heart-centered brands and holistic small businesses to amplify their reach and positive impact on the world.

Lauren lives in upstate New York with her two kids, husband, and their dog Hudson.

www.discoveressenza.com

in linkedin.com/in/ltatro

TWENTY-THREE

Shirley Wantland

#MORELOVELESSFEAR

I'm not an addict, I'm not a therapist, I'm not an entrepreneur. I'm a thirty-two-year-old Vietnamese female six months pregnant with my second baby, in the middle of a move from San Francisco to Marin County with my husband and two-year-old daughter. So why did I start an addiction consulting business in the midst of all this? It's the reason we do a lot of things: because I **needed** something different. I had been working for corporations my entire career. Blame it on the raging pregnancy hormones, but benefits like health insurance, paid time off, and a paycheck every other week no longer felt secure but suffocating. The thought of finagling my upcoming maternity leave left me gasping for air. Two years prior, when I was discussing my maternity leave with my manager at the time, he asked me if I thought **one month** was "enough time." One. Month. I sat there in the conversation imagining myself still wearing a giant phonebook-sized pad between my legs, bleeding, going back to work, fearing I had no other choice. That was a common occurrence in my life—having *no choice*. I did what I needed to survive and keep moving forward. I knew my inherent work ethic and high standards were lost on and exploited by this company. They would squeeze every last ounce of work they could out of me, and when I reached or exceeded my goals, they would raise the bar, to mitigate compensating me for my worth. This relationship was no longer working for me.

While working at this last company, I collaborated with therapists, psychiatrists, and interventionists (think the A&E show Intervention). One of those interventionists threw out the idea of he and I starting our own company, helping people navigate their sobriety and recovery. When he first brought this up, my initial response was, "Thanks so much for your generous offer, but I can't do that." As I was driving, the thought kept gnawing at me, *Well, why **couldn't** I do that?* To counter my excitement, my mind spun up endless reasons why I couldn't and shouldn't: *You've never started a business before. You don't know what you're doing. You're not even in recovery!* And then the questions started: *How would we set it up? How would we get business? What would we call the company? How do we get payments from people? How does one even form a company? What if we don't get any business? What if we don't make any money? What if we fail? What if **I** fail?* I calmed my nerves with a heavy dose of logic (my go-to!). My business partner had been in business for over three years, so he clearly knows how to do all this. He's in recovery himself, so he must have all sorts of networks to garner business from. What was there to worry about? I had a *partner*.

Fast-forward eighteen months into this venture. We were gaining traction (and business!); although it was lean in the beginning, we were making money! It should have been a time to celebrate the success. Instead of celebrating, I felt exhausted and resentful. I did almost all the work—coming up with the name, finding the graphic designer for the logo, the website, finding an accountant, finding a business photographer, marketing, networking, business development, and *everything* in between. I was even flying on red-eye flights to New York and driving to Connecticut, where there were potential opportunities —all with a toddler and newborn at home. I was growing increasingly angry and resentful but felt like I had no other choice but to continue.

It wasn't until I had lunch with a dear colleague, who's a therapist, that things changed. We were catching up, and she was asking about the business. Eventually, she asked how my business partner and I divided the responsibilities. Sitting there, I was momentarily paralyzed and couldn't come up with an answer. Everything I wanted to say sounded like I was throwing my partner under the bus. Although she was a friend, she was still a colleague, and I didn't want to come across unprofessional by airing all my dirty business laundry.

Struggling to come up with a diplomatic answer, I looked up at her and said, "I do…all of it."

She said, "I know. Why?"

I didn't have an answer for her or myself. Wrapping up my lunch, I remember getting in my car and the resounding "why?" from the conversation was deafeningly loud. It was the first time someone was giving voice to the chatter that had taken residence in my mind over the last year. Sitting in my car, I knew what I needed to do. I immediately texted my husband telling him I'm thinking about breaking away from the business partnership and going solo. I was a little nervous at what his response would be. Would he be disappointed? Would he think I failed at my business? Would he think I was incapable of success?

His response was: "What took you so long? I fully support you, baby. You got this."

Well, now that I had decided I wanted to go solo, how do I actually *do* it? I had no credentials, no multi-million dollar business to stand on, and I wasn't in recovery myself—who would pay me to work with them? Maybe I'd been lucky this whole time in the partnership and that luck would run out if I went out on my own. The reality of going out on my own was equally terrifying and exhilarating. There was nowhere to hide. It was just me. All me. The feelings of immense freedom pushed out the doubts and fears and made way for new ideas to emerge and take shape.

I had a feeling my business partner wasn't going to take the news well and it would be met with anger. After all, I was his golden goose, and now I was telling him I didn't want to share my eggs anymore. I was anticipating the lashing out that would inevitably happen and remembered why I had avoided this topic all together. I went into deep research mode to come up with a plan—how I was going to bring it up, how we would logistically split up the company equitably, and a million other items. And then the questions came again: *Would I really be able to do this on my own?* He was the one with the recovery experience, he was the one who had a company before, he was who I was leaning on. *Wasn't he?* I remember taking a trip to Disneyland with my family, all the while, so preoccupied with this impending conversation. I had scheduled a time to meet with my business partner upon my return from this trip. Driving to that meeting felt like I was getting ready to skydive. The meeting itself was as unpleasant as I had anticipated. My business partner—scared and hurt—flung insults and called me names. The silver lining was we reached an agreement, and I was on my way to becoming the sole proprietor of Recovery Consultants. As I was getting into my car, relieved the grueling ordeal was over, my phone rang with my first new client, and I never looked back.

Six and a half years later, reflecting on the experience, it was one of the *best* decisions I've made, and I'm reflexively kicking myself for not having made the decision sooner. But as I've come to adopt the universal law that "everything happens for a reason," I look back at the partnership and have such gratitude. Without my business partner's initial suggestion and prompting, I may not have had the courage to start the business—on my own or otherwise. I could see that it was all part of my journey.

It was empowering to forge forward with *my* ideas, vision, and execution. The business was in a place where it was humming along. I had a full client caseload and was making good money. Over the past few years, I had visions of growing a team but always stopped once I thought about who could step in and do the job *like me*. After all, this business was my third baby—would someone else love, respect, and treat my baby the way I did? My ego (and fear) convinced me that no one else had the "Shirley secret sauce." It was a tall order, and short of inventing ways to clone myself, I was convinced the vision I had wasn't realistic. Surrounded by fear, I forged forward; alone. I was a lot of things to a lot of people, and I was getting *burned out*.

My parents were Vietnamese refugees who came to Oklahoma City in 1980. A Baptist church in Oklahoma City sponsored refugees from the Vietnam War. Without the currency of language, education (American education, that is), or support network of friends and family, my parents worked several jobs to make ends meet and survive. This meant that I was left to figure a lot of things out on my own. I was sent to the local elementary school in my neighborhood not knowing any English, and without even a backpack! Self-reliance and resourcefulness were survival skills I adopted early. My difficult experience growing up in a majority caucasian demographic with Vietnamese immigrant parents has shaped myself and my business today.

I took a lot of pride in doing things myself and didn't ask for help very often. My difficult childhood experiences formed the belief that there weren't many people that could *effectively* help me. Either they didn't have the knowledge, experience, understanding, skill set, or capacity. So I stopped asking and took on more and more myself. My entire life was built on self-reliance and resourcefulness; it fed the part of me that felt like I had to prove to the world that I was *worthy*, and it weirdly made me feel safe. I could do it all because I was Superwoman, right? So I *did* do it all—running around stressed and overwhelmed, I was running my business, raising two kids, planning, and controlling life. I had it down. I was *doing it*. Wasn't I? The "successes" gave me the illusion I was in control and abated the fear that if I *didn't* do it all, who was I? What would my worth be? It became increasingly stressful and overwhelming to stay on top of everything, all the time. Some crisis would inevitably occur (my industry has a propensity for crisis!), and I found myself surviving life rather than living it. I knew this was (probably?) not sustainable long-term but felt powerless. What else could I do? If I wanted to grow the business, I had to keep taking on more clients. I didn't have the kind of money to hire dedicated employees—I couldn't see another way, so I just did more.

Then a duo of Lindas came into my life and upended the way I viewed myself, my business, and the world. The first Linda approached me about joining a network of female leaders who supported one another, called LeadHERship Global. How had she been fooled into thinking I was some sort of "leader"? Sure, I had my own business and some success, but a *leader*? I kept thinking she had mistaken me for someone else. A leader was someone who was a total badass, running huge companies with teams of people, with bold and innovative ideas, and not afraid to speak their mind confidently—it wasn't me. I was just a mom running this little boutique consulting company. Admittedly, I thought it was going to be another one of those memberships designed to take my money with nothing tangible to show for it. Despite my jaded mentality, something urged me to take the leap of faith. It was that single decision that changed everything.

After joining LeadHERship Global, I still couldn't believe that this company's mission was *really* to help female leaders and entrepreneurs accelerate their growth—it was not just lip service. This was reaffirmed in my first few conversations with Linda 1, where she asked me what I wanted for my business. I shared my fears—I wanted to grow but felt limited in the resources I had in place and unsure of how and where I could find the right kind of support. In a warm and compassionate manner, she was able to show me how I was operating from people-pleasing (i.e., fear) rather than doing what's best for my company. That conversation gave me the strength and a template to have those necessary conversations and start building toward my vision.

Through LeadHERship Global, I met the second Linda, who would challenge my understanding of *everything* I knew to be true. Linda 2, was a coach who talked about concepts like self-limiting beliefs, feeling not enough, and imposter syndrome—I felt like she was peering into my soul and speaking directly to me. She offered an eight-week beta group course. Even though it was more money than I felt was responsible to spend at the time, I heeded the call and took the course. That course catapulted me into another orbit entirely!

Through Linda 2's course, I was introduced to spirituality concepts like universal abundance, scarcity, fear-based actions (and results), and subconscious limiting patterns of beliefs. It was *incredible* and made so much sense to me. I'd never seen these concepts so seamlessly integrated into such a practical approach. I'm someone who has worked alongside many therapist colleagues in my business and personally.

Why hadn't I ever heard of these things? Everything was so logical and I had a whole new understanding of myself (and others!). Why I was the way I was—all from my past traumas and life experiences, shaping my subconscious fears. As someone who has always searched for truth, I was an eager sponge soaking it all up! Within six weeks of starting the course, I started getting new clients. And then *more* clients; *big* clients. As the number of new clients soared, I was excited but conceded it was probably a fluke, right? It just *happened* to be during the same time I'm doing this course.

It didn't make any sense! My business multiplied by three, and eventually five. Could this be true?! I had been in business for eight years, and in the matter of a few months, the business grew exponentially. Although very excited, I was afraid that none of this was real and it would eventually disappear. My mind teeter-tottered between skepticism and exhilaration. I went back and reminded myself to embrace it —be present and *enjoy* it. What I ultimately learned from this (continued) work is: the only thing that changed was my perspective; and the energy I put out in the world has an effect. Linda 2 explained that the universe is infinitely abundant and full of love; **we are the ones who limit ourselves by letting our fears dictate how much abundance we** *deserve*.

In this new inside-out paradigm, I realized the way I had been living was ruled by fear, expressed through perfectionism. I was planning and controlling every possible outcome of life, which I became quite adept at, but it had a cost! I was endlessly trying to attain external things in order to be successful and happy. When I was able to let go of my grip on fear, I started seeing the truth, which is I *am* successful— and I would effortlessly attract external things once I *believe* I am. Linda 2 explained that it is a continual *choice* to believe the truth, rather than the other seventy thousand thoughts and stories my brain engages in any given day. This model gave me opportunities to see when I'm not aligned to love; and how coming from fear inherently limits my capacity to tune myself onto the right "channel" to receive love and abundance.

For much of my life, I was so caught up in concepts like "right" and "wrong"; "good" and "bad". In my continued growth work, I can see how those concepts not only limited me but additionally lent itself to judgment when outcomes fell into the "wrong" or "bad" categories. Through my coaching and work, I can see that there are no mistakes, only information. When you're able to muster the courage to take a new action, it will yield valuable information, which you can use to adapt and evolve. I can see where I've wasted so much time and energy playing into my fears and doubled-down on "perfect"—gathering endless amounts of data to avoid "failure." I wanted to have everything perfectly planned, executed, and answered before I would even take any action. And when the outcome wasn't what I had planned in my head, I judged myself as a failure and abandoned ship rather than seeing it as invaluable information. Ultimately, it limited me from being fully present to understand what's working and what isn't.

Looking back, I can see that I was *always* a leader, I just let my fear convince me my vision and ideas weren't valuable because I didn't accept **myself** as valuable. It was only when I was brave enough to *take action* despite being afraid, that I could see the truth on the other side. Which is that everyone is a leader when they can bypass fear and step into their inherent power. You don't have to run a Fortune 500 company—it can be how you lead yourself, your family, your job, your passions, your community, or how you see yourself in the world. It takes courage and authenticity to accept who you are. If you have the audacity to do something that brings you joy, you will attract success.

Today, the vision for my company—the one I thought was impossible —is unfolding before me. I have a team of incredibly talented women and now have a template to grow the business, outside of me, without cloning technology! I never thought it would happen. What I ultimately had to let go of is the control (i.e., fear) that anyone joining my team would need to have the "Shirley secret sauce." Each person brings their *own* secret sauce—my job as a leader is to recognize my team's unique talents and be a champion of their growth. And I don't have to have it all figured out, but I can co-create this role *with* my team not *for my team*.

Can you fathom the impact we could have if we operated with more love and less fear? It isn't an easy ask (what worthy goal has ever been easy to achieve?). It's the commitment to myself, my family, the people in my life, and those I have yet to meet—to take the courageous leap outside of fear and to step into love, ultimately *trusting* that it's **all going to work out**. It's a gift to be present to experience all the love, joy, abundance, ridiculousness, pain, grief, heartbreak, and laughter on this wild roller coaster ride called life we're all on together. I see you and honor the journey you're on. What's holding you back?

About the Author

Shirley Wantland is the co-founder & principal of Recovery Consultants, LLC, which provides a full continuum of recovery services to individuals and families struggling with substance use disorder and mental and behavioral health issues. She graduated from Southern Methodist University in Dallas, Texas, with a bachelors of science in biology and psychology. She has been in the healthcare industry for the past nineteen years with experience in the pharmaceutical and behavioral health industries.

She is dedicated to serving and advocating for those who feel shamed and stigmatized by addiction or mental health issues. She believes in compassionate, non-judgmental care and helps illuminate a path for people to reach their true potential. She helps people navigate resources, creates unique treatment recommendations, and coaches people through their limitations.

Shirley has served on the board of directors of Center for Open Recovery & Sky's the Limit Fund, two nonprofit organizations where the aim is to end the stigma of addiction and help families in crisis gain access to wilderness therapy programs for adolescents and young adults.

Originally from Oklahoma, she has enjoyed her relocation to the San Francisco Bay Area. She resides in Mill Valley with her husband, two daughters, and dog, Mochi. She enjoys cooking, entertaining, hiking, traveling, all things fashion and beauty-related, spending time with friends and family, and *growing*.

~

Website: https://recovery-consultants.com/

facebook.com/recoveryconsultantsllc
twitter.com/WantlandShirley
instagram.com/recoveryconsultants
linkedin.com/in/shirley-wantland-31869415

About the Publisher

Founded in September 2020 by Kayleigh O'Keefe, Soul Excellence Publishing has quickly built a reputation for helping over 350 Fortune 500 executives, CEOS, and community leaders share their perspectives on the topics that matter most in best-selling books, such as:

- *Leading Through the Pandemic: Unconventional Wisdom from Heartfelt Leaders*
- *Significant Women: Leaders Reveal What Matters Most*
- *The X-Factor: The Spiritual Secrets Behind Successful Executives & Entrepreneurs*
- *Black Utah: Stories from a Thriving Community*
- *STEM Century: It Takes a Village to Raise a 21st-Century Graduate*
- *Greener Data: Actionable Insights from Industry Leaders*

Soul Excellence Publishing is a hybrid publisher that makes it rewarding for executives to share their stories in multi-author collaborative books, individual thought leadership books, and corporate team books.

We do things a little bit differently around here, by design.

We help you marry your business expertise with your soul's big vision through your writing, setting you up to spark a movement through book.

∾

Website: https://soulexcellence.com

Made in the USA
Middletown, DE
25 October 2023

41369202R00179